Building and Maintaining a European Direct Marketing Database

For Bart and Ian with love and thanks

BUILDING AND MAINTAINING A

EUROPEAN DIRECT MARKETING DATABASE

GRAHAM R. RHIND

Gower

Published by
Gower Publishing
Gower House
Croft Road
Aldershot
Hampshire GU11 3HR
England

Gower
Old Post Road
Brookfield
Vermont 05036
USA

British Library Cataloguing in Publication Data

Rhind, Graham R.
    Building and Maintaining a European
    Direct Marketing Database
    I. Title
    658. 800285

    ISBN 0–566–07471–0

Library of Congress Cataloging-in-Publication Data

Rhind, Graham R.
    Building and maintaining a European direct marketing database/by
Graham R. Rhind.
        p.   cm.
    Includes bibliographical references.
    ISBN 0–566–07471–0
    1. Direct marketing–Europe–Databases.   2. Database management-
Europe.   I. Title.
HF5415. 122.R5   1994
025.06'65884–dc20

94-174
CIP

Typeset in Palatino by Raven Typesetters, Chester and printed in Great Britain
by Bookcraft Ltd. Midsomer Norton

▌ Contents

Figures and tables

Figures

Table

Maps

Acknowledgements

This book could never have been written without the help of a great many people who have provided me with the information and skills required to compile especially the chapters on individual countries. I am especially indebted to Ian Morris and Bart Lauwereins, whose considerable language skills and willingness to chase after information for me about anything from Andorra to Zetland at the drop of a hat I could not have done without. For your support, my friends, I dedicate this book to you. Thank-you.

Many others have contributed to a greater or lesser extent, and though I would like to name them all, I am sure to fail. For those whom I omit, forgive me, and believe that I extend my thanks also to you. Thanks to Jeannet Aalberts for her contribution on The Netherlands; Mr Rients de Boer of the Fryske Akademy in Ljouwert; Arnold Bonemeyer for his help with The Netherlands and for knowing the difference between a doctor and a dokter; Maria-Paolo Eusepi for her help with Italian; Joan-Carles Ferrer i Pont, for his help with Catalan and Catalonia; János Friss for his Hungarian input; John Harris for his help with the Scandinavian languages; Marketta Herttua for her help with Finland; Katy Iliopoulou for her help with Greece; Verena Krawinkel for her help with Germany; Christiane Lokcick for her help with Luxembourg; Carine Magdelijns for her input on Dutch and Italian; Mihály Matura for his help with Hungary and Hungarian; Marco Orlandi for his help with Italy; Mrs M.D. Pattison of the English Place Names Society; Gabriela Ribeiro for her help with Portugal; Klaus Riedmann for his help with Germany; Eveline Strudler for help with Austria; Sabine Vandecauter for her help and criticism, in being the first person to read the finished product; the Information Service of the Embajada de España in Belgium; the Nederlandse Taalunie, The Hague; the staff of the post offices of Belgium, Malta, The Netherlands, Norway and Switzerland, and Touring-Wegenhulp, Brussels.

I would especially like to thank Ruth Lancet for her support, and John Windle of State Street Consultants Inc. of Boston, USA, without whose initial question about database management this project would never have been started.

▌▌ Author's note

Every effort has been made to ensure that the information provided in this publication is entirely accurate. Should you, however, notice any errors, or have any other comments about the book, I should be very glad to hear of them from you.

The chapters on individual countries cover 33 European states, including those of the European Union, EFTA and some Eastern European and Mediterranean states. In the countries of the ex-Soviet Union and the Balkans civil unrest and/or rapid political and socio-structural changes have dictated their omission in the current edition of this book.

I provide an update service so that you can keep up to date with changes within each individual country, and also software tailored to European database management for direct mailing. If you are interested in either of these services, please send your name and address to:

Graham Rhind
Postbus 112
3000 LEUVEN 3
Belgium

Introduction

Everything I say is obvious, although I like to think that some of the obvious things I have said were not quite so obvious until I said them

(Clive James, *May Week Was in June*, p. 241)

Creating a database, especially an address database, is one of those tasks that everybody thinks is so easy that anybody can do it. After all, one only has to create a few fields using any off-the-shelf database package, and then start to type in the names. Right?

Wrong. Many companies have made half-hearted and badly planned attempts to build direct marketing databases, and, having been frustrated in the attempt, have given up. Creating a database which will be of optimal use to you needs more than a little attention. It need not be so difficult, but there are many potential pitfalls. The idea that creating a database is easy has exacerbated the problems that many companies have unnecessarily encountered with their databases. I have often seen company managers sweating over their databases and sometimes spending small fortunes correcting faults which could better and more cheaply have been dealt with at the outset.

There are thousands of address databases being used increasingly heavily, nationally and internationally, for a whole range of direct communication activities. Direct mailing, telemarketing and so on have been enjoying a boom in recent years throughout Europe, and much attention has been given to improving the effectiveness of direct marketing campaigns. Despite this, and despite the significant technological advances which have been made to hardware and software in recent years, database management techniques have not enjoyed the same attention, remaining largely ignored and certainly underfunded.

The database is the core of all your direct marketing work. Without it, there would be no direct marketing. If it is bad, so is your direct marketing. In my opinion it is the single most important factor in influencing the effectiveness of any direct marketing activity. It must be given its due attention.

There are masses of books covering the essentials of direct marketing – why you should do it, how your artwork should look, where to buy your lists, how to test your response and so on. What you will not find is a book which tells you, in practical terms, how to build your database. Even those books professing to deal with this topic seem to gloss over it in the minimal number of pages. Whether this is because people still think that it is too easy to bother with, or whether it is that for those in the know it is too difficult a topic to tackle I could not say. This book is intended to fill the gap and to provide the knowledge which is missing from other sources. It does not examine the importance of direct marketing, its advantages and disadvantages, its legal aspects and so on; these matters have been dealt with at length by many better authors before me, and will no doubt be tackled by many after me. This work continues from where the others have left off. It gives the reasons for treating your database with respect and giving it the attention which it deserves. It explains database structures and general guidelines for good database management. It advises on the best ways to treat the data which is found specifically in databases dealing with direct marketing, and provides suggestions for effective deduplication. Finally, for a series of European countries, practical information is provided to allow effective direct marketing and database management in each country.

Greatest attention is given to business-to-business databases as opposed to consumer databases. Contrary to popular belief, business-to-business databases are more difficult to build successfully than consumer databases. For a start, businesses are usually a good deal more complex than households. They usually contain more people, whose relationship to each other can change regularly (which is not the case in households). People also move out of and between businesses more often than they do between households, and more people belong to more than one company than belong to more than one household. Good business-to-business databases are more difficult to find than good consumer databases, which can be built from ready-made sources such as electoral lists. All this means that business databases tend to lack the depth of consumer databases.

Although the text gives most attention to business-to-business databases, it is true to say that most of the points raised and guidelines provided are equally relevant to consumer databases.

As the title of this work specifies, it is concerned with database management for direct marketing, and therefore it concentrates on databases which contain names, addresses and telephone numbers. These databases are those which are used for direct (as opposed to mass) communication (buying or selling or information-gathering) with an individual at a particular location in space and time, be that a particular address or the end of the telephone line. In other words, whether you use your database for direct mailing, telemarketing, market research, sending out magazines or members' newsletters or whatever, provided that communication will be direct by mail or telecommunications, the principles will be the same, and this book will be useful for you.

1 ┃ Why bother?

It is a lie to say that information is power. It is what you do with the information that counts.

Companies and institutions keep address databases for any number of reasons. The most common in the business environment is the database for direct marketing, but address databases might just as easily be kept to contain records, for example, of publication subscribers or an organisation's members. What most address databases have in common is that the addresses or telecommunications numbers are used, at one time or another, regularly or rarely, to communicate information of some kind, be it a sales pitch or a newsletter, directly to the people whose addresses or numbers are in the database.

This is the common factor in any address database – the use of the addresses or numbers to send communications to those addresses. Regardless of what you keep in your database apart from the addresses or numbers, or what you do with it outside of direct marketing, your database and your relationship with your prospects, customers, subscribers and members can benefit greatly from the guidelines laid down in this book. Some aspects might be less important to your circumstances than others, but every guideline is relevant to every database containing addresses which are used for mailings.

The reasons why you should give your database the attention it needs to produce its best in return are outlined in this chapter. Again, although reference is made to databases for *direct marketing*, the principles are valid for any database used for direct communication with individuals, for whatever purpose.

Direct marketing does not deal with consumers as a mass or as segments, but creates an individual relationship between you, the company, and the recipient of your message. You target your message to the individuals you choose and ignore others; you model your message according to the type, depth and stage of your relationship with that individual. Marketing and communication stop being a hit-or-miss affair – you, the message-maker, regain control of your market. If you are in marketing, you are also no longer reliant on the goodwill of your brokers in the market, your salesforce, who previously owned the relationship with the customer. The management of this relationship returns to you.

As a company, institution or individual you will already have recognized the tremendous advantages that direct marketing has over certain other marketing and communications techniques. By its very nature, direct marketing allows you to direct your advertising, information and sales efforts as precisely as possible to those people who are most likely to respond, increasing sales with decreased outlays. You can customize your advertising and your message to the individual, basing your choice on any number of statistics available, referring to the individual now or based on his or her past behaviour. Not only can you communicate more effectively but you can also monitor every move that you make with every reaction which your customers give to improve communication in the future. Direct marketing is, in short, direct.

1

The database is also the raw material which can be used to give immediate and accurate feedback on cost and effectiveness of campaigns. Other marketing techniques would require slow and expensive market research to give even an indication of effectiveness. A database controls the surge of information about your suspects, prospects and customers from a mass of sources and makes it manageable.

If you are working in direct marketing, you will already understand the importance of the package which you send – the artwork, the message, the medium. Spending money on these aspects of your mailing or telecommunications is worthwhile because they will increase your response rates.

This book aims to draw your attention to the best methods for managing lists of addresses, and the importance of the database and its correct management in direct marketing. What distinguishes direct marketing from other forms of marketing is that it requires the existence and maintenance of a database. The database is what enables the user to *direct* the mailing to where it should be going. The database is not only the foundation and first stage of any mailing or direct marketing system, it is its heart and soul, the single most important factor in its success.

That said, it is also the case that the database is the least understood aspect of virtually every direct marketing campaign, and it is given the least attention and the least resources. It is usually underrated and underdeveloped. Spending astronomical sums of money on artwork, design, printing and mailing for a direct marketing campaign will be throwing good money after bad if you fail to give your database the same amount of attention, because no matter how good your offer and no matter how arresting your creative work, you will not sell if you make the offer to the wrong people and thus negate one of the most powerful advantages of direct marketing.

If you don't have a database, you don't have direct marketing. If you have a bad database, you have bad direct marketing. Rubbish in, rubbish out. Treating the database, upon which your direct marketing and communication depends, as a poor relation will only be to your disadvantage.

Why is the database so important?

> I won't say that we can pick out immediately all the indigenous depressives with blue-eyed grandmothers who were born in wedlock because we haven't coded information about grandparents. But anything coded can be extracted without trouble.
>
> (P.D. James, *A Mind to Murder*, 1963)

That excerpt was written in the days when computers were transistorized monsters, and it refers to the old punch card indexing system where you made your choices by pushing a series of metal rods through the holes punched in the cards. But what was said all those years ago is as true today, even though the storage method for our databases has changed from cards to disks, tapes and compact disks which store the data digitally. Computers give us the power to conduct direct marketing from large and complex databases, but they also make it much easier to break the rules which we need to follow in order successfully to manage our databases which in turn will result in successful management of our direct marketing. Alas, it is more often the case that these rules are not followed, and the results are seen everyday – badly addressed letters, doubles, wastage. In order to be able to say in all honesty of your database that anything coded could be extracted without problem; that you were able to make macro-level changes to the data effortlessly; that you were able to find an enquirer's details in the database without them having to root through their rubbish bin to find a label with their match code on it – this requires that you give the form and structure of your database more than superficial attention.

Many companies, when conducting direct marketing, rent one or more lists from list-brokers which are then merged, the duplicates removed and used for a single campaign. Keeping your own company database for direct marketing involves a fairly high initial cost outlay, but has innumerable advantages, especially if you are dealing with a limited section of the market. Information can come from many openly available sources, such as list-brokers, directories, membership lists, electoral rolls, exhibition visitor lists and so on, and these are often used by list brokers to make their own listings. What list-brokers cannot do is make use of the overwhelming amount of information which flows constantly in and out of your company. Only you will know who your customers or subscribers are, which people have filled in answer forms from newspapers or magazines, who reacted to the last campaign, which packets were undelivered and undeliverable, which people complained about receiving a mailing, which people requested your catalogues, etc. Some companies let this information go to waste, but by integrating it into a database you can make your mailings a great deal more effective. Your own database may not be sufficient on its own, but can be used in conjunction with bought lists which can be cleaned and updated on the basis of the invaluable information contained in your own database.

Most companies have systems of one sort or another to manage their databases and remove duplicates, but most give less attention to the database than to any other aspect of their operation. If your database is small, then remember that your database is never too small to bother. Lists of only a few hundred records will invariably contain duplicates. If you expect your company, number of subscribers, number of members or number of customers to grow (and who doesn't?) then your list will grow with it. Providing your database with a healthy structure when it is small is a great deal easier than having to impose one when the database has outgrown a strait-jacket structure. If your database contains only the names of your clients, then you should give your database loving attention to make sure that you are able to *keep* those clients. If your database is a subscription list, then you don't want to waste money by sending people two copies of each issue. In effect, it doesn't matter who you are, what you mail and to whom, the database remains the most important part of your system. Cherish it and it will deliver the goods. Abuse or abandon it, and your success will be diminished.

So you should bother because the success of your direct marketing depends on your database, and this is generally recognized by most database users. Less obvious is the fact that your database can *improve*, or at least *protect* your company's image.

You are doing a mailing. You have spent hundreds or thousands of your local currency on creation, consultancy, printing, mailing, and even, if you are sensible, your database. What happens to your mailing when it lands on your recipient's welcome-mat or in-tray? Do they shut their eyes, feeling their way into the envelope until they are ready to feast their eyes on your fabulous creation? No, of course they don't. They progress through a whole series of processes before they read your information or fill in the order form to buy your product, but of initial importance to the database manager is what they do first – *they look at what is printed on the front of the envelope.* They will want to know whether it is for them or somebody else in the organization or household, and even people who live or work alone will often check the name and address instinctively. Everybody will check that the package is intended for them, *and they will check that you have got your facts right*. The impression that your target audience gets when it looks at the address will be one of the first impressions that it has of you, of your company, and of your product.

Nothing is likely to give the recipient of your mailing a worse impression of your company than seeing a label without salutation, with an incorrectly spelt name, inaccurate address and line upon line of match coding. An electrical company which often sends mailings to me addressed in this way sends me three of everything it mails. This is painful, not only to me because it is irritating, but for another reason which should give you plenty of incentive to pay attention to the structure of your database – it can be *very costly* not to do so.

An American company once sent a mailing to my workplace – in Brussels, Germany. I do not think that there is a Brussels in Germany, and if there is, I do not work there. Furthermore, my name was spelt wrongly. In this case the label distracted my attention completely from the contents of the package, and this can as easily happen to the recipients of your mailings.

When you buy a product you will often be highly influenced by the image which you have of the company selling it. You might frequent one shop instead of another because the staff are friendly and helpful, or because the decor gives an image of professionalism, or for some other, intangible reason. Recipients of your mailings will equally be affected by the image of your company as projected by the mailing, and the first influence of that image is the care which has been taken to ensure that their personal details are correct. Direct marketing creates an image. Remember that when you send something to somebody, they get the whole package – good and bad. You also know that you have to work hard to remove the bad, because, in the eyes of the recipient one bad will outweigh the ten goods in your mailing.

For obvious reasons I take a good look at any envelope I receive, but most of the people you mail to will not. A well-printed address, correct in every detail, may not solicit a positive response from potential buyers, but it will not distract them in their progress towards opening the envelope, reading the contents and perhaps buying your product. You can be sure that some degree of negative feeling will occur when something is wrong with the address, and your chances of making the sale or just giving a good impression will be slightly (or greatly) diminished.

Returning to something that probably gained *your* attention, in an earlier paragraph I mentioned saving money. Imagine that you have a mailing list with some 20 per cent doubles (a fairly low average according to some authorities). If you produce a mailing run of 20,000, you'll be paying to have 4,000 mailings printed and posted which are not only unnecessary, but are also an irritant to the recipients, perhaps reducing the chances that they will buy your product. Fill in your own costing figures, and you will see that the cost soon builds up. Similarly, if you don't keep your database in optimal order – flagging nixies (undelivered or undeliverable returns) to prevent them from being mailed again and ensuring that your database is structured in such a way as to ensure the maximum targeting effect – it will cost you money. Make no mistake, making the best of your database can be a costly business, especially in the initial period, but you will later save money hand over fist through your initial investment.

You *need* to make that initial investment if you want to make direct marketing work for you in the way that mass marketing techniques do not. Direct marketing does not beam amorphous messages to all of us in the form of a television advertisement or an insert in the newspaper, hoping to hit its target (if we are watching at that time or reading that newspaper) in the process; it is direct. It is addressed to a person, a human being, a suspect, a prospect or a customer. And direct mailing allows us to decide *who* the people will be who receive our message – in other words, it allows us to **target**. Just as with the P.D. James quote above, if you have a mailing which you want to send to blue-eyed *Sun* readers who own Alsatian dogs, then you can do it, provided that the information is coded. In every respect and facet in which your database fails to allow you to target your mailings, without errors, doubles and undeliverables, it is bringing you further away from the goal of direct marketing and closer to that world of mass marketing from which direct marketing is aiming to escape. Only mail which is sent to people for whom it is inappropriate (or which is sent to people twice) is junk mail, and only those people will consider it as such. To those people who have been properly targeted, your mailing is an offer, something of interest, not junk. It is pointless, wasteful and irritating to mail an invitation to join your book club to somebody who has just left that same club.

You should never underestimate the importance of the human element when you mail to people. Indirect advertising techniques catch the attention of some people and pass unnoticed by others in anonymity. Direct marketing and communication are different. You address a person, an individual, with a mailing which is addressed to that person individually – a message from you to him or her. It is much easier to cause personal indignation in this way than through mass-marketing techniques.

You will not only be placing yourself at a disadvantage by failing to manage your data properly, you will also be doing a disservice to the whole of the direct marketing industry. You need to increase the amount of your direct marketing which is relevant to an individual and decrease the amount which is, for him or her, rubbish. People are very quickly irritated by direct marketing, probably because it is unsolicited. Some recipients feel that it is an invasion of their privacy that personal details are used in this manner and will grasp every opportunity to complain about direct marketing. Direct marketing is currently self-regulated in most countries, but the expansion in the amount of direct marketing is leading to increased interference on the part of legislators, whose effect can only be negative. In some European countries, individuals and companies have the right to demand to have their details removed from a database – they are added to a so-called 'stop list' – and it is therefore essential to have a well-structured and well-managed database to allow names to be 'stopped' without these same people being sent mailings from duplicate records or by their reintroduction into a mailing database from an external source. It is in the interests of the whole industry that every company which mails direct takes as much trouble as possible to prevent the unnecessary irritation of the recipients.

Do you still need persuasion that looking after your database (better?) is a good idea? In commercial terms, the breaking down of internal barriers within the European Economic Area and the European Free Trade Association (EFTA) from 1994 is a filip to good database management. There has been an increasing tendency in recent years to undertake cross-border marketing, and many companies now have international as well as national market-places. Their databases will contain addresses and telephone numbers from many different countries. The prevalent method of handling foreign addresses, unfortunately, has been the rather imperialistic one of treating them as if they were a colony of the mother country – same addressing, same salutations, same language. It is remarkable that when you are exhorted to do more cross-border mailings, you are assured that so-many per cent of the population speak English (for example), so it is worth your while. It is remarkable that sight is so quickly lost of the aims and advantages of direct marketing. Mailing in English to a population where 20 per cent *do not* speak English when a mailing in French to the same population would reach every individual is irrational in the extreme.

Foreign addresses need to be handled differently. Not in terms of the data itself – if you build your database properly it will be flexible enough to be used for a mailing in Ulan Bator – but in terms of the way in which this data should be output. Addressing German businessmen as Mister instead of Herr, structuring their addresses incorrectly and giving their towns English names will not be appreciated by the recipients, whose confidence in you as a company and/or in your offer will be impaired by your inability to treat them and their data correctly.

Apart from all these other advantages, you might like to consider that it is so much *easier* to get it right the first time. Structuring your database well, and ensuring that data added is not only consistent but also correct can add to the cost of database maintenance, but only in the short term. Remember, you are dealing with the heart and life-blood of your direct marketing activities. Deduplication and merging programs will be more successful. Input and output will be simpler. You will have fewer problems finding individual addresses within your database. Your increase in sales and decrease in wasted production and mailing costs will more than cover the increased costs of database management, and, as will be explained later, in the long term the database will become easier and cheaper to manage.

So do the job properly – the whole job.

Back to my initial question – *Why bother?* Well, if you don't care about the response which your direct mailings achieve; if you don't care about the image you convey to the people to whom you mail; if you don't care that you are irritating the people to whom you are trying to sell; if you don't even care about the cost of mailing twice or three times to the same person – then you need not bother.

Otherwise, you should bother for the following reasons:

- You can **target** better.
- Your **image** improves: *irritation* decreases, *self-regulation* works.
- It is **easier** to get it right.
- It is **cheaper** to get it right.
- Other national markets in **Europe** are beckoning.

2 ‖ The database and its structure

The database which you create will contain information about individuals and groups of individuals in households or companies. For each of these 'addresses', the database will be a receptacle for the information required for you to maximize and optimize your marketing communication with them. Each 'address' will be a record of a person, household or company in time and space.

The concepts and principles behind direct marketing and communication are easy to understand but difficult to execute. Neither this nor any other book can tell you precisely how to structure your database. Every company, whether selling widgets or magazines, lawn-mowers or china thimbles, will have different targets and different information requirements. However, every database being used for direct communication has certain common elements. It will contain names and addresses and a certain amount of information common to most databases. It will also need to be:

- Relevant
- Up to date
- Accurate
- Free of doubles

It needs to be **relevant** so that your marketing can be targeted, that is, direct: no relevant information, no direct marketing. It needs to be **up to date** because both your company and your contacts do not remain static – they change, they move, they develop and your database must do the same. It needs to be **accurate** so that you do not waste your money sending mailings to people who are not interested, and to prevent your potential and existing customers being irritated by errors. And it needs to be **double-free** to prevent you wasting your money whilst irritating your contacts by sending duplicate mailings.

Knowing, however, that your database needs to be, for example, free of doubles is not enough. You need to ensure from the beginning that your database is structured and built in such a way as to make these aims *achievable*. This can be accomplished by following certain guidelines which are outlined in this chapter and the following chapter.

If your existing database does not conform to these rules, then you might profitably consider making the necessary investment in time and money to initiate these changes. If your database is not well-structured but this causes you no problems, consider changing the structure in any case because an inflexible structure could cause many more problems and cost more to correct in the future as you develop and grow. If your database is small there is equal reason to follow the rules given here because they will allow your database to grow unhindered. Waiting until your database outgrows its structure will increase the costs of improvement, and cause disruption to the information flow into and out of the database during the transitional period.

Before you start

Thought and planning are needed to ensure that the building of your database runs smoothly and efficiently. In-depth discussion and planning will be needed to specify the aims and needs of the database, and from these the form which it will take. Avoid leaving this planning stage to a single person or to too few people. A team for planning a database project should consist of a number of users and the people who will build and/or maintain the database. People who know both the technical and the marketing side of a project are ideal members of such a team.

The right person for the right job – peopleware

Remember that although many people think that creating a database is an easy task, this is not the case. Equally, not everybody could start on such a project and make a success of it, or be flexible enough to change along with the database. Database creation and maintenance is a job for professionals, and you should ensure that the team handling your database is sufficient for the task. Do not pump millions into your direct marketing activities only to have the whole project ruined or severely limited by allowing a jack-of-all-trades amateur to execute the database building and management programme.

Resources

A direct marketing database should be controlled by the marketing or sales divisions of your company. Though it should be linked to other data sources within your company to allow an efficient data exchange, it should not be pushed into second place nor have to compete for resources with other databases such as the accounting or order-processing system.

Furthermore, you should regard your database as an integral part of your business. It is your tool and weapon, ensuring better and more effective communication with both your existing customers and your suspects and prospects. Do not treat it as an afterthought or starve it of financial, computing or 'peopleware' resources. Ensure that the information exchange within the company feeds the database with the information which it needs. If such ongoing commitment is not made, the value of any initial burst of investment is quickly eroded. A database can never be a finished product; it must grow and change and mature to continue to be useful.

When considering your database structure you need to start with the basics, clearing your mind as much as possible of the structure which you currently use. Initially, we must consider the term 'database'.

What is a database?

Some authorities would have it that a database (in direct marketing terms) is no more than a posh word for a list, or what you would do with a list once you have got it. This is not the case, and it is short-sighted to regard your database in this way. A list is something static, an unchanging report giving certain limited information about certain addresses. A database has to be much more than this if you do not want to waste your time and money.

As previously mentioned, each 'address' in your database is a record of a person, household or company in time and space. In its use as a tool to optimize the effectiveness of your marketing interaction with the people whose names are stored in your database, it must contain information about the 'address' now and in the past, and must be able to be used to predict the behaviour of each individual in the future.

The age-old (if simplified) definition of a database is that it is a structure for the storage of data. This is not the full story, though this is evidently how many people see it. It *is* a structure for storing data, but if you view it only in this way then you may encounter problems when you come to create your database. Storage is only a short stage in the database cycle. If all you did was *store* your data, the information stored would become out of date very quickly. A database must evolve. In fact, the development of a database involves the following processes:

- Input of data
- Manipulation of data
- Measurement and assessment of data
- Storage of data
- Output of data.

This may seem obvious, but it is surprising how many people fail to appreciate the significance of each of these stages when they design their databases.

Databases contain data in **fields**, each field of a given type and length designed to store one piece of data per record. The number and type of fields, and the data stored within them, gives the database *depth*. A **record** is a collection of fields pertaining to a single address, contact name, equipment piece or whatever. The number (and quality) of the records gives a database *breadth*. A **database file** is a series of records, and each database file can be linked to other database files to make a complete (related) **database.**

Database? Interface!

It is important at this stage to draw your attention to the difference between the database, the receptacle which contains the data, and the interface, the program which is used to access the information within the database. The database manager will, of course, have access to the raw structure and data of the database. The user will usually have access to the database through an especially written interface which will allow input and access to and output of certain pieces of data whilst hiding or protecting other pieces. Unless otherwise specified, I refer in this book to the database rather than the interface. However, the guiding principles of address database management apply as much to the user-interface as to the database itself. A database with a super-flexible structure and fantastically consistent data which can only be accessed by the user through an inflexible and awkward interface is as useless as an inflexible and inconsistent database.

Data only

The use of the word data, rather than 'address', 'customer', 'information' and so on is deliberate. Although each piece of data for each person in your database represents something as tangible or fixed as a telephone, a house, a car or a date of birth, and though you must be aware of what it is that each piece of information represents when it is entered into the database and what it will represent when it comes out again, what the computer deals with is data, and that is what your information is whilst it is in your database.

Computers do not manipulate addresses or names or telephone numbers; they manipulate data, strings and variables. Treat all your information in this way and you will not go far wrong.

Let me give you a by no means exceptional example. In negotiating to buy a database from an American company with a great deal of experience in building and managing databases, I asked why the database contained telephone numbers (as an example) in a single field and in an inconsistent format. There was (01) 123–4567, 011234567, 01–12.34.56.7, 00–44–1–123–4567, etc. The answer was that as telephone numbers, the data had to be recognizable only as a telephone number. If it could be read and dialled, the format was irrelevant. In this, they saw the database as a receptacle, a storage medium, for *information* rather than *data*, and their consideration was for the *present* rather than the *future*. The problem is, of course, that whilst we can recognize each of the above formats and make something of it, the computer cannot. A telephone number must go into the database and a telephone number must come out of it again, but we must not neglect to remember that during its period in the computer it is a piece of data only. As the world changes and telephone numbers (and other pieces of information) change with it, it is necessary to manage the data in the database. Were the numbers consistently added to the database, changes (such as changing the area code in London from 01 to 071 and 081 and adding a 6 in front of all subscribers' numbers in The Hague) would have been easy to make. Changing the telephone number in the inconsistent formats above, however, would have been time-consuming (and therefore costly), and would have degraded the database in terms of accuracy and timeliness.

Which database structure should you use?

Before you start creating your database, thought must be given to the form that it is to take. There are four main types of database structure:

1   Simple.
2   Hierarchical.
3   Network.
4   Relational.

The simple database

In a simple database, all the information that is required, name, address, contact names, equip-

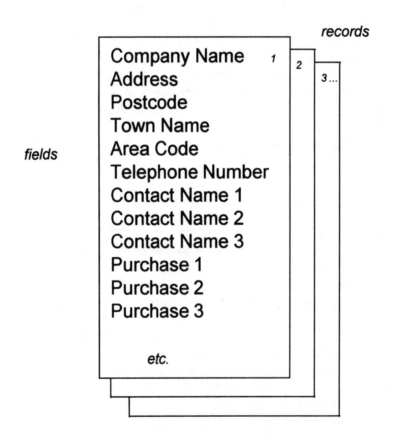

Figure 2.1   *A Simple Database*

ment ordered and so on, is stored in a single database file (see figure 2.1). Most marketing databases begin life in this way, and even when the borders of usefulness of such a system have been reached, most businesses are slow to change the structure, drastically reducing the usefulness of the database and causing problems during the transitional period between systems. This structure is usually adopted because it is easy for non-programmers to create and manage such a database system. The problems of this system are as follows:

- It is space-wasting.
- It restricts the amount of information that the database can hold.
- It is inflexible, making manipulation difficult.

In your database you have, for example, three sets of fields for contact information (customer names and job titles, or householder names and positions, etc.). These names are located in the same database as the rest of the information about the address, so relating pieces of data to each other could not be easier. You will not, however, have three contact names for every address and for those companies without three names the empty fields will, in some database systems, use disk space, which is at a premium, and will slow the system down. There are also addresses where you have information for more than three contacts. (You may feel that you only need the name of one contact, but you should never restrict the use of your database by fencing yourself into such restrictions – consider always your potential future needs.) These extra names cannot be accommodated, which indicates immediately the invalidity of the system. You are also forced to search three sets of fields every time you want to find a name or count the number of Managing Directors in the database, that is you must count all the Managing Directors in the first, second

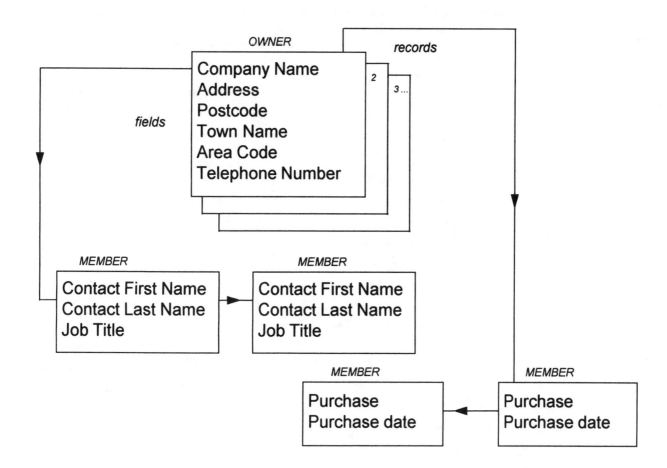

Figure 2.2 *A Hierarchical Database*

and third title fields, which can be rather time-consuming. The same American gentleman who had such problems with his telephone numbers used this structure with his large database. He had allowed three fields to list the makes and models of a particular equipment type. All fourth, fifth and further pieces of equipment had to be ignored. This meant not only a reduction in accuracy and fullness in the database, it also meant that I (or he) could never be sure whether companies with all three fields filled had three or more than three of this equipment type. In thus compromising the quality of the database, the quality of your link with each person in the database and therefore the directness and usefulness of the database are also compromised.

Hierarchical databases

As the name suggests, links in this databasing system are purely hierarchical (see figure 2.2). Records are represented as having 'owners'. Each record may have only one owner, but may have more than one 'member'. Imagine that a customer has ordered two sets of goods from you. A link would be made from the company information (the owner) to the first record with the goods information (the first member): then a horizontal link would be made to the second piece of goods information (the second member). This system doesn't contain the intuitively obvious linkage system which relational databasing does, and creates complexities and inflexibilities. It is not suitable for address databases.

Network databases

Network databasing is rarely used as a way of storing address database information, but is often used as a method of linking direct mailing databases to other databases which may exist within a company. Thus, the direct marketing database, which itself may have a relational database structure, might be linked to other databases, such as the accounts database, the orders database and so on (see figure 2.3). These network databasing systems, often mainframe based, allow users to

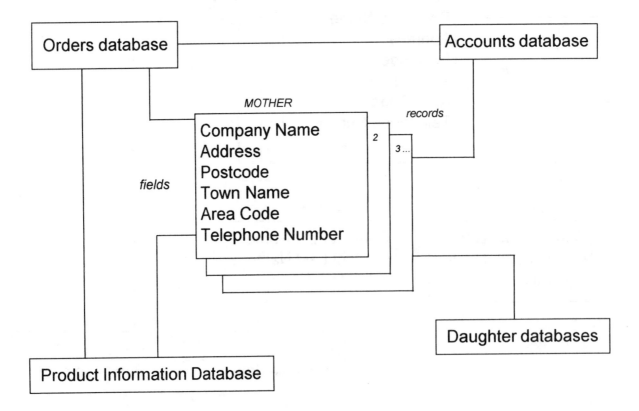

Figure 2.3 *A Network Database*

access the data in each of the networked databases from a variety of platforms, through a network of linkages created between the different data groups. Again, users must know which links exist to use the system effectively.

Relational databases

In this structure the data is held in more than one database file (a 'mother' and one or more 'daughters'), these being related to each other by an identification number or code unique to each record in the mother database, but which may not occur at all or may occur more than once in the daughter databases. For example, the name and address of the customer might be stored in the mother database file, and the purchases that the customer has made in the daughter database file. For every sale made to that customer, a new record can be made in the daughter database file specifying the details (type, quantity, date, etc.) of the purchase. This contains the unique identification code of the customer in the mother database. As many records as one likes may be added to the daughter database file to refer to the single record in the mother database file. To then find out, for example, how many and which customers have bought the left-threaded widget within the past month, the daughter database is searched for this information and then the related records from the mother database are extracted.

The relational database system is the one which you should generally adopt for address databases used for direct marketing and communication. The reason is that in direct marketing there is one piece of information which is unique – the person's address to which you are sending your mailing (note that it is the *address* which is unique, not the *occupants* or *contacts*). This address should and need appear only once in your database. You then have information in varying amounts which relates to this address information: occupants/employers (in any number); items bought; competitors equipment installed; turnover per year and so on. These items are put in daughter database files, as shown in figure 2.4. This system is exceptionally flexible, allowing no

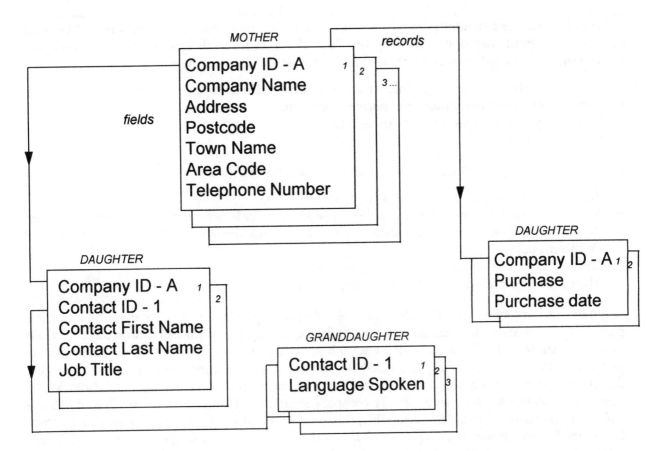

Figure 2.4 *A Relational Database*

limit to the amount of information added and allowing easy access to the data. The linkage is evident and intuitively obvious and the system is comparatively simple to use. Furthermore, you only create a record in the mother and daughter database files when the information is available, making disk-space usage more efficient. It does, however, require a certain amount of programming knowledge to put the system to its full use.

What information should you store in a database?

I cannot tell you what information to store in your database, you must decide for yourself basing your decision on your marketing strategy. I have concentrated on the information which you *must* have in any database to make it useful for direct mailing: the names of the people/businesses and their locations. From this basis you can build up any length of list of data to include. John Fraser-Robinson (1989), for example, splits the data stored in business databases into the following categories:

- Corporate data
- Operational data
- Corporate relationship data by individual
- Personal data by individual
- Cumulative previous data from previous employees

He gives a list of 53 items for possible inclusion. For the consumer database, he suggests the following categories:

- Operational data
- Relationship data
- Personal data

Forty-five items are listed for possible inclusion. I shall not reproduce his ideas here, but I would suggest a different way of categorizing the data. All data for both businesses and consumers which you would want in your database fall into the following categories:

- Who/what they are (demographics/psychographics – the human dimension)
- Where they are (geographics – the place dimension)
- When they were/are/will be (the time dimension)
- Operational data.

Furthermore, each piece of information in the database will be either:

- Single occurrence and unchangeable (e.g. date of birth)
- Multiple occurrence and unchangeable (These are usually lists giving a historic view – the list cannot be changed, but can be added to, e.g. addresses already inhabited, date of births of children, etc.)
- Single occurrence and changeable (e.g. main residence)
- Multiple occurrence and changeable (e.g. cars owned)

Singular pieces of information (such as date of birth) belong in the mother database file; multiple pieces of information (like car ownership) and singular pieces of information related to these multiple data (e.g. model of each car owned) belong in daughter database files. The process of putting multiple data into daughter database of files, linked to a mother (which itself can be a daughter) containing the single piece of data to which it is related, is called normalization. A fully normalized database can have a fairly complex structure. Although as a principle databases should be normalized as much as possible, this process should not be at the expense of database flexibility. If a maximum of two pieces of data might be related to a single other piece of data, it might be as useful to store all the data together in a single database file for the purposes of flexibility as to store the related data in a normalized daughter database file.

I shall discuss each data grouping in turn.

Who/what they are

This demographic and psychographic information allows you to target your recipients. What information you will include depends heavily on the message that you are trying to convey and on the way in which you want to target people (now and in the future). Examples of this type of information include the following:

- Name(s)
- Gender
- Date of birth
- Telephone number
- Marital status
- Residence type
- Car ownership
- Customer type
- Language(s) spoken
- Job title
- Buying patterns
- Corporate ownership pattern
- Turnover
- Business type
- Equipment ownership

Where they are

Although you keep a database because you are interested in people, because it is people who are going to decide whether or not to buy your product and it is people who read your magazine, geographic information is an essential factor in database management. People are not unique, and they may fulfil several requirements at once. Someone is male and 40 years old. He is also bearded and has a dog. He is also a Protestant with a Mazda. However, he is and can be in only one place at one time (however many residences that he has). Geographical data will therefore often be the basis of much of the manipulation of your data, whether it is to change telephone numbers, give correct address formats, or to classify areas by socio-economic factors. For this reason you would be well-advised, as with provision of demographic information, to be as generous as possible when adding this sort of information to your database – it also dictates the success of your targeting. Geographical data might include the following information:

- Address
- Telephone area code
- Postcode
- Country code
- TV area
- Sales area

When they were/are/will be

To fully appreciate the power of a database, one must see it not merely as a mailing list but as a history of a person, and as a history of the *relationship* between you and that person. This category is rarely given the attention it deserves in databases. Data items to note include the following:

- Purchase history
- A record of every communication between you and your customer
- Source history (where each mention of your recipient was found, and when)

- Turnover, capital investment, profit, etc. history
- Date of last (each) employment change
- Date to which employee number information refers
- Year equipment installed
- Dates mailed
- Date of last (each) house move

Knowledge of this sort of information gives a deeper insight into the nature and characteristics of the people with whom you are communicating, and can be used to prevent such irritating occurrences as inviting someone to join your book club a month after they have left it, or offering someone an overdraft at advantageous rates when, after numerous threats from the bank, they have just finished paying one off, and so on.

Knowledge of the history of recipients, and their current status will help you to predict their future behaviour. Knowing what they have bought, for example, will help to indicate future purchasing patterns.

Operational data

This data is what is needed to run the database effectively from the operational point of view. It will include the unique identification code in both the mother and the daughter database files to allow them to be linked and related properly; fields serving temporarily to flag records, store data for alterations to be made to it before output, and to sort data, etc.

3 | The principles of good database management

When you know what sort of database structure to choose and you have an idea of what information you need to include in your database, your next consideration is how to put this together in the most successful way. As I mentioned at the beginning of the previous chapter, your database needs to be :

- Relevant (by making it
  flexible and
  accessible)
- Up to date
- Free of doubles (by making it
  consistent)
- Accurate

These results can be achieved by carrying out the following procedure:

- Flag and code the data (segmenting).
- Fragment the data.
- Relate the data.
- Give the records fullness.

All of these factors are intimately related. Adding flexibility, for example, will make your database potentially more accurate and up to date; consistency will aid flexibility, accuracy, accessibility and deduplication; and so on. Work on one of these factors and you will automatically contribute to fulfilling one or more of the other factors.

Flexibility

One of the greatest problems which companies face is the failure of their databases to live up to their requirements. The root of this problem lies in the quality and the flexibity of the database files, which are not specified to sufficient levels of detail or accuracy, and/or do not have the flexibility to be tailored and updated to meet detailed requirements.

Every database contains information which refers to a current situation. It will, in the best case, contain information currently relevant to the addresses within the database – marital status, company name, address, car ownership, number of employees and so on. The structure of the database and the applications written for it will all be subservient to a marketing plan or working procedure in which the database has a specified place and purpose. But the world doesn't stand still; it changes. Your customers and potential customers will change, and, hopefully, your company will change and progress. Your database, an expensive tool to set up and a valuable asset to any company or institution, must be able to change with it.

Let us take an imaginary case which, you will agree, is certainly not a far-fetched example. Your company sells electronic widgets. Twenty-five years ago these widgets stood in large air-conditioned rooms, watched over by three widget-operators. Very few companies could afford to buy a widget, and it was unheard of that anybody would own more than one widget. So you put the information about the installed base of widgets in a simple database, allowing only one entry per company. Of course, the only person who used the widget was the Widget Director, so you only allowed space for one contact name in your database.

Then the price of widgets began to fall. They became smaller. Companies began to buy two widgets, linking them together. The Widget Director was no longer the only person using them – there were Widget Managers. Then even smaller widgets were brought onto the market, and these were given to secretaries. Then all executives wanted a widget, and by this time the price of widgets had fallen so much that the buying decision for widgets had been relocated to each branch and each department. Then along came widgets which were portable enough for salespeople to carry so that they could widget in the field. Then there were lap-widgets, palm-widgets, widgets which fit onto the wrist and around the neck. You get the picture. The world changes. Your customer changes. Your product changes. You change. If your database is not capable of following (or, ideally, leading into) these changes without you effectively having to re-build and re-structure it each time, then your database is not flexible enough.

Whilst you want to keep absolute control over your database, you must never build your database into a strait-jacket structure or place it under a rigid interface which will have no other effect than to give you problems. Let us take an example. For thirty-two years Germany's postcodes were easily assigned and simply formed. Each municipality had its own 4 digit postcode, beginning with a number between 1 and 9. On 1st July 1993 the German postcode system changed to a street-based system which has 5 digits, the first being any digit between 0 and 9. Although these sorts of change do not occur often, there has been a great deal of uproar, wringing of hands and weeping into keyboards because many companies have inherited a database or interface which which allows 4 digits only in the postcode, the first digit of which may not be a 0. Those companies with flexible databases were the quickest and best off the mark when the changes were introduced.

How do your make your database flexible?

Your database can be made flexible by ensuring that it is:

- Consistent
- Flagged
- Fragmented
- Related

These factors are discussed in more detail below.

Accessibility

By accessibility I simply mean that access to the data should be easy and efficient. You, and other, perhaps non-technical colleagues, want to be able to access all the data, and tricky combinations of data, as easily as possible without having to re-program or follow through time-consuming procedures. Accessibility is intimately tied up with the concepts of flexibility and consistency – if your database is flexible and consistent, it will automatically be accessible provided that you don't put a restrictive interface between the user and the database.

That said, accessibility to the database for all the users means that the data can be easily accessed and used, but this does not mean that it should be allowed to be easily or uncontrollably *changed* except where this is desired. When one has worked hard to ensure the consistency and quality of a database, unacceptable changes to data formats and so on must be avoided. Such changes can be prevented by, amongst other things, building templates into the database interface system to prevent 'illegal' formats from being entered, and by not allowing changes to be made to some data. An 'in-tray' system, where changes made are first stored in a file which can be programmatically and manually checked for bad formatting etc. is also a useful option. In any case, when designing or purchasing a database management system or interface, consider not only the user but also the quality and protection of the data.

Timeliness

A database is not out of date as soon as you enter the data into it as most people would have you believe – in fact the data is usually out of date before you even receive it. Did you know. for example, that 16 per cent of Danes, 14 per cent of Finns and 20 per cent of Swedes change their address annually? This is certainly not a purely Scandinavian phenomenon! Did you know that 30,000 postcodes are added or changed in The Netherlands annually? You must ensure that the data is checked and, if need be, corrected as often as possible. To keep an eye on the timeliness of your whole database, and on individual records in particular, always remember that a database has three dimensions:

1   The human dimension – the people to whom you are mailing.
2   The geographical dimension – where they are.
3   The time dimension – when the data was received and to when it refers.

In reference to this last dimension, you should note in your database not only *when* records are updated, but also keep a history of updates. The more often you find a recipient in databases similar to your own, the more relevant that contact is likely to be for you. You must also ensure that all time-bound pieces of information are dated. You needn't, for example, time-mark date-of-birth information, because it is unchangeable. But knowing that a company has 50 employees is of little use if you don't know whether that was in 1981, 1991 or is an estimate for 2001.

Consistency

Even if you choose to ignore everything else which is written in this book, take at least this piece of advice – be consistent in absolutely everything that you do when working with databases. Keeping entries consistent to begin with can be irksome, but the effect that consistency has on the flexibility, timeliness and accuracy of the database can never be underestimated. Remember also that computers work logically and not intuitively. The more consistent your data, the easier it is to manipulate and manage on a computer.

What is meant by consistency is simply following a set of rules when adding information into the database and when manipulating the data. You may be adding everything wrongly, but at least you are adding everything *in the same way*. You may call every male contact person who speaks French Mr instead of M, but when you discover your mistake, it is extremely easy to change all the *Mrs* to *M* for all French-speaking males.   Add all telephone numbers as 071–123–4567 if you want to, or even (071)1–2–3–4–5–6–7 if you really feel so inclined. Provided that you are consistent, you can change the data quickly and efficiently.

Let us look at an example. You have already read the story about the American database with the inconsistent telephone numbers. The problem with this database was not that telephone numbers were added with full stops, dashes, spaces and brackets, but that they were added *inconsistently*. If the area code had *always* been enclosed in brackets and a space was *always* left after the first 3 digits of the subscriber's number then it would not have been a problem to manipulate the numbers with a short program and to merge them into another database. As it was, this was impossible. This same company provided postal codes *either* with the international sorting code in front (e.g. GB-WC1 2AB) *or* without. And when the international sorting code *was* added, it *sometimes* had spaces around the hyphens and *sometimes* did not.

Using the example which we introduced above of the German postcode changes, the postcodes in Germany changed from being based on municipality to being based on either postbox number, large-user deliveries, or groups of addresses. To enable companies successfully to assign a new postcode to each address, the Bundespost produced large databases containing the new codes along with the addresses to which they referred.

Whichever format the Bundespost chose to use for its addresses – Strasse written in full or as Str. or as Str, etc. – database managers with consistently formatted databases could, without too much difficulty, make any changes necessary to their own databases or that of the Bundespost to make them consistent with each other, and therefore could successfully assign the new postcodes to each address using the computer. The managers of databases without consistency did not have this luxury, and expended much time wastefully looking up postcodes manually.

Another great advantage of being consistent is that it is the best way to ensure that deduplication and merging programs do their job properly. The more consistent you are, the easier it is to find similar records and therefore the fewer doubles you will have in your file.

Being consistent will make it a great deal easier to find an individual piece of information, record or set of records within the database.

Finally, and in summary, consistency aids control. A database can potentially be very large and unwieldy. Consistency reduces problems arising from this to relative insignificance and allows you to concentrate time and energy on other matters.

The usefulness of consistency should already be obvious. Address formats rarely change, but postcodes do. As do telephone numbers, area codes and fax numbers. The golden rule to beat all golden rules is **be consistent**.

Accuracy

You should be consistent, and if you are going to be consistent you might as well be accurate. This has less to do with the way that your database is held together and can be used on a day-to-day basis, and more to do with the way the information will appear on the label or in the letter of the mailing you send. Ensuring names are correct, the street name is correctly spelt with the house number in the right place, the postcode is correctly formatted and in the right place, the salutation and surname are correct – it all simply makes it easier for you to sell your goods or ideas to the recipient , and that, after all, is what it is all about.

Flagging and coding

This is often referred to in the literature as *segmentation* though I prefer to speak about *flagging*. Segmentation suggests that you are splitting addresses up into categories. Considering that every address is a unique mixture of characteristics, and that each communication with the address may require a different mix of characteristics to be taken into account, segmentation into a series of hard and fast groupings is not advisable. Advice to split customers from prospects, for example, is often given, but a simple flag or code to indicate status makes this task unnecessary and irrelevant.

Flagging, more accurately, suggests that you mark an address if it fulfils a particular role or has a particular characteristic, like belonging to a computer wholesaler or someone who is deceased, or being a detached house. Flagging this sort of data allows categorization at the output stage of manipulation, where for one mailing you may want to know which people have dogs and live in detached houses, whilst the next mailing is to readers of a particular newspaper. Flag and code, therefore, dog-owners, detached-house inhabitants and readers of each newspaper without segmenting them into groups.

Coding is exactly what it says, and this you reserve for areas where any number of categories might be needed, such as business type, the function of the contact within a business, social group, language spoken. Flagging is where you want to give a yes/no, 1–2–3, A-B-C type indication, such as whether a particular mailing was sent, whether a mainframe computer is installed at that site, whether the installed photocopier works in colour, or whatever you feel that may need to be known in order to **filter** the contacts when an output is needed from the database.

You should make a habit of coding and flagging as a norm – it greatly increases the flexibility and usefulness of the database. Most list–sellers, for example, correctly code business contact functions. This is because of the large number of job titles which proliferates in the business world. If you have only noted the function title of the contacts and you wanted to mail to Managing Directors, you could always check through the database for those records with the title 'Managing Director'. This would, however, mean that you would miss those people with their titles written as 'MD', 'M.D.', 'M D' (it's the consistency story again) 'General Manager', 'Company Manager' or, if you're mailing to other European countries 'Geschäftsführer', 'Algemene Directeur' or 'Gérant'. Just selecting all the contacts with the function code 1, 2 or whatever you choose to code it would be easier, more efficient and more accurate.

Although when you use your database you usually check for qualifications which a person or address should fulfil, do not neglect the fact that every positive qualification can have its negative equivalent. Flag companies which are to receive a particular series of mailings, but flag also those who must *not* receive that mailing. Flag residents who are pleased to receive your mailings and buy your products, but flag also those people who do not wish to hear from you again. Flag telephone numbers which are known to be good, but flag also telephone numbers which are known to be bad.

Take care, therefore, when using Boolean fields in a database. These fields allow only two options: true or false (sometimes expressed as yes or no, or 1 and 0). If a Boolean field used to indicate telephone number status, for example, defaults to true (the telephone number is good), then you can see which telephone numbers are definitely not good as the Boolean field will be set to false. However, you will no longer be able to distinguish which telephone numbers are definitely good (you have called them and got through to the correct person/company) and which numbers have an unknown status, as all have the Boolean flag of 'true'. Use as a preference a character field, where more than two status possibilities are allowed.

Flagging is a necessity, not an option. Consider the insurance company who wished, for various reasons to retain the names of people who had died. Instead of giving these records a flag to indicate their status, and to enable a stop to be put on the record being used for mailings, the company simply wrote '(deceased)' after the name of the person. Their next mailing was characterized by a number of distressed widows and widowers receiving a mailing about life insurance for their late partners and addressed to 'Mr. A.N. Other (deceased)'. This was flagging in a way, but such data should be *fragmented* (see below) into different fields. A simple 'Y' or 'N' flag in a 'Deceased' field, or a code in a status field, would have sufficed.

You may also code business type – use a code like the SIC (Standard Industrial Classification) or NACE (Nomenclature des Activités dans les Communautés Européennes) code to do this – but always try to combine this with flagging. The great beauty of direct marketing, as I have mentioned, is that it can be highly targeted, and the more that you know about the person and company whom you are contacting, the more cost-effective and efficient your communication will be. It is therefore good to know that your recipient is a fruit-juice processor, but it is even better to know that their oranges come from Spain, they add no artificial sweetener to their juices, and that they currently package only in bottles. All this information can be indicated through flagging and coding, making the database much richer and more useful.

When choosing a coding system, you are advised to choose the 'finest' (that is to say, most detailed) system possible which does not have an unduly negative effect on time and financial considerations when using the database. A 4-figure industry coding system, for example, when you currently only have need for the first 2-digits is advisable if there is a chance that a finer degree of coding will be needed in the near future. It is easy to get a 'rougher' degree of filtering from a 'fine' coding system, but this does not work in reverse.

Fragmentation

Fragmentation should be practised to aid database manipulation, and to improve output flexibility. It aids consistency, and also aids in deduplication processes.

Fragmentation is the splitting of data into separate fields down to the lowest suitable variable. Any macro changes would affect each variable independently of the other variables.

Let me illustrate this. A telephone number is a telephone number, but it consists of a country code, an area code and a subscriber's number. The contents of each field can alter individually, or each can change on a macro level as a series. All of the subscribers' numbers in a single area might change (all adding a 6 at the beginning, for example), or the area code might change (e.g. from 01 to 071 and 081), or the individual subscriber's number might change. You should therefore 'fragment' the data into several fields, one for the country code if required, one for the area code and one for the subscriber's number.

Fragmentation will aid consistency and is the ideal way to enable quick and easy macro changes to data. In turn, it makes the database more flexible and aids in the location of duplicates. It will also enable an envious flexibility of output. Let's look at the example of contact names. A name will consist of a salutation (Mr, Mrs, etc.), first names, a surname and possibly some letters indicating qualifications. You could, of course, put the whole name in one field (most companies do). After all, being able to put 'Mr A. Smith' on the label is all you want to do, isn't it? Well, what about the salutation? Doesn't 'Dear Mr A. Smith' grate a little? Wouldn't 'Dear Mr Smith' be better? Well, of course you can do that by just taking the first and last words. Fine, except that Mr van den Broek will end up as Mr Broek. He won't like that.

The book club which I left knew my name, but I recently received a mailing which took personalization just a little too far. It read:

Mr Rhind Graham, perhaps you are already £1000 richer!

Dear Mr Rhind Graham,

It went on to mention my mangled name a further seven times in full. Apart from putting my surname and first name in the right order, fragmented contact name data would have allowed them to insert 'Mr Graham Rhind' where that was relevant and 'Mr. Rhind' where *that* was relevant.

You should therefore strive to fragment data into its lowest common denominators and put the data into different fields.

Fullness

The building of any database should be undertaken with cost-effectiveness in mind. One must choose what is to go into the database to ensure that the data can be put to the maximum use, and achieve the best return on investment, for the minimum cost of entry. One must, therefore, make choices about adding some data whilst omitting other data.

Not entering certain data into the database can save data-entry time, disk space and disk access time/program running time. However, although one must recognize the need to make decisions on the inclusion of data into the database, you would be well-advised always to err on the side of 'fullness', that is, to put *more* rather than *less* into the database. The reasoning behind this is that, as mentioned above, the world, your customers and your product will change. The database must be able to encompass change not only in terms of its flexibility but also in terms of the data it holds. Taking the example of the widget which we used earlier, when the widget was a large machine in an air-conditioned room, you only needed the name of one person in that company – the Widget Director – for your mailings. However, most bought databases or lists from directories and so on would probably have contained other contact names for the same company – Managing Director, Financial Manager, Sales Manager and so on. The short-sighted Database Manager would have added only the information for the Widget Director to the database. When widgets become smaller and more accessible to other members of the company, and when the decision process itself moved to other members of the company, you would have liked to target them with your widget sales campaigns. If you had not included their names in your database, you would have to enter these names before the campaign could be held, and this would result in delay. As data held in databases rapidly becomes outdated, it is pointless adding data which is only likely to be needed in ten years time. You should, however, always strive to make sure that your database, in terms of fullness, stays at least one step ahead of your marketing strategy.

You should also be aware that it is quicker to add information while building the record initially than to append information later, because you have to locate the original record and possibly scroll through existing information before changes can be made.

Let us take as an example the first name of a contact. Let us say that our contact is called Mr Andrew Smith. Well, we don't use the first name on our labels, and we salute him as 'Mr Smith', so let us save time by putting him into the database as:

Mr A. Smith

or just Mr Smith. That is fine for what you want to do *now*, but what happens when you *do* want to use his first name in a mailing? Or when you want to check to see whether A. Smith (Andrew) is the same person as A. Smith (Alan) in the company? The fact is, if you don't want to put 'Andrew' onto the label you don't need it – you just lift the first letter of his first name and follow it with a full stop. You can easily make names *shorter* using computers, but it is *impossible* to program a computer to know that A. Smith is Andrew Smith.

Incidentally, if you don't think you'll ever use a first name in a mailing, how about this:

Dear Mrs Smith,

Having two lovely children under the age of five, Tony and Celia, must be a great joy to you, but I'm sure that it causes problems on wash day when you try to get their clothes stain-free . . .

I made that up, and you can see that I am no creative genius, but just suppose that you wanted to mail such a letter. It would be impossible without the full first names of all the children. (Obviously, you will 'train' your output program to know when the first name field is either blank or contains an abbreviation (or when one or more child's name is missing) so that a more generalized, less personalized sentence (excluding the first names) is produced for those households/ businesses.)

Although this may sound like heresy to those used to talking about careful planning and cost-effectiveness, a full and flexible database will be far more cost-effective than any half-full and inflexible equivalent.

You should note that fullness does not mean repetition or unnecessary data entry. You must allow in the database structure the ability to add relevant information automatically, but you should not force operators to enter information twice, albeit in a different form. Let's look at some examples:

1 The country code. It is very important to know in which country the address is, but you only need to know it once. If you have given an indication that the country code is 'BEL' for Belgium, then don't give the country telephone code (32) or the international sorting code (B-) because they all indicate exactly the same information, and these can be added, if necessary or desired, automatically or on output, by the computer. That is what computers do well.
2 The telephone area code. If every area code in a particular country begins with 0 why bother including it? Omitting it will save data-entry time and a little bit of disk space, and every little bit helps.

3   Customer or non-customer? This is a very important flag for mailing purposes, of course, but if you register the equipment that has been bought, do you also then have to register that it is a customer? No, of course not – leave your computer to do that in a batch job. Not only does this save time, it also avoids the chance of human error.

Following these simple guidelines will make life easier when you come to use your database. Here are another couple of hints.

Deletion – a dirty word

'Delete' is a dirty word in database marketing, but most authors do not mind using it. The literature is smattered with the word, telling you to delete this or that, and most database managers follow this advice with relish.

A golden rule in database management is never to delete, but instead flag a record until such time as it has been flagged as being invalid and has been unaltered for at least n number of years. The size of n depends on the data concerned, your product and your database sources.

Your database should not only be used to record customers and prospects. It is equally relevant to note ex-customers, incorrect addresses and the names of people who do *not* wish to receive your mailings.

The reason is evident. What could happen to a business, for example? It could go bankrupt, close down or move. It could even just change its trading name. When this happens, what do you do? Delete the old record? You could do that. But, as you know, no database and no directory, in fact, no database source, is ever completely up to date. If you delete the record and then buy a list with the old (incorrect) address in it, your deduplication and merging program will not find the old address and will add it as being new. You will then waste money mailing to an address which you know is incorrect, and in deleting the same record twice or more times from your database. You should flag all records as being either okay, bankrupt, closed-down or moved, for example. In this way your record will be found when duplicating and merging, but your output programs will filter on these flags to ensure that these addresses are not mailed.

The book club, which asked me to become a member a month after I had left it, had deleted my name, bought a new source, removed the names of *existing* customers, and then mailed away. This cost the book club money, will cost it more every time that it mails to me, and causes me irritation.

You might also like to bear in mind that ex-customers can be a very useful and highly profitable source of information. By contacting them and finding out why they have become ex-customers, you are able to build up a profile of addresses with which you have *not* been successful and this is a powerful marketing tool.

Remember, the address becomes an address only when it is output – before that it is data, only data, and very useful data.

Non-business consumers are the same, except that they don't close down; they die. For your own sake, don't delete names when somebody dies – flag them. Otherwise you might find yourself sending Christmas cards to them, and there is nothing more embarrassing.

You should also bear in mind that each address in your database will contain a wealth of data from any number of different sources for a person or set of people. This wealth will be lost if you delete the records containing this information. Whilst a person may die, his house remains standing. When a company moves, it takes its equipment with it – delete its record and you will no longer know what that equipment is. When companies go bankrupt, your database could give you the chance to analyse what types of company are failing. The possibilities and the opportunities are endless.

Nixies (undelivered packages returned to you, the sender) can be flagged in your database according to why they are nixies. You will want to handle records differently according to whether the potential recipient has died or moved. On the one hand, you will want to keep the record open to allow for new address information. On the other hand, you will no longer need the information on the deceased recipient but need to retain some information to prevent him or her from being mailed again. In most European countries, each returned package will either have a sticker or a stamp indicating the reason for the return, in the local language and in French. Translations of these return texts in six languages are provided in Appendix 1.

Finding your records – identification

The problem of finding records in your database, to wheedle out returns for example, or to register a telephonic enquiry from a prospective customer, has been a problem since databases began to be built on computers. Most companies give each record a complex code, based on the address information (as with the match code suggested by Shaw and Stone (see Chapter 4)), customer number, VAT number or whatever. The trouble is that none of these systems use intuitive data, so that if you want to register a customer you have to ask them for their number, and in order to register nixies, you must either open all the returns to find the code or put the coding on the label. This is unacceptable to any self-respecting company that is serious about what it is mailing, and doesn't want its labels to look like the one below.

00054241080500002 910506
   9053760205 0070
   601511 335M68
   RHIND   GRAHAM
   A VERRESTR   190

   3012   WILSELE

This sort of information is fine if it is held within your database, but it really isn't necessary to plaster it on the label. Why? Because your label already contains information which can not only be used to find a record, but is also intuitive. The label contains the name of the customer and the address in exactly the same format as it exists in the database. (If you do change the output when mailing, you will have made a consistent change, such as putting the international sorting code in front of the postcode, and this can be taken into account when searching for the record.) You can search on any part of this address. You might have a program, for example, to list on the screen all pertinent information for all addresses which start 'A VERRE' within the postcode region 3012 and which then allows the operator to choose the correct record via the identification code.

Even if you have found a foolproof method of finding recipients based on a code, don't rest on your laurels. How often do people write to you without quoting their reference number, or plea that they have mislaid their letter, or 'they haven't got it with them' when they call you? Do you then respond 'Well, I'm sorry, I can't help you'? That won't improve either your sales or your image. People will forget your identification code but they will rarely forget their own name and address!

You will read in Chapter 4 about my colleague who was receiving two copies of a magazine from a company in the United States of America (USA). She rang them up to inform them of this without having the address labels to hand. The difficulties which this caused were incredible and unnecessary.

Your identification code need not, therefore be complicated. It must be unique to the record (which is a danger when using match codes – however complicated their construction, there is always a chance that they will double for another address) so that it can find related records in other databases, and it should be easy for somebody to type in (and you should therefore think hard before using long strings of numbers). Otherwise, you can basically choose any system you like for identification. Use IDs to *link* records, use personal information to *find* records.

4 ‖ Deduplication and merging

Deduplication and merging are not exact sciences – they are art forms.

When designing a database, and deciding in what format to add different data to the database, it is important to consider what you need to do with each piece of data while it is in the database. Deciding on formats and structures which are optimally suited to input, storage, manipulation and output is fraught with difficulties because each of these functions will often require that data is stored or treated differently than it is for the others.

Two of the routines which you will certainly need to execute on your database are **deduplication** and **merging**. Before looking at each data type in detail, therefore, we must look at the demands and methodologies behind optimal deduplication and merging procedures, and the demands that these make on database structure and format.

Deduplication and merging, together known as merge-purge, or mark-merge, are the processes by which two or more databases can be merged together into a single database, marking or purging duplicates as they do so and usually producing pages of statistics and counts referring to the process and the final database. Deduplication and merging are processes that you must regularly instigate in order to save yourself money and your contacts irritation. The procedures which you use to implement your deduplication and merging will be largely dependent on the way that you approach your mailing or other communication and the importance that you attach to good relations with your targets.

Deduplication and merging procedures are perhaps the most misunderstood procedures in the whole process of database management for direct marketing purposes, yet they are probably the most important procedures that you will ever need to apply to your addresses. These procedures are increasing in complexity but, alas, not always in efficacy.

Companies without their own databases, or companies using externally rented listings for a single mailing will usually entrust their deduplication and merging to an external bureau. The customer will have ranked the quality of the lists given to the bureau. A computer will be used to locate duplicate records in the highest quality list (let's call it list A) and in the next highest quality list (list B). Where a duplicate is identified, the address is retained in list A but is *purged* from list B. The remaining addresses in list B are assumed not to be in list A and are added to it. This is the *merging*, so the process is called **merge-purge**. This process is repeated for each list until a single database file remains.

The treatment given to lists in these cases is fast and easy, but is usually highly inefficient. Large numbers of doubles slip through this net, and there is usually little human intervention in the workings of the programs. No list, you will be aware, can be duplicate-free, but the fact that many businesses have been happy to accept lists which are no more than 70 or 80 per cent duplicate-free either demonstrates how little is understood about the procedures necessary for deduplication, or, sadly, demonstrates yet again how little appreciated is the rôle that a well-managed database can play in the success of any direct marketing exercise (and in keeping down the cost of making the contact while boosting its effectiveness).

Companies with their own databases, where the records can be used many times for many purposes and the number of records is probably not so high as to require the database to be sent outside for deduplication, should put greater emphasis and care into deduplication than outside bureaux. Computers can do a great deal of our work for us, and they are ideal number crunchers, but they cannot think, consider and make value judgements. In this respect they are not always ideal for locating duplicates in something as potentially inconsistent as an address. When you have control of your own database you can put into practice its better management by letting the computer do what *it* is good at, and by allowing humans to fill in the gaps in its abilities.

As you will need to use the data in your database many times over, and as it will contain a greater depth and variety of data than can be gathered from any one of the contributing sources, you should practice a procedure slightly different from the merge-purge procedure described above, which I will call **mark-merge**.

As with merge-purge, duplicate records in two different database files are identified, but as the data within them is required, they are not purged but marked. This is the *marking* or *deduplication* stage. The records which are not identified as duplicates are added to your main file from the file being imported. The records which are identified as duplicates are then compared and data from the record being imported is written to your main file when this data is missing in the record in the main file, or is incorrect. This is the *merging*, and differs thus from merge-purge because merging occurs on a field and record level as well as on a database file level, and no purging is involved in the process. It is with mark-merge that we are interested in this chapter, and though it is the single process of bringing two or more database files together into a single file, it consists of two distinct stages, deduplication and merging, which are discussed separately below.

Deduplication

Remember P.D. James's card classification system, mentioned in Chapter 2, where lists were produced by pushing a number of metal rods through the holes in punch cards? When lists were kept on filing cards and were sorted methodically and laboriously by hand, duplicates didn't occur very often. Lists had, of necessity, to be small, but the fact is *there is no better way to find doubles in a file than by hand*. The human brain, a magnificent piece of biological engineering, works using a brilliant mixture of logic and intuition. A computer is based only on logic, and its only intuition is logic-based. The human brain will never be matched by a computer in terms of the pure intuition and subjective decision-making which is required to identify a duplicate record. You can program a computer to take into account any number of possible combinations of format, misspellings and case structures, but it will never be able to take into account all that the human brain can at a glance.

When deduplication was done by hand, doubles were rare. When the computer came along database managers, as they were to become known, dropped their index cards with a sigh of relief and turned the whole process of deduplication over to the computer. The computer is able to handle enormous amounts of data fast. Its ability, however, to remove duplicates is lower than that of any human being, a consequence accepted by most direct marketing managers as an inevitable compromise. When dealing with the extremely valuable information available in your company database, it is a mistake to leave deduplication entirely to the computer, feeding the data in at one end and receiving a cleaned but not clean enough list at the other. Both deduplication and merging require decisions to be made, and computers are not good at decision-making.

You might also note that many consumers who regard your mail as junk, equate their being sent the mailing (or two of the mailings) with that amorphous evil 'the computer'. The fact of the matter is that they are usually right. How often do they have to hear 'Sorry, it was a computer error'?

How do you identify a duplicate?

With any database, you will have to decide how to process the data to identify duplicates. What should be the basis of this deduplication process? Which data should you compare to have the best chance of finding the double? Should it be the individual or the company to whom you are mailing? Some methods of identifying doubles sacrifice efficacy for speed and ease, and you must decide how much effort you wish to put into removing doubles. Generally, the more effort that you put in, the better the results which you achieve, to the benefit of the recipient, the response and your bank account.

One of the main problems with deduplication procedures is the necessity to take the contact name and/or company name into account. This is an unavoidable evil. Names are not unique; thousands of us share common surnames, first names and initials. Equally, not only are company names often shared by different companies or different locations of the same company, but company names can be written in a bewilderingly wide range of formats. That said, other parts of addresses are simply not unique enough in themselves, or in combination with other address variables, to be used without the company or individual's name in deduplication procedures. Contact names or company names must therefore be used, but ensuring data consistency and taking certain precautions in setting up the deduplication parameters will increase the number of duplicates found.

An address, you will remember, is what locates a person uniquely in space and time, and a person can only be in one place at one time. What is of interest to you, therefore, in terms of the database is not so much the uniqueness of the person but rather the uniqueness of the location of the person at one time. A mailing sent to the same person at two different addresses, and which will therefore be seen by the recipient on two different occasions, will be only a fraction of the irritant of receiving the same mailing twice at the same place at the same time. It is therefore logical that it is upon the *location* of a person in space that one must attempt to identify duplicates. That said, one must remember that many households contain more than one person and many addresses contain more than one business. Addresses are not only the logical reference point for deduplication, they also have fairly rigid formats which can easily be given an increased measure of consistency through computer programs. This is not the case with company names or contact names, where the permutations are endless.

Equally, other aspects such as telephone number are good indicators of duplicates. Each telephone line has a unique number assigned to it, although not all households have telephones and not all addresses in your database may have a known telephone number.

What is a duplicate?

Robert Shaw and Merlin Stone, in their book *Database Marketing* (1988) consider the question 'What is a duplicate?' and give the following example:

Pair 1	J. Roberts 46 Cranbrook Road London W4 2LH	J. Roberts 46 Cranbrook Road London W4 2LH
Pair 2	Bob Shaw 46 Cranbrook Road London W4 2LH	Dr K.R. Shaw, 1 Surrey Street London WC2R 2PS

It would seem to any deduplication program, and to the human eye, that pair 1 are the duplicates and that pair 2 are the addresses of two different individuals. In fact, say Shaw and Stone, the first pair are brother and sister Jim and Jean, whilst the second pair are the private and business addresses of the same person.

Apart from the fact that this example supports my earlier recommendation for *fullness* in your database (giving the names Jim and Jean in full would have solved the problem), this sort of duplication, where an identical mailing is received in two different places at two different times, is, as I have mentioned above, hardly a problem except in terms of cost, and it will occur only rarely. Equally, even if one J. Roberts was removed by a deduplication procedure, the mailing (or telephone call or whatever) would still arrive at the single location of both J. Roberts and would either be looked at by both or passed from one to the other should it appear that the package is intended for, or more appropriate to Jim and not Jean or vice versa.

A duplicate, for our purposes, is two records both of which refer to the same person or company at the same location in space.

How do deduplication programs work?

All deduplication programs recognize the importance of the address in identifying a duplicate. Looking at the whole address is to tempt fate – a single typing error could be the difference between finding and not finding a double. Most programs therefore base their search on a number of characters taken from elements of the address which are the most likely to be unique but which are the least likely to vary between databases.

Using this information alone, however, is not sufficient. Some street names, such as London Road or Bahnhofstrasse occur so often in addresses that using only address elements will result in a number of non-duplicates being identified as doubles. Because most deduplication programs do not allow human intervention and rely on the computer to find doubles based on a number of variables, it is necessary to add elements to this search string from other parts of the address and name in order to be sure that when a duplicate is found, it really is a duplicate. This search string is called a **match code**. Let us look again at Shaw and Stone:

A match code may be created by the software to represent a customer. The match code is an abbreviated form of the address. An example of a 14-digit match code derived from a name and address is as follows:

ADDRESS	ITEM FROM WHICH CODE TAKEN	VALUE
Addison Lee	Outward postcode	WC2N
45–64 Chandos Place	Number of Characters in name	7
London	Name (1st, 3rd, 4th)	ADI
WC2N 4HS	Number (1st, 2nd, 3rd)	45–
	Street (1st, 3rd, 4th)	CAN
Derived match code	WC2N7ADI45–CAN	

Match codes derived from databases in mixed upper and lower case should be made into upper case to eliminate potential problems stemming from case differences and other inconsistencies.

As already stated, the great advantage of this method is that if you find two match codes which are identical using this system, then you have probably (but not definitely) found a double. This means that you can leave the computer to find the duplicates, making the system relatively quick and easy. What the system is not, however, is effective. Look, for example, at the manner in which an electronics company, which sends me three of all its mailings, addresses me:

RHIND
A VERRESTR 190
3012 KESSEL-LO

GRAHAM RHIND
A VERRESTR 190
3012 KESSEL-LO

RHINO
A VERRESTR 190
3012 KESSEL-LO

It's evident that deduplication has been implemented on the basis of my name or on a key which included a substring from my name. This has failed to find these duplicates.

Here is another example, from a customer database. This company also sends me three of all its mailings, also uses a match code, and also fails to find these duplicates:

Mr. G. Rhind
Albert Verrestraat 190
3010 Kessel-Lo
BELGIUM

. G.R. Rhind
Albert Verrestraat 190
3010 Kessel-Lo
BELGIUM

Mr. Rhino
Albert Verrestratt 109
30010 KESSEL-LO
Belgium

For deduplication programs to be successful at finding increased numbers of duplicates using a match code system, the way in which the match code is built must be much less arbitrary than that mentioned above. If you have worked to make your database consistent, then the parts of any field which will be least consistent will be the non-alpha-numeric characters, i.e. punctuation and spaces (ASCII code of 47 or lower), and the letters which can be accented in the language concerned. Taking the first point, consider, for example, the BBC, which you might find as BBC, B.B.C., B B C , B. B. C. and so on. It is programmatically possible to reduce the last three to the same format, B.B.C., but the computer cannot recognize BBC as an abbreviation, and reducing all abbreviations to the same format as BBC would be unwise because you would incorrectly change other abbreviations like names (e.g. G.R. Rhind to GR Rhind). It is, however, not necessary if you use a match code creation program which will ignore all punctuation and spacing. In this case, all four forms of the abbreviation BBC will end up the same. Accented characters might appear with their accent, without it, or an equivalent letter combination. So, for example, Ü in German can be found as U or as UE.

It would therefore follow that match codes are best created without taking punctuation or letters which can be accented from the address. Whilst the former is largely true, as is demonstrated in the example later in this chapter, ignoring letters which can take accents can prove a double-edged sword, and a decision on whether to take this approach depends on your knowledge of the level of inconsistency between your database and that to be imported. So, for example, ignoring accented letters in Germany would find a company located at

Koelnstrasse
Kolnstrasse and
Kölnstrasse

which no other match code creation methodology would identify. Equally, ignoring the i, j and y in a Dutch database would find

Dijk and
Dyk

On the other hand, this method would fail to find

ABC and
ABC Printers

which would add BC and BCP to the match code respectively, whereas this duplicate could be found using other methods. For this reason, care should be taken in ignoring accented characters when creating match codes.

Short match codes for deduplication of databases containing company names can be very effective. The most effective formulation of a match code for this purpose which I have found to date is formed as follows:

4-digits of postcode + 3-digits of company name + 2 digits of address

The match codes used in the examples below are formed in this way. Making the match code any shorter by, for example, reducing the number of characters taken from an address from 2 to 1 results in an increased number of non-duplicates found and ultimately to a lower deduplication rate.

Let us consider:

A.B.C.
11–17 London Road
Oxford
OX9 6RY

Match code : OX9 A.B11 – or, without punctuation, OX96ABC111

ABC
11/17 London Road
Oxford
OX9 6RY

Match code: OX9 ABC11 or, without punctuation, OX96ABC111

As you can see, the address can be identified as a duplicate by a computer only by using the match code which ignores the spacing and the punctuation. Therefore I would strongly advise against using the number of characters in a field or name, as has been used in Stone and Shaw's example for company name database deduplication. Abbreviations, punctuation and typographical errors (typos) will alter this and make a match impossible.

If your data is consistent and punctuation is ignored, there is also no reason to take the first, third and fourth characters, for example. The first three of the string will suffice.

What is also essential when writing or choosing a match code programme is that it selects a different part of the street address from which to take the characters depending on the country. The example above works well for the United Kingdom (UK) and France, for example, because the house numbers are situated before the thoroughfare name, but in Germany, The Netherlands and elsewhere, the opposite is true, so that the match code must take characters from the end of the street address string rather than the beginning.

In some countries with long addresses, where information is often added in different places in the address, such as in the UK , there is no reason not to make more than one match code per address, for example one using characters from the first street address line, the second using characters from the second street address line, and then comparing both of those with both match codes from other records. If you have a match with one, you have found a duplicate. Consider the following:

ABC Ltd
Lotus House
17 St. Helen's Avenue
London
SW1 4WW

Match code : SW1 ABCLO

    ABC Ltd
    17 St. Helen's Avenue
    London
    SW1 4WW

Match code : SW1 ABC17

In the normal course of events, this duplicate would not be identified. However, giving the first address a second match code, based on the second line of the address, would give it an identical match code to the second address, allowing the duplicate to be identified.

Better still is a match code system which will ignore certain text strings which it comes across. Certain text strings should always be ignored, such as articles (the, a, an) and thoroughfare names if at the beginning of a string (rue, avenue, viale). Other exceptions will depend on the contents of your database. If you sell flour to bakers, then your Dutch database will probably be full of company names starting with the word 'bakkerij', such as

    Bakkerij Dehaene

and somewhere else in your database will probably occur

    Dehaene, Bakkerij.

A simple match code creation program will not find this duplicate. A match code generator with a look-up table which is asked to ignore the word 'bakkerij' (as well as spacing and punctuation) will ensure that this duplicate is given the same match code and can be identified and flagged.

In summary, then, match codes for company name database deduplication are best created by ignoring punctuation and spacing, common text strings and, in certain circumstances, letters which can be accented.

Deduplication programs based on such match codes will undoubtedly find a large numbers of doubles. But the number of doubles which are missed can also be very large. In using a match code, you are gambling not only on the accuracy and correct format and typing of one part of an address but on many parts of an address. A single difference in any of the character strings used in the match code will result in the match not being found. This methodology removes the definite doubles but leaves the doubtfuls behind.

Another method of identifying doubles is to use fuzzy logic by taking all of the components (characters) of all (or a selection) of the name and address items, juggling them around and then assessing the *degree* of similarity between this address and other addresses. The customer can decide to what degree it wants to accept the similarity as a double. For example, accepting 90 per cent similarity would find fewer duplicates, whilst accepting 70 per cent would find more duplicates but would also remove a number of good addresses. This method can find certain duplicates which cannot be found using match codes because it does not need to take account of the order of letters, making typos less influential in the deduplication process. Furthermore, a degree of intelligence can be built into such programs by allowing them to identify sound-alike characters (c and k for example) and giving them the same value; to ignore certain strings (like Ltd, Bakkerij, etc.) and to identify common short forms of names (Bob for Robert for example). Using this form of deduplication does not in any way negate the need for consistency within a database. Consistently writing certain information in the same way is a great asset when using this deduplication system.

When the list to be used does not belong to the company doing the mailing, or the amount of importance given to the customer irritation factor and cost of mailing doubles is low, match code or fuzzy-logic deduplication procedures are practised so that the process is fast and labour extensive.

Companies should show more appreciation for the effect that their mailings have on the people receiving their package. Not only can doubles cost a lot of money, they irritate to the extent that pressure is rising for increased legislative controls on mailings throughout Europe. Unless companies put more effort into removing doubles from their lists and become less interested in the *total* number of communications made and become more interested in the total *effective* number of communications made with a greater than 80 per cent deduplication rate, then the choice may be taken out of their hands.

How do you increase the number of duplicates found?

High double rates are, amongst other things, the result of losing the human element in deduplication procedures.

Let us look at an example where the procedure goes wrong. A colleague of mine subscribed to an American magazine from a company which did not structure its database flexibly or consistently, and had no idea of the differences between European countries and between Europe and the USA. My colleague was receiving two of every issue of the magazine, which is rather expensive for the publishers and also rather irritating for my colleague. The envelopes were addressed in this way:

900880 SIT AVEREG92   095H

RUTH SMITH   MAY 92
SINCAP EUROPE SA B1050   AIR0
AVE REGINE 150
BRUSSELS BELGIUM

900889 SIT 1050B094   095H

                                       MAY 92
RUTH SMITH   AIR0
1050 BRUSSELS
SINCAP
AVE REGINE 150
BELGIUM

Apart from not respecting the rule of the exclusiveness of each field for the data intended for it, the company obviously did not know which information belonged where in the address. It was inconsistent (note the postcode – 1050 and B1050), and the result is that its match codes (SIT AVEREG and SIT 1050B), evidently based on the surname and parts of the address, will never identify this double.

My conscientious colleague rang up this company to inform it of its expensive error. She was informed that it could only find her in the database if she could quote the match code on the label. Of course, she no longer had *either* of the envelopes. In some organizations she would have received only the contents of the envelope in any case, it being opened by a secretary or assistant, and even if she received the mailing whole the chances that she had kept one of the envelopes would have been small, even had I not myself retrieved them from her waste bin to use as an example in this book. To add insult to injury, when taking my colleague's details to try to trace her in another way, she was asked 'Could you spell Belgium for me please?'

It is true that in any mark-merge program you will be gambling (after, of course, taking the necessary precaution of being consistent) that the data is correct. And running, deduplication program based on a match-key form like that described by Shaw and Stone above will have the effect of flagging a certain number of your doubles. But it won't be enough, and you should not stop your deduplication process there as, unfortunately, do most companies. You should continue to locate duplicates which have slipped through the match code net by *checking other address elements in turn* rather than gambling on only a single check on a multiple element as in the match code above.

By this I mean that you should continue your deduplication procedure by looking at the postcode, the telephone number and/or the single address element most likely to make a match – the street address. That is, you check a string of the street address, for example, against all other equivalent street address strings. The smaller the string that you take, and the larger the number of different address aspects that you compare, the more doubles that you will be able to find but the longer the procedure will take. The amount of effort you put into this depends on your commitment to database quality, but the effort will be worthwhile to you and to the people whose names are in your database.

As previously explained, locating duplicates on an address string only and using exclusively a computer will result in non-duplicates being identified. Using this procedure, therefore, will require the re-introduction of a human decision element into the process. The computer can find the potential duplicates, but a human being is needed to decide whether or not the records actually are duplicates. This process takes time and carries obvious costs in staff overheads. Again, doubling the number of doubles found in your database could save you much more than you spend on human resources merely in terms of packages, postage or telecommunications costs, and may result in higher response rates to your mailings or calls.

How do you actually deduplicate and merge?

Any successful procedure to deduplicate and merge two databases will require the following steps:

1   Run programs over the databases to give the data consistency. These programs can recognize and correct commonly found inconsistencies. Other inconsistencies can be found by the following methods:

- Sort the incoming database, for example on town and address, to enable manual checks for consistency differences between this and your database, or between this and another incoming database.
- List the contents of the database (on hard copy or onto the monitor).
- Check which elements of the data need to be made consistent.
- Run programs over the database for each country represented to make the data consistent. Use the guidelines provided for each country in the later chapters of this book.

2   Identify doubles using a classic match code system (ignoring punctuation, spacing, common words and, in certain circumstances, letters which can be accented).
3   Identify further doubles (in certain countries only) by comparing on postal code. Allow manual confirmation, and flag duplicates, filtering out addresses already identified as doubles.
4   Identify doubles using the telephone number (where available).
5   Identify doubles using one element of the address based ideally on a match code created from the address element concerned, ignoring punctuation, spacing, vowels and (potentially) accented or easily confused consonants.
6   Repeat 5 for other parts of the address.
7   Append non-duplicates to the new database.
8   Ensuring that you specify which data should be merged, merge duplicates, using manual intervention where necessary.

In more detail, these steps involve the following. Your first action is to get all of the data in the new file into the same **structure** as that in your own file. This will involve fragmenting where necessary, such as splitting surnames from first names. You must then make sure that the data is in the same **format** as that in your original file. Chapters 5 and 6 'Handling the data in practice' and the chapters on each European country will suggest how best to do this. Put the telephone number in the format you desire, the street address in the correct version with consistent (and preferably correct) abbreviations (or full names) used for the street type, check that the cities are spelt correctly and so on. There are certain inconsistencies which will occur regularly (such as, for example using the abbreviation Str for Strasse in Germany), and you might like to write or buy programs which you run over address lists as a matter of course. After that, however, check your data by making a hard copy (or list the fields onto the monitor). You might be surprised just how inconsistent inconsistencies can be. Sort the file, ideally on the field which you are checking for inconsistencies, and make a listing of the file. In this way you can, with a little studying of the list, put that magnificent machine, your brain to work and ensure that a magnificent database results.

Once you have completed this, and you are satisfied that the data in your new file matches the format of the old, you can set to work on the flagging of duplicates. Deduplication programs do not necessarily need much computer memory, but they do need some time to run because they must constantly access the disk. Keep both files apart until all marking has been completed.

After running a classic deduplication program based on a match code over the database, you can then continue your search using parts of the address. Start by using the postal code in some countries, such as the UK and The Netherlands, where each postcode represents either a single user or a limited number of addresses. After that, take the telephone number, if it is available, and then the street address. As an example, let us say that you search on the first 10 digits of the address (ignoring punctuation and spacing). Take the first 10 digits of the address of the first record of your old file and have the program search for an identical string in the address field of the new file *within the same country* (this reduces the amount of unnecessary checking by the operator). If the computer finds a match, you need to check that it is, indeed, a duplicate. You might do this by bringing the name and address from the old file and the match from the new file onto the screen and basically ask a single question : 'Is this a double?' Your operator can then indicate a Y or N (or a 0 or 1, for example, which are closer together on the keyboard). The computer then searches for the next incidence of the string in the new file. When no more incidences are found, the computer takes the first 10 digits from the address field of the second record of the old file and so the process continues. Deduplication in this way is actually made much more effective if a match code is made of the address element, without its vowels, punctuation or any consonants which can be accented in the language concerned, and then by comparing a shorter string, say 5 digits of the address element match code rather than 10 digits of the unchanged address element. So, for example,

    Koelnstrasse 51 and
    Kölnstrasse 51

will not be found unless a match code ignoring the vowels (being KLNSTRSS51 in each case) is used.

Note that if your database contains business addresses, you will often find more than one business registered at the same address. This might be the same company operating under a different name, a related company, or an entirely different company. We could flag these as doubles and therefore remove them from the database, but this would be short-sighted. These businesses, even if both are arms of the same business or otherwise related, might be slightly different legal entities or have slightly different activities, which are highly relevant factors for your direct marketing purposes. Perhaps more importantly, you should not delete but *flag* such occurrences. If a company has been found under two different names or under two different variants of the same name, then the chances are that it presents itself to the world in both ways because the original information must have come from somewhere. This being the case, the best chance to avoid deleting them and then re-entering them later from another source is to flag these records as being *related*. This increases the efficacy of deduplication procedures whilst enabling you to prevent sending two of the same mailing, for example, to related companies.

Note also at this point that in The Netherlands and Germany, mailing addresses (i.e. postbox numbers) have different postcodes to street addresses for the same company. As businesses in these countries commonly have two addresses, one mailing and one street address, your database will end up with at least 50 per cent duplicates if this is not taken into account at the deduplication stage. Without looking at the company name as a string, or the telephone number, these duplicates are very difficult to locate, and are impossible to locate using a match code only.

Within each phase, when the computer program or operator indicates that a double exists, the double in the new file is marked as such, and the identification code of the old record is copied to the new so that they can be easily found when the marking part of the process is over. As this double has already been found, it is no longer checked in the other stages, making each stage progressively easier and quicker.

You can limit the number of non-duplicates located by allowing a filter on country code or postcode area, provided, of course, that you are sure that this information is correct. Every use, however, of other data within the database as a filter will inevitably reduce the number of doubles found as the chance of an error or typo increases.

When all the addresses have been checked in this way, re-check the records not already paired with a duplicate on another variable such as postbox number or company name (another good reason to ensure that this information is added consistently and correctly). In this way you will find many more duplicates than any system using a single match code.

This is monotonous work, but your database is the heart and soul of your direct marketing business, and it is what makes direct marketing unique. It is worth every bit of effort that you put into it. Using this system you can check a database containing 30,000 names in a single day (although running the computer programs to make data consistent etc. will add to this time). That single day's work could find you many more duplicates than another way of working. If 10 per cent more of the records are found to be duplicates, for example, this saves you not only the irritation of 3,000 of these recipients, who might buy your product and make the whole process doubly worthwhile, but it will also save you the cost of printing and posting 3000 mailing packages. That is certainly a worthwhile result!

When you have finished the flagging, you can simply append the non-flagged records to your original database. They are already consistent with your existing data formats, and are ready to fit neatly into your database and work for you.

An example of a deduplication exercise

To give some ideas of how these factors can affect the number of duplicates identified, let me describe a test case. Two lists were chosen for Belgium, one of 5,595 records from a highly respected Belgian list supplier, and one of 3,180 records from an American supplier. It was expected that a high number of duplicates would be found. These two databases were chosen not to show the greatest possible difference between traditional match code techniques and those discussed above, but to show the *least* possible difference. Belgian addresses are highly structured, and both databases were already fairly consistently formatted. Furthermore, the American database contained a very high number of typos which cannot be affected by improving database consistency or changing the way in which the match code is produced, and the bilingual street addresses were also impervious to these changes.

My aim, then, was to show the minimum difference that can be made by taking the measures discussed above and applying them even to consistent databases where the changes would not be expected to make much difference.

The 9-digit match code was created on the basis of the first 4 postcode characters, the first 3 company name characters and the last 2 street address characters (in Belgium the house number follows the street name). After the match code had been used for deduplication, checks were made using a human-interface on the basis of the first 14 characters of the address and company name, on the first 7 characters of a match code formed from the company name and then from the street address by ignoring punctuation, spacing and letters which could be accented, and on the complete subscriber's telephone number. The process was then repeated using a match code created without punctuation, and then again using a match code without punctuation and ignoring certain strings found in the company name, such as words indicating the type of company (e.g. baker) and definite and indefinite articles.

Next, the data was given a measure of consistency by putting the house number in its correct place in the address where necessary, making all thoroughfare type indications etc. consistent,

Table 4.1   Deduplication rates

Before the data was made consistent

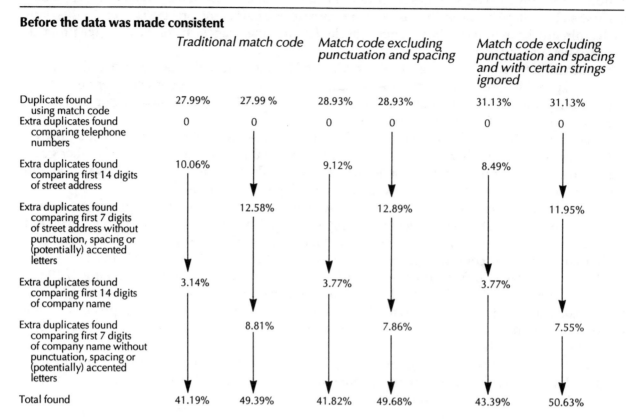

	Traditional match code		Match code excluding punctuation and spacing		Match code excluding punctuation and spacing and with certain strings ignored	
Duplicate found using match code	27.99%	27.99 %	28.93%	28.93%	31.13%	31.13%
Extra duplicates found comparing telephone numbers	0	0	0	0	0	0
Extra duplicates found comparing first 14 digits of street address	10.06%		9.12%		8.49%	
Extra duplicates found comparing first 7 digits of street address without punctuation, spacing or (potentially) accented letters		12.58%		12.89%		11.95%
Extra duplicates found comparing first 14 digits of company name	3.14%		3.77%		3.77%	
Extra duplicates found comparing first 7 digits of company name without punctuation, spacing or (potentially) accented letters		8.81%		7.86%		7.55%
Total found	41.19%	49.39%	41.82%	49.68%	43.39%	50.63%

After the data was made consistent

(The telephone numbers in both databases were inconsistently added, and therefore no duplicates were found on the basis of the telephone number in the case above. After they were made consistent, many duplicates were identified on the basis of telepone number. To make this section more comparable with that above, the figures in brackets show the number of duplicates found when the telephone number was not used during deduplication.)

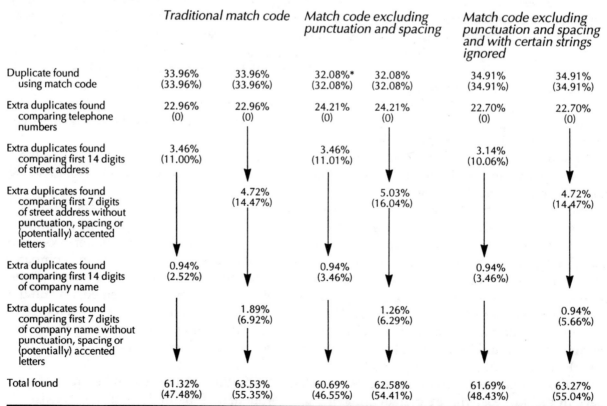

	Traditional match code		Match code excluding punctuation and spacing		Match code excluding punctuation and spacing and with certain strings ignored	
Duplicate found using match code	33.96% (33.96%)	33.96% (33.96%)	32.08%* (32.08%)	32.08% (32.08%)	34.91% (34.91%)	34.91% (34.91%)
Extra duplicates found comparing telephone numbers	22.96% (0)	22.96% (0)	24.21% (0)	24.21% (0)	22.70% (0)	22.70% (0)
Extra duplicates found comparing first 14 digits of street address	3.46% (11.00%)		3.46% (11.01%)		3.14% (10.06%)	
Extra duplicates found comparing first 7 digits of street address without punctuation, spacing or (potentially) accented letters		4.72% (14.47%)		5.03% (16.04%)		4.72% (14.47%)
Extra duplicates found comparing first 14 digits of company name	0.94% (2.52%)		0.94% (3.46%)		0.94% (3.46%)	
Extra duplicates found comparing first 7 digits of company name without punctuation, spacing or (potentially) accented letters		1.89% (6.92%)		1.26% (6.29%)		0.94% (5.66%)
Total found	61.32% (47.48%)	63.53% (55.35%)	60.69% (46.55%)	62.58% (54.41%)	61.69% (48.43%)	63.27% (55.04%)

Note: *This unexpectedly lower figure was due to the very large number of typos and errors pertaining to the thoroughfare type in the American database. This has less effect on the match code created with punctuation included because this usually contained only the house number and a space. As ,with the space being ignored, the last digit(s) of the thoroughfare type was included in the match code, the typos lowered the number of duplicates found.

correcting postcodes and so on; and then the process was repeated. The results are shown in Table 4.1.

With the inconsistent data, checking the data on various address strings following the match code checking process succeeded in this example in finding about 45 per cent more duplicates in each case than we found using the match code alone. When the address strings without punctuation or (potentially) accented characters were checked, the number of extra duplicates found rose in each case to about 55 per cent.

Using an unimproved match code on consistent data found 21 per cent more duplicates than when the data was inconsistent. Interactively checking address and company name strings on the consistent data after the match code checking process almost doubled the number of duplicates found. Where the telephone number was not used for deduplication, the use of an address and company name string without punctuation, spacing or (potentially) accented characters had an especially significant effect on the results.

The difference between the lowest number of duplicates found (traditional match code only on inconsistent data) and the best (match code excluding punctuation and certain strings, plus interactive string checks on address and company name excluding punctuation, spacing and (potentially) accented characters, on the consistent data) was a massive 126 per cent. Even excluding telephone numbers from the equation, the latter still found 97 per cent more duplicates than the former. This may not seem an excessively high figure, but it can have a significant effect on costs, and this figure may be a great deal higher for databases which are less consistent to start with or contain fewer typos and no bilingual addresses. Also, as the way in which the match code was created was improved, the number of doubles found using only the match code increased, decreasing the amount of work needed to locate extra duplicates using interactive checking of address and company name strings. Again, it must be emphasized that the increased number of duplicates found using these methods can be much higher. A database for the UK, for example, containing 25,000 records and deduplicated in this way was shown, using telemarketing, to contain less than 2 per cent duplicates.

Internal deduplication

This discussion has referred to 'external deduplication', where two or more databases are being compared to each other and then merged to make a single database. If this database is used only once, and the process is repeated for each direct marketing action, it is the only form of deduplication that you need to practise. If, however, databases are being imported into a central database which is to be used over and over again, it is essential that *internal deduplication* is also practised. This, simply, is deduplication within a single database, and is necessary because external deduplication processes are never 100 per cent effective. If each import of an external database brings 2–3 per cent duplicates with it, after many imports the number of duplicates within the database can become unacceptably high. These duplicates were not found the first time around for a reason – a typo, for example – and will not be found the second time around if no change has been made to the record within the database. However, as your database is being used, corrections and improvements will be made to each record – a typo corrected, a telephone number added, a format corrected and so on. Each change or correction will increase the chance of finding the duplicate, so internal deduplication will become an effective option. Internal deduplication requires no re-structuring or making consistent of the data (as this should have been done on import), but the rest of the deduplication procedure remains the same. You can either compare each record with each other record within your single database, or make a copy of the database and treat the process as an external deduplication (with the difference that each record must ignore its twin in the other database).

Merging

As I have already mentioned, merging can take one of two forms – retaining one record in its entirety whilst ignoring its duplicate completely (as practised in most merge-purge routines) or merging data from a record in one file into its duplicate in another file (as in the mark-merge routines). It is the latter form which you should practise if your database contains more than just name and address information. You will want to make a database which is richer than any one of the contributing sources, containing selected information from each. Some data will be more trustworthy than others, but no source will be so good that you will want to replace your existing information willy-nilly.

You can update all information for merging by hand. This would make the maximum use of human intuition and would certainly result in a good database. But this method is exceptionally time-consuming, and unsuitable for any database with more than, say 10,000 entries in total.

You should therefore be able to tell your merge program which items you do want to replace and which items you would prefer to retain provided that they come from a particular source. This is one of the reasons that you are advised always to source code all pieces of information in your database file. Choose in any case data which improves the fullness of your database, for example, choose the first name of your contact from the database which gives the whole name rather than just the initial.

Having taken this initial step, you could leave the computer to do its work, but it will be to your advantage to remember the value of human judgement in merging. From the marking stage of the procedure each record now contains the identification code of its duplicate in the other file, so finding the matches is a simple matter. You could programme your merge file to bring certain relevant fields with their source information from the old and new file up onto the screen when there is a variance of more than a certain percentage. For example, your old file notes that there are 50 employees in a company, whilst the new claims 60. Bringing these onto the screen and asking which is most likely to be correct requires little effort but adds enormously to the quality of the database.

Evidently, if you are handling databases containing hundreds of thousands of records, this method of deduplication and merging will not always appear suitable, and it is certainly more applicable to databases with a maximum number of records in the tens of thousands. Remember, however, that the more attention that you give to these processes, the more doubles you will find and the more money you will save. The amount of money that you will save will be greater the higher the number of communications made. Minute attention to detail in your database is never wasted.

5 ‖ Handling the data in practice - general principles

The demands on data of input, storage, manipulation and output will often be widely different, and therefore recognizing and putting into practice the optimal method of treating each data type is not easy. You will make errors and have to make alterations, but hopefully the guidelines which follow can help prevent you from falling into too many traps or spending time and money exploring blind alleys.

Although you will have to handle each piece of data according to your own needs, certain rules will be relevant to, and certain pieces of information will be found in, every mailing database. This chapter suggests the best ways to manage some of these data types and forms, adhering to the guidelines laid down in the previous chapters, to give you a well-structured, easily used, accurate and duplicate-poor database to enable you to derive the most from it for direct marketing activities.

It is important at this stage again to make the distinction between the three stages in the life of a piece of data as far as your database is concerned, namely the way the data is entered into the database, the way it is stored in the database; and the way it comes out of the database. That data will often exist in three different forms during each of these stages must be recognized and kept in mind throughout the database-building and maintaining process. Data to be added to the database will virtually never be in the form in which the data should be stored, which in turn will need another transformation for output. Take, for example, the telephone number. A telephone number in the form 071-123 4567 may preferably be output as (071) 123 45 67, but whilst in the database it is better stored in two fields as 071 and 1234567. Whilst planning and structuring your database, you must consider that your data must be able to move through each of these stages without problems or hold-ups, whilst maintaining a form which will allow optimal use and management. Any structure which prevents this movement will be detrimental to your system and to the quality of your data. No attempt will be made here to advise on the type and nature of the interface between the database and the users. Information is provided instead on the data management system itself, the preferable **structure** of the parts of any database containing the different data forms mentioned; and the **form** in which the data is best stored.

Gleaned from experience with dozens of imported databases, knowledge of correct output formats and internal database management, I have provided below some general guidelines and specific examples on the best way to handle particular types of information and data in your direct marketing database. Whilst this information concentrates on the way the data reaches you, and the way your database can best store it, consult Chapter 7 and the chapters on individual countries to discover the best way to output the data for each European country.

Remembering always the principles of database management outlined in Chapter 3, one can distinguish between the management of two data-field types: those needing to be designed to ensure accuracy and maximum utility; and those needing to be accurate but which will also be used in an operational manner to help in such procedures as deduplication. Knowing which fields will be used operationally will very much dictate the way in which a database is best structured.

Database structure and field exclusiveness

Keep in mind at all times the guidelines listed in Chapters 2 and 3. As a general rule you should allow a separate field for each piece of information required. This must especially be the case where different parts of a compound piece of information can (consistently) change independently of other part(s), such as the area code and subscriber's number in a telephone number.

Maintain always each field exclusively for the data for which it was intended. Avoid, therefore, not only putting more than one piece of information into each field, but also spilling over from one field to another. If a piece of information is too long for its field, either shorten the information (in a consistent manner) or increase the capacity of the field. Failure to do so will destroy consistency in the database. If you wish to add information for which no field exists, add a field rather than adding the data to a field meant for other data. Ignoring field exclusivity will, after a time, make a database as useless for direct marketing as a listing on paper.

Allow space in the database not only for the *storage* of information, but also for 'working' fields, where data can be set temporarily or flags activated or deactivated during programs as necessary.

Database importing

Whatever the source of data for your database, every record acquired externally, whether from directories, business cards or databanks, will eventually end up in a digital format and will need to be integrated into your existing database, using the deduplication and merging procedures discussed in the previous chapter. When the data is in a digital format, procedures need to be followed to make the structure and the data compatible with your database. Do not cut corners at this stage. Imposing the same level of consistency, fragmentation etc. on the data in the imported database before attempting to integrate it with your own database will only be to your advantage.

Though each incoming database will have to be inspected individually to see what needs to be changed or manipulated to bring it into line with your own database, certain procedures will almost always be needed so a number of standard programs, once written, will remain very useful. These programs are best written on a country-by-country and language-by-language basis, as most address idiosyncracies are found on these levels.

Program Structure

It is best not to embed ephemeral information into programs, but to use a set of look-up tables which are easily changed and expanded as necessary, as address conventions, postcode patterns and so on change and develop. Look-up tables are themselves databases containing information which the program 'looks up' when running. For example, a look-up table to change town names in The Netherlands might be structured in this way:

	Correct Name	Incorrect Name 1	Incorrect Name 2, etc.
Record 1	Den Haag	's-Gravenhage	The Hague
Record 2	Vlissingen	Flushing	Fléssingue
Record 3	Den Bosch	's-Hertogenbosch	
etc.			

The program would locate incorrect town names from the look-up table in the database and then replace them with the correct name, also from the look-up table. This means that a single program can be used for all countries – the town names do not form an integral part of the program, and this in turn means that the look-up table can be added to and modified easily and quickly using an interactive database program as you find new idiosyncracies or as changes are made in the countries concerned.

For example, German postcodes prior to 1st July 1993 contained 4 consecutive digits starting with any number between 1 and 9. Many database managers used programs which had this information embedded within them, thus the program allowed only 4 digits, the first of which could not be zero. Other database managers kept this information in a separate database which the program looked up when checking postcode formats. The latter could easily change their look-up database, using an interactive database program, when the postcodes changed to 5 digits, beginning with any number including zero. The former, having often only a compiled program rather than the source, had more problems, having to rely on the company which wrote the program, if it was not their own company, to make these changes for them in the programming itself.

Upper case or lower case?

Externally acquired databases will often contain data in upper case. Almost equally often they will contain the data in mixed upper and lower case. Changing all data to upper case is very easy. Changing all data to mixed case is much more difficult. This poses a problem.

'Dear Mr. GRAHAM'

my credit card company, which should know my surname , wrote to me recently,

' blah blah blah .... We thank you, Mr GRAHAM, for your trust. . . .'

Personally, although I like letters to begin with my name (my correct name, that is), I must say that I find it distinctly irritating to be reminded of it throughout the letter. Accepting, however, that this form of personalization works and is therefore here to stay, it is made much worse when it screams from a page of mixed case in capital letters. It is difficult enough to keep your recipients' minds where you want them to be – on the fantastic offer you are making – without having their names jumping out of the page in capital letters wherever they look.

The human eye, in the head of the recipient of your message, usually prefers to see information in mixed case, especially when embedded in a message which is already in mixed case, as in the example above. This might suggest that you should store the data in your database in mixed case, but, as has already been mentioned, the way data should be stored in a database is often different from the way in which it should be output. Whichever way you choose to store the data, you will have problems, and therefore, for the sake of smooth database manipulation, I would advise that you store the data in upper case. If you are importing data in upper case, and your database is in mixed case, you will have to translate the upper case data to mixed case. If your database is in upper case and you wish to output in mixed case, you must do the same. The process is the same, but moving the case change process from the input to the output stage and storing data in upper case provides a number of advantages:

- Easier data entry – errors in case are avoided at this level.
- Optimal data manipulation opportunities without the chance of error or difficulty caused by mixed case.
- It aids consistency, which in turn greatly increases accuracy, flexibility, accessibility to and usefulness of the database.

Programs can be made which will output your upper case words in lower case, forcing lower case between extraction and printing. If necessary, your word-processing program can force lower case in the mailmerge file. Forcing lower case, however, involves more problems than you might imagine, as you will have to train your program to recognize certain capitalization rules, and there are different capitalization rules in different names and languages. Although real names in English are usually spelt with a capital letter, in many languages this is not the case. Equally, prepositions are usually not capitalized, and must therefore retain lower case letters which means that your programs should be able to recognize the prepositions in the language of the address information. In German, all nouns are capitalized; in Dutch not all parts of a contact name are capitalized; and in French and Spanish, the names of thoroughfare types begin with a lower-case letter. So, for example,

Mr. A. van den Broek; and
17, rue de la Montagne.

Abbreviations, such as PLC, must also be retained in upper case, and where these are not separated by full stops or spaces, they cannot be programmatically identified. The British Post Office, for example, sends letters to me as

Mr GRAHAM Rhind
Malpotom Europe Sa

The 'Sa' is an abbreviation for Société Anonyme and should be written SA. If you want a program to take these idiosyncracies into account, you have to be able to 'train' it to recognize them. The chapters on individual countries explain as much as possible capitalization rules for each language.

Note also that many standard database programs do not automatically alter the case of accented letters. So, for example, 'ü' would be retained as such and not changed to 'Ü'. You should also note that many lower case accented letters do not have an upper case ASCII equivalent. You can create an 'í' but not an 'Í' These must therefore be handled separately for each letter and for each language (as upper case equivalents which cannot be formed with an ASCII code are treated differently in each language). Rules for each European language are given in the chapter 'Accents and ASCII Codes'.

Numeric or character fields

As you are probably aware, fields in databases are given a particular type: character (alphanumeric), numeric, date, Boolean and so on. For the fields containing the name and address information with which we are particularly concerned in this chapter, you will usually be making a choice between character fields or numeric fields.

It is important to realize that it is not so much the *contents* of the field which are important when deciding on a field type, but *what you are going to do with them*. As a rule, data should only be stored in numeric fields if the intention is to carry out one or other mathematical operations on that data. So, for example, a company's profit is best stored in a numeric field because you will want to add data from one record to that of another, or show this data at different exchange rates for different currencies. On the other hand, no one will ever want or need to add up or multiply postcodes or telephone numbers, so even if the data itself is numeric, it should *always* be stored in character fields. When Germany introduced postcodes with 0 as the first digit, those people who had stored postcodes in numeric fields had to change this to a character field (and alter the related programming) as numeric fields do not allow numbers starting with 0 to be stored with the initial 0.

Address language

Virtually all countries in Europe contain people who speak more than one language. In some countries, such as Belgium, this language differentiation has sharp geographical boundaries. In other countries, like Spain and Switzerland, the boundaries between language groups are fuzzy and ill-defined, but there is, nevertheless, a definite geographical expression of this language. Other language groups, like Romany speakers and speakers of new immigrant languages such as the people from North Africa and Turkey, have no territorial basis.

It is always necessary not only to define the language of the contact name (as discussed below) but also, where possible, to define the language of the address. This can usually (but not always) be made on the basis of postcode. In borderline cases, or in bilingual areas such as Brussels, it is often possible to recognize the language of the address based on clues given within the street address, such as the thoroughfare type names used. Knowing the language of the address is useful for determining correct formats, correct town names and so on. For example, the abbreviation 'str.' in Belgium will mean 'straat' in the Flemish-speaking areas but 'Strasse' in the German-speaking areas; the address 'Avenue Louise' in Brussels would need the town name 'Bruxelles', whilst 'Louizalaan' would require 'Brussel'. In those countries, therefore, where more than one territorially-based language exists, coding of address language is strongly advised.

Abbreviations

Abbreviations and acronyms will usually appear in one of eight ways: with full stops, spaces, both or neither, in upper case or in lower case:

AGM
agm
A G M
a g m
A.G.M.
a.g.m.
A. G. M.
a. g. m.

Most delivered databases, in my experience, form abbreviations in one or more of the first four forms shown in the example above. I cannot say what people prefer to see on their address labels – it seems to depend on personal preference – but it is more accurate to add full stops to abbreviations and this also helps in case manipulation – single letters before full stops can be identified as needing to remain in upper case for output. This same action cannot be carried out for all letters preceding a space or all letters preceding other letters. It is easier to remove elements from character strings in a database than to add them – making spaces and full stops into strings without either full stops or spaces, or full stops into spaces is far easier than vice versa, but whilst a company may not object to being addressed as 'ABC' instead of 'A.B.C.', an individual will sometimes object to being called 'GR Rhind' or 'Gr Rhind' instead of 'G.R. Rhind'. The difference between a company name abbreviation and personal initials cannot be recognized by a computer.

In company types, street addresses and contact names, many abbreviations such as PLC, Ph.D. and BA regularly occur, and as such can be recognized and changed by a computer program. In the name of companies themselves, however, this is not the case. Although the problem of inconsistent abbreviations can be circumvented by ignoring punctuation and spacing in the deduplication procedure, the rules of consistency and accuracy apply, not least because it helps you to find companies more easily in the database. For this reason, it is possible and recommended to give abbreviations a consistent format, preferably with full stops, which is more accurate, or with spaces. Removing both full stops and spaces is a mistake because this process is irreversible. You will be unable to change abbreviations with neither spaces nor full stops into abbreviations with spaces or full stops except manually where an abbreviation is recognized as such.

And, & and +

Company names will often contain the word 'AND' (or its local language equivalent) and the symbols '&' and '+' interchangeably. The symbol '+' often appears in German company names. These can be made consistent. It really does not make too much difference in some languages whether you change 'AND' to '&' or vice versa. The word 'AND' on its own will very rarely mean anything else in a company name, neither will '&', so changing one to the other should not present problems. On the other hand, in some languages, like Italian (where 'AND' is 'E') and Spanish (where 'AND' is 'Y' or 'E'), it is absolutely impossible to change all free-standing examples of the local word for 'AND' to '&' because by doing this, a person's initials, parts of abbreviations and so on are also (incorrectly) changed.

Deduplication programs can best be trained to ignore all occurrences of each version of 'AND'. (The chapters on individual countries provide the translation of the word 'and' into the local language(s).)

Articles

Definite articles ('THE') and indefinite articles ('A', 'AN') will very often appear in company names, unfortunately in any number of formats. They might appear in front of or at the end of the name, after a comma or between brackets. Although a good deduplication program can be trained to ignore articles, most will not, and the general need for consistency remains. You should therefore strive to put the article always at the front of the name, or always at the end, and in a consistent format.

Putting the article at the end tends to be favoured by some managers because it leaves the company name proper so to speak at the beginning of the field, upon which a match code will be made. On the other hand, this strikes a false note and can cause irritation when output for the recipient of your mailing. An article's natural place in a sentence is before the noun to which it refers, and my preference is to put it there and to use better deduplication procedures which can recognize and ignore articles to overcome any problems that this might create.

One way that many database managers avoid this, and other, similar, problems is to create two fields for such data, one to contain the original data, and one to create data which can be used operationally. In this case, for example, one field can contain names with the articles in front, whilst a second, used for creating match codes for deduplication, contains no articles or has the articles at the end of the string. This is certainly a solution but it has two consequences. The first is that it tends to distract attention from other factors relating to the data, such as the need for consistency. The operational field is made consistent whilst the data field itself is largely ignored. Secondly, the inevitable consequence of this is a reduction in the accuracy of data. A data field containing all of the articles in front of the company name, for example, is consistent and accurate, and effective programs can be written to ignore the article when this data is being used operationally. If a second field is not strictly necessary, it is better to keep to a single field.

The chapters on individual countries provide the translation of articles into the local language(s).

Accents

Most European languages contain accented and unique letters. Not all of these letters can be created on a computer. Some acquired databases will use an accented letter, some will use a correct ASCII equivalent whilst others will use an incorrect equivalent. Kölnstrasse, for example, might be found in a database as Kolnstrasse or Koelnstrasse. It is impossible to know that either of these should, in fact, be Kölnstrasse. Accents should, as much as possible, be retained in address databases. They do make it a good deal easier for the user of that language to read a text, and give no cause for indignation in that user. Operationally, the consistency problems that this may produce can be overcome by ignoring letters which can be accented in the creation of match codes etc. during deduplication. In any case, you should satisfy yourself that the accent situation is satisfactory before you purchase a database. Another alternative is to store data in two fields: one with the correct accents, in the other the same data with correct non-accented equivalents.

Using the example of the German postcode changes in 1993, the database provided by the Bundespost to aid in the assignment of new codes contained two fields in this way, one with the correct accents, the other with the correct non-accented equivalents for operational use. Databases which contained no accents and no correct equivalents would have, to a greater extent, had to have been assigned their new postcodes manually.

It is easy to alter accented characters to their correct equivalents but more difficult to reverse the process. Ü in German is easily replaced by UE, but all UEs cannot be changed to Ü because UE exists as a letter combination in its own right.

It is not necessary to retain two fields for town names. There are more limited numbers of these, and they can usually be identified by postal code. You know, for example, that Koln and Koeln, in postal code area 5, refer to the city of Köln, and you can alter your database as such (using a programme based on a look-up table).

Quotation marks

Addresses, especially those containing house names, will often contain quotation marks, thus:

'The Laurels',
14 The Footpath

If you can train your deduplication program to ignore these quotation marks, all well and good, but their presence destroys consistency and can make other operations more difficult. Again, you cannot programmatically add quotation marks, because you cannot train a computer to know where they should appear. Quotation marks are not really necessary and are best removed from addresses.

Apostrophes

Bought databases will often omit apostrophes. In English, where apostrophes indicate missing letters or possession, these cannot programmatically be added and must equally not be removed. In other languages, such as French, apostrophes appear where certain words occur before a vowel and a letter is dropped. Because these occurrences are not difficult to locate, it is possible to write a program to add apostrophes where they have been omitted and replaced with a space. This improves the appearance and the readability of your communication for the recipient of your mailing.

The identification code

As already discussed in Chapter 2 direct marketing databases are best kept in a relational database structure, and each record within these databases needs a unique identification code to link it to records in every other database.

Although this means that each record in the mother database has a unique code, this is not the case in daughter databases where more than one record can belong to a single mother, and therefore each have the same linking code. As you may wish to use data in daughter databases (such as one containing employee names) for activities such as mailings or telemarketing, and because the daughter database files may themselves be the mother of another daughter database file, you also need to give each record in a daughter database a unique identification code alongside the code linking the record to the mother database to be able easily to re-integrate data, mailing replies and so on, into these databases. Thus records in daughter databases should have two identification codes – one to make the link to the mother database, the other a unique code within the daughter database.

The unique identification codes are *not* the same as match codes created for deduplication, and you should avoid the temptation to treat them in the same way. Match codes are not necessarily unique, and when a piece of information changes in a record, so does the match code. Identification codes should be treated as unique and unchangeable.

The record status

Good database managers do not delete records; they flag them. Your records should always therefore contain fields which indicate the status of aspects of the address. You might, for example, flag the street address itself as being correct, incorrect, moved, bankrupt or closed down; the telephone number as being correct, incorrect or incomplete; a contact name as being correct, incorrect, no longer at this company or deceased; and so on. Flagging in itself gives you endless opportunities for preventing shoddy direct marketing and making the most of the database, but flagging instead of deleting addresses and contact names has the added advantage of preventing the re-integration of this same, incorrect, information from other databases into yours, and it preserves the wealth of each record, which can be very useful for follow-ups and analyses.

The source history

It is beneficial to know from where the information on a particular person or company has come. This shows the amount of synchronicity between different sources, enabling a better management of sources, and also gives an idea of the quality of the information contained within the record. You might store the date and source for every change that is made to a record in the database in a daughter database, for example. When a corresponding data record is located in the database and an external source, but no changes are made, you should still habitually note the source and date of the external information source for the appropriate record. Omitting this might suggest that a record which has remained unchanged for so-many years is redundant whilst in fact it is up to date and accurate, but not flagged as being so.

It is also worthwhile to note the sources of important pieces of information in the database such as numbers of employees in a company, individual contact names, turnover and so on. By so doing, rather than allowing any merge program simply to overwrite existing data willy-nilly, a set of priorities can be built in to reflect the confidence which you have in different sources. Thus an import might overwrite data from one less reliable source but not data from another source which you consider to be more reliable.

Data entry using templates

Programs can be devised which will make existing data consistent and accurate. If your database requires manual data entry, you can assist the data entry staff and guarantee certain aspects of consistency at the input stage by programming into your interface a number of templates allowing only correct data patterns. Thus, for example, a telephone number in France must have eight numeric digits whilst a postcode in Germany must have five. This also reduces the chances of typing errors. These templates must be easy and quick to alter as data formats change regularly.

6 | Handling the data in practice - data types

Certain data types can be managed and manipulated in specific ways which increase the value of your database. Each data type common to all direct marketing databases is discussed here in turn.

The company name

Databases will invariably be supplied with the company name stored in a single field. Fragmentation of this data is, therefore, impossible unless data is to be gathered and entered only within your company, in which case business name and business type (Ltd or PLC for example) can sometimes be distinguished.

It is very difficult indeed to bring absolute consistency into company name fields, as this information is so often written differently according to source. The problems often revolve around abbreviations (with or without spacing or punctuation), and articles and words (before or after the rest of the company name, in different formats) indicating company activity and form. Thus, names could be written:

AGM STATIONERS LTD or
A G M STATIONERS LTD or
A.G.M. STATIONERS LTD
or
THE BEEHIVE or
BEEHIVE, THE or
BEEHIVE (THE)
or
BOULANGERIE DUPONT or
DUPONT (BOULANGERIE)

and so on. For these reasons reliance upon using only the company name in operations like deduplication should be avoided. However, as efficacious deduplication of business databases is not possible without using the company name, attention must be given to achieving consistency in terms of abbreviation punctuation and word order. If your deduplication and merging program takes these differences into account, you should still pay attention to these details: database consistency makes data more easily accessible and this information will appear on address labels and within mailings where its accuracy will avoid irritation to the recipient. A rule of thumb is to follow intuition (making access to the data by the users easier) and write company names as much as possible as the companies would wish them. Thus

49

THE BEEHIVE and
BOULANGERIE DUPONT

are often preferable and more intuitive than the alternatives.

One aspect of the company name that can be made consistent is the business type (i.e. Ltd, PLC, SA etc.), where a limited number of options are available for each country. So, for example, 'Limited' can always be written as any one of 'Limited', 'Ltd.', 'Ltd', 'LTD.', 'LTD' and so on. The most common business types for each country are listed in the chapters on individual countries.

Where possible, you should ideally also attempt to make abbreviations consistent, put the articles in the same place in relation to the rest of the company name and make the word 'and' consistent, as discussed in the previous chapter.

Contact names

The names of individuals usually consist of one or more of the following parts:

- A salutation (Mr, Mrs, Dr, Lord, etc.)
- The first name and/or initials
- The surname
- Suffixes (BA, Ph.D., MBE, etc.)

Although this is a whole, and none of these parts can *consistently* change independently of the other, it is best to store each of these parts in a separate field because you will want to use different parts of a name in different circumstances on the label or within your package.

Consistency in the abbreviation of the salutations is advisable, as is adding first names in full when you know them, enabling you to extract the first initial only where required or the full name in personalizations or on labels.

It is not possible either to deduce gender from salutations or salutations from gender. Some salutations are the same for both sexes (Dr, Professor, etc.), others are optional (Miss, Ms etc.). Equally, it is not always possible to identify gender on the basis of first name, as some names, especially outside the UK, can be used for both genders.

With business contacts, reserve a field for the job title (for labelling) and a different field to code these functions. Coding functions is essential to enable use to be made of a certain type or class of employee only. This is impossible on the basis of job title alone due to the range of versions of each job title and the different languages which will be used, although a look-up table containing job titles to which additions and changes can be made can be used initially to code a proportion of the functions.

Thus, for example, you could build a look-up table which automatically assigns the code '1' to all contact names it finds with the titles 'Managing Director', 'MD', 'M.D.', 'M D', etc. After running this program, uncoded titles can be coded manually, if necessary updating the look-up table in so doing to reduce on each occasion the need and time taken for manual coding.

The bias of your contacts file will reflect your business activity, but the table in the chapter on job titles gives an indication of the most common job titles and their translations into the major European languages.

It is sometimes the case that a single person fulfils more than one function within a company – the Commercial Manager might also function as the Financial Manager, the Managing Director as the Production Manager and so on. You need to flag both of these functions for this person to ensure that any mailing directed at either one of the functions will reach him or her. You might allow more than one field for function coding or, given the strength of relative databasing and the weaknesses inherent in spreading similar information over more than one field within a single record, you might be better advised to add the contact again in a new record with a different job title and function code or create a daughter database for the daughter database containing the person's name. These records can be flagged to show that they are not doubles but a single person doing more than one job, and this flag can also be utilized in a properly constructed output program to ensure that a mailing to be sent to both commercial directors *and* financial directors, for example, would be sent only once to a recipient fulfilling both functions.

Contact languages

Remarkably, proponents of direct mailing will exhort you to attempt cross-border mailings, and assure you that so-many per cent of 'business' people speak English, so you can mail away in English with a clear conscience. Apart from the fact that most of the time this percentage of English speakers is over estimated, it is remarkable how the aims and advantages of direct mailing are so quickly forgotten. One would rarely consider broadcasting an advertisement in English in a non-English speaking country, and never without sub-titles, so why do the same with direct mailing? You will waste a lot of money in this way, and your recipient will be much less receptive to the message which you are trying to convey, as we all are when addressed in a language foreign to us. Mailing in English to a population where 20 per cent *do not* speak English when a mailing in French to the same population would reach every individual is certainly irrational.

You would be well-advised to ensure that you note the language of the respondent. Do not assume that everybody living in France speaks French, for example. Apart from countries which have more than one official language (Belgium, Switzerland), there are also countries with language minorities (France, Spain, Italy, Finland, The Netherlands, Great Britain etc.), and the already significant numbers of non-nationals living in each EEC country will have begun to increase dramatically since 1993. Where mailing is to businesses, bear in mind that a large amount of commuting occurs over language borders within Europe. Note the real language of the respondent, not the language in which you will send him his information. It comes down again to the concept of fullness. You may now have brochures only in English, French, German and Spanish, but if a person speaks Catalonian as a mother language, then note it as such. It is not difficult for you to ensure with your program that people speaking Catalan receive a brochure in Spanish, and your life will be a great deal easier when, with trade to Barcelona increasing dramatically, you decide to produce a brochure in Catalan. To be flexible is to be prepared.

The Street address

The street address will in most cases consist of any number of the following elements:

- A floor number and/or a unit number
- A house name
- A street name
- A thoroughfare type string
- A house number
- A box number and/or a staircase/flat number
- A postbox number
- The name of an industrial or residential estate

Again, fragmentation of these different parts of the address into different fields would be ideal but is hardly practicable unless you are dealing only with data gathered internally – externally gathered data will almost always provide this data in two or three fields in the same order and format as would normally be printed on an envelope. The postbox number is often listed in a separate field, but this is certainly not always the case.

Fragmenting all street addresses for all databases which you are importing and merging into your database would require much work and would rarely be worth your while. However, ensuring that street addresses are added consistently and unfragmented will ensure that when you do need to fragment (albeit temporarily) the street addresses, that this can be achieved without too much trouble.

Taking the example again of the change in German postcodes from 4 to 5 digits, the assigning of the correct new code required the program to know the street name and the house number separately. The Bundespost database stored this information separately, and companies updating their databases had to fragment their addresses in the same way to identify successfully the new postcode number. This is easier to achieve when the street address data is stored in a consistent format.

Attempting to split the house number from the street address is full of problems, and is very difficult to do programmatically, especially considering the fact that street addresses will often contain a whole range of numbers. The house number will often be followed by a box number, a flat number or a staircase number. Street addresses, especially in France, will often contain numeric dates, such as 'rue de 11 novembre 1914', and others, for example in The Netherlands, will contain numbers indicating the *street* number rather than the *house* number, for example '1e Egalantiersgracht'.

Fragmenting addresses can cause extra problems in label printing. Each country has its own way of formatting the street address, which has to be taken into account in the output program. Countries with more than one format of output, such as Switzerland, have to have their format dictated by language, which could either be dictated by postcode or by the contact's language, neither of which are always available in a database. It is therefore better to put street addresses in their correct format at source rather than at output.

If you do, in any case, wish to try to identify and isolate the field containing the street address (as opposed to a house name, unit number and so on), a part of the address which nearly always exists in a database address, and to use this in deduplication, you will need to search the fields for strings containing thoroughfare type strings such as Road, avenue and Strasse. Lists of these thoroughfare type strings are provided in the chapters on individual countries.

When adding addresses, bear in mind that sometimes much of the address can be largely irrelevant, especially in the UK, where some addresses are more a route description from the nearest large town to the house than an address. Knowing that X house, in X street, off Y avenue, in Z, near A in the county of B is informative but largely irrelevant. A street address, town name and postal code are usually more than enough.

Though addresses are difficult to fragment, they often fortunately follow very strict format rules which, provided you ensure that certain consistencies are maintained, can be very reliable when used operationally such as during deduplication. For example, addresses in The Netherlands and Germany are always formatted as:

Street[ ]number

for example,

Molenstraat 51
Bahnhofstrasse 25

whilst those in France are usually

Number[,]street

for example,

19, rue de la Reine

These addresses will often be incorrectly formatted in bought databases, especially if the database was built in a different country to that to which the data refers, in which case it often follows the address format of the country where it was created. It is relatively easy to run programs over street addresses to put data into these correct and consistent formats, in terms of the positions of the different parts of the street address (number, name, thoroughfare type), the punctuation and the consistency of any abbreviations used. Attention should be paid to giving a consistent rendering of the thoroughfare types, such as Road from Rd, Strasse from Str. and so on, using, where known, full words or correct abbreviations, as listed in the chapters on individual countries.

Although correcting street formats programmatically is not difficult, it presents some problems and requires a certain amount of human intervention. An address such as

Mill Road 23

in the UK will require that the number is moved from the end of the street name string to the beginning, but there are addresses where more than one number exists in the street address. How do you tell a program where to split the following address?

rue de 11 novembre 1914 23 boite 17

There are also many cases where the number *should* be at the end of a character string, such as:

Unit 25
Studio 3
Block 2
Suite 7
Number 9
Factory 1
Rear of 17 . . .
Building 3
Floor 5

A well-written program to correct street addresses can be trained (via a look-up table) to recognize these words and not change the format, but this does not help in some cases such as where numeric dates or street numbers rather than house numbers are integral parts of the street address. In these cases, human intervention is needed to tell the computer at which point in the field the split for changing the contents of the field should occur.

The greatest possibility for error in the address lies in the house *numbers*, especially for businesses which occupy more than one number in a street. The address might be given as 41 or 43 or 45 or 41–45 or 41–43 or 43 & 45 or 41/45 or any other combination involving these numbers and the numbers in-between. If possible, identify all possible formats and change them to a single, consistent format such as

number–number, for example 41–45

Another inconsistency is the *dropping* of numbers, such as:

21–3

where 21–23 is meant. As no address is ever written with the highest number first (i.e. in the example above, it is inconceivable that the '3' refers to the real number '3' because in that case it would be written '3–23'), it does not present any problem programmatically to change such occurrences to their full (i.e. 21–23) versions. Some house numbers are followed by letters, which can be written as follows:

41A or
41 A

These, also, can easily be given a consistent format (either with or without the space).

Consistency in address punctuation is also essential. In some countries, no punctuation exists in a street address. In others, such as Spain, it is virtually obligatory. In yet others, such as France and the UK, a street number may be followed by a comma, but does not have to be. Any program which you use to make addresses consistent should ensure that the same punctuation form and format is used throughout for each country or language region.

The Mailing Address

Even when postbox numbers are not separated in the file, it is relatively easy to identify and move this data to a separate field as, mis-typing apart, postbox numbers are always preceded by a word or abbreviation indicating that they are postbox numbers, such as PO BOX, POSTBOKS, CASE POSTALE and so on, upon which you can search. Lists of these are provided in the chapters on individual countries. It is highly desirable to retain both the mailing address and the street address in two separate fields. The latter is, of course, what your salesperson needs for prospecting, but the former is preferable for mailings. In some countries, such as The Netherlands and Germany, the postbox addresses have a different postcode and sometimes a different postal town, so it is necessary to have fields available to store this information. In these countries, where the street address *and* the postbox number are given on the same envelope, the post office concerned will usually try to deliver the package *only* to the postbox at the given postcode. If these do not correspond (i.e. the postcode refers to the street address) then the package will be returned as undeliverable.

The postcode

The postcode is very important to you and for your database. Not only is it of primary value to the post office of the country concerned for delivering your package, but it can also be used by you to identify any number of aspects about the people living there, ranging from their likely socio-economic class to the language that they probably speak. For this reason consistency and accuracy should be striven for in the postcode field of your database, and you should not allow it to be filled with unnecessary data such as the postal sorting code, as given below:

    B-1080
    GB-WC1 2AB

As this code is always the same for every address and postcode in a country, it need not be added to the database at all – it can be added on output dependent on the country concerned. Be aware, however, that imported address lists rarely store postcodes consistently, and some will be preceded by the sorting code in one of two formats:

    B - or
    B-

These you should remove.

Postcodes are highly formatted, and corrections can be made during batch jobs or during data entry, when a template can be used to ensure accuracy. In countries where a single postcode represents a municipality, it is possible to check the settlement name against the postcode for errors.

Most of Europe's smaller countries belong to the postal system of one of their larger neighbours. Thus Liechtenstein belongs to the Swiss postal area , Monaco to the French, San Marino to the Italian and so on. If you buy a database for France, you will often also get a number of addresses for Monaco. Equally, databases can also contain addresses from overseas territories, such as France's West Indian départements. On the basis of postcode, it is possible to identify and flag or re-code these addresses, if so desired. Where one country belongs to the postal system of another, this is specified in the chapter on that country.

Postcode fields in databases should always be character fields. Some countries have postcodes beginning with 0, and these would be lost if entered into a numeric field. Postcode layout and convention is explained for each country in the chapters on individual countries.

The town name

Although at first glance town name would appear ideal for operational use, for sorting and list-ings, and possibly for deduplication and merging operations, this data is not always as consistent as might be required. The first problem is that it is not always obvious in some countries, such as Great Britain, which name should be used where more than one is given. When an address ends Benson, Oxford; Birkenhead, Liverpool; or Sale, Manchester, which should be used? The com-puter cannot decide, and operators will often be unaware that Benson is a small village, Sale a large suburb and that Birkenhead has nothing much to do with Liverpool except in terms of prox-imity.

The other problem is that towns are not often known by a single name. You have the autochthonal name (that used by the inhabitants), that used by speakers of other languages, pop-ular misspellings and then complexities added by the addition or removal of accents, hyphens or spaces. You could, for example, find Cologne in your database as:

Köln
Koeln
Koln
Cologne
Keulen , etc

It is, nevertheless, to your advantage in terms of flexibility as much as possible to control and make consistent these names, and from the point of view of your recipient and of the post office of the country to which you are mailing that the autochthonal name is used. This will often be the name used in databases acquired from the country concerned, and there is no good argument against using this form. These names, along with the alternative foreign language names in six European languages, are provided in the chapters on individual countries.

Other aspects of a town's name may also require some work before it becomes consistent. A common source of inconsistency, for example, is the word 'Saint', which is often found in European town names and in any one of a number of forms. Equally, hyphenation and spacing can cause problems. In some countries, such as the UK, there is no rule about hyphenation, but in other countries, such as France and the Benelux countries, town names are always hyphenated except following certain words. These names can therefore programmatically be given the correct hyphenation. The rules, where applicable, are given in the chapters on individual countries.

Although rare in some countries, other countries add a number or string (indicating the rele-vant postal sorting office) at the end of a town name. For example, you might find

1020 Oslo 2

These numbers or names should be used but *should be stored in a separate field* to prevent the incon-sistent sorting of town names during operations. Splitting this second part of the postcode from the town name also allows you a free hand when replacing incorrect town names with correct town names. Do not forget to split off this second postcode/region, which is important for deliv-ery purposes, before overwriting the contents of the town field with other data.

Provinces

The UK, Italy and Spain are the only European countries where province names (counties in the

UK) are used in the address. Counties are often used in British addresses, but are not strictly necessary. In Italy and Spain, however, it is still the preferred way of addressing, with a 2-letter abbreviation indicating the province (in Italy) or the full name (in Spain) being added in brackets at the end of the town name, e.g.

MILANO (MI)
ELCHE (Alicante)

For the operational reasons already discussed, this province information should be stored in a second field.

If these regions do not already exist in the address, they can usually be assigned on the basis of postcode. Where this is the case, this information is provided in the chapter on the relevant country.

In other countries, you may find province names specified where, in fact, it is undesirable. In Switzerland, for example, the canton name or abbreviation is often given with the town name, but the Swiss post office prefers it not to be used, and it should therefore be removed.

The country code

It is essential that the country in which the address is situated is coded in some way, as this information will be used to dictate, for example, address and postcode format.

There are a number of ways of coding countries, and much of the data which you have in the database can be used in one way or another to indicate the country, such as the international dialling code or the postal sorting code. You need, however, only code the country once – any other information indicating country can be re-added, if necessary, on output.

You could code the country, for example, by one of the following methods:

- Telephone code (44 for the UK, 49 for Germany, etc.)
- Car registration number (GB for Great Britain, D for Germany etc.)
- The first three letters of the name, or an abbreviation (UK for the United Kingdom, GER for Germany)
- The postal sorting code (GB for Great Britain, D for Germany etc.)

The choices are manifold. Be aware, however, that you are best served choosing a system where you are sure that every country is or can be part of that coding system. Albania, for example, has no telephone dialling code, neither does Liechtenstein nor a host of other countries, and it would be short-sighted to ignore this point just because these countries are small or perhaps currently unimportant to you. Many other countries do not have an international sorting code. Consider also your system's users, and choose a system that is intuitive. Not everybody knows the international dialling code for Iceland by heart, but most people can spell 'Iceland'. A system using letters from the country's name, therefore, might be the best option.

Telephone and fax numbers

As I have already suggested, where individual portions of a piece of data can change consistently but independently of each other, these should be fragmented in the database. Such is the case with telephone and fax numbers, which comprise an international dialling code, an area code and a subscriber's number, all of which can change independently of the others.

It is not necessary to store the international dialling code, as discussed above, because this can always be added on the basis of the country code on output, or added automatically to the database via a batch program. Numbers are much easier to enter and are then much easier to manipulate if they are entered without punctuation or spacing. In the case of the area code, the first digit of every area code within a given country will always commence with the same digit – usually 0 or 9 in Europe, in which case you may consider this digit also redundant in data entry and storage.

In some countries, such as France, all numbers have a specified length, which can be used as a format check on data entry. In some countries also there is a strong correlation between region and telephone number, which can be used as an accuracy check. In France, for example, you can see whether your postcode is correct by checking the first two digits of the telephone number, and vice versa.

In Summary

A final point. If you do decide to follow the suggestions made in these chapters, be aware that you must pay attention to the **order** in which the programs are run over a database, to prevent the destruction of data which you may need later. The order in which you tackle each point will depend on the country in which the addresses are. If you are checking address formats, then you might first have to assign a language code. If you are assigning a language code, then you will first need to bring consistency into your postcodes.

In general, you should make changes to the **form** of the data (case changes, accent corrections) and **fragment** data (postbox and telephone area code to a unique field) before making changes to the **contents** of a field (town name corrections, overwriting county names).

Finally, remember that consistency is the watchword in everything that you do with the database. It should be considered whenever and whatever you add or change in the database.

7 █ Outputting the data

Up to this point you have read about the theory and practice of effective address database management, giving you the background which you need to set up a database and to input and manipulate the data whilst it is stored in the database.

The purpose of any direct marketing database is, however, not to store data but to use the data to communicate with people, your suspects, prospects or customers. In other words, you will regularly need to output data from the database.

At this point the need for consistency, flexibility and so on all take a back seat to the need for accuracy. Not only do you want to enable the post office of the country concerned to transfer your package to its recipient as quickly and as efficiently as possible, but you also want to make sure that the data on any address label is as accurate as possible to avoid any unnecessary irritation to the recipient. It is very unfortunately the case that, even where companies commendably spend time, money and effort in building up a quality database, the output stage receives the least attention. Tatty and skew-whiff labels containing address details in the wrong order and the wrong format are, alas, all too common.

For this reason the rest of this book comprises information which will enable you to store, manipulate and output data to ensure maximum positive impact for 33 European countries. Information has been provided on a language and country level as these are the lowest common denominators for formatting information.

The following chapters bring together that information which can be acquired only by delving into a number of different sources or for which specialized language-knowledge is required. They are not intended to provide alternative postcode listings or telephone code listings to those published by the relevant institutions in each country as these are easily available and are also subject to frequent alteration. Where this information equates to another important factor, however, such as language spoken, the link is explained and the relevant listings provided.

The information provided, the way it is laid out, and the reasons for its inclusion are detailed below.

Accents and ASCII codes

Almost every European language contains accents and/or letters which are not found in English. For database input, manipulation and output you must be prepared for each of these to ensure that they are added as consistently and accurately as possible. This chapter provides a list of the accents contained within each language, their ASCII codes where available, and any alternatives which might be used.

Job Titles

When mailing to a foreign country, you will immediately be faced with the problem of knowing the function in a company of the names within your database when the job titles are in a language foreign to you. For this reason, translations of a large number of commonly occurring job titles are provided in twelve European languages. A table is also provided of the correct salutations which should be used on the envelope of any mailing for each language.

Country information

This table provides the name of European countries in the language or languages of its inhabitants and its translation into six European languages, as well as suggesting some possibilities for country coding.

Chapters on individual countries

Each country is considered separately.

General formatting rules

Because each European language has its own alphabetic ordering, all listings have been provided ordered according to the English alphabet to create the minimum of confusion. Accented letters are treated as their unaccented equivalents. So, for example, Ü is treated as a U and not as a UE as it would be in German. The German ß is treated as ss. Punctuation and spaces are ignored.

The country names are given in English, but where the inhabitants give their country a different name, this is written below the chapter heading.

Where formats are shown, information between square brackets ([]) should be written exactly as shown, whilst information between braces ({}) occurs in some but not all addresses. So, for example,

postcode [ ] Settlement Name {[Cédex]}

means that there is an obligatory space between the postcode and the settlement name, and that the settlement name may, in some addresses, be followed by a space and the word Cédex. A 9 or an n is used to indicate a numeric character, an A is used to indicate a letter.

If the word in the format is in upper case, the information should be printed in upper case. If the first letter only is in upper case, the first letter of the text must have an upper case initial letter. Correspondingly, a lower case first letter in a format means a lower case first letter in the text. So, for example,

number[,]thoroughfare type[ ]Thoroughfare name
SETTLEMENT

may equate to

17, rue de Paris
LILLE

When common abbreviations are given, they are given in only a single form. Readers should bear in mind that they can appear in a number of formats, and remember that when using the abbreviations provided.

Languages

Only a tiny minority of European countries do not have significant indigenous language minorities, and it is important that the database manager knows which languages are spoken, where and by whom, to allow accurate output, either ensuring that the mailing, or at the very least the address information, settlement name and so on is in the language of the recipient.

Company names

This section provides, where relevant, the layout of the company name in terms of the company *nature* and the company *name*. The company *nature* is the word or words in the complete name which indicate the activity of the company, for example Baker, Stationer, Printer and so on. The *name*, on the other hand, indicates the unique part of the company name, often the name of a person, an abbreviation and so on.

Company types

Company type refers to a word or abbreviation indicating the legal status of the company, for example Ltd, SA, PLC, etc. It is useful to be able to recognize these so that they can be given a consistent form and put into the correct position within the complete company name or moved into a separate field where desirable.

Contact names

This section contains information which is of importance when using salutations or for changing upper case names into a correct mixed case format. In some cases it also gives naming conventions which can alter in different countries for married women and for children.

Addresses

This section is very important for ensuring that address data can be stored consistently and that it can be output in the correct language and format. In this section, the words *street address* refer to the part of the address which contains the thoroughfare *type*, the thoroughfare name and the house number. The term *street name* is used to indicate the thoroughfare name and type together. So, in the example

12 Green Street

the *12* is the house number, *Green* is the thoroughfare name, and *Street* is the thoroughfare type. The street name in this case is *Green Street*. Lists of commonly occurring thoroughfare types and their abbreviations are provided to allow recognition of this part of the address so that its format can be corrected, the strings within it made consistent, and, if desired, its components moved to different fields.

This section also contains lists of nouns, adjectives and prepositions which will be found in company names and addresses. These are provided to aid recognition of these parts of addresses which are common yet often inconsistently written. Recognition of prepositions is also important when changing from upper to mixed case as most prepositions should retain a lower-case first letter.

Postbox

This provides the word used for postbox in the appropriate local language(s).

Postcodes

This section is important in that it provides the formatting rules for the postcodes of the country concerned, and gives in some cases the numbers of postcodes which are *not* used, thus allowing basic computer checks for invalid formats and postcodes. Furthermore, the postcodes of the regions where minority indigenous languages are spoken are provided to allow output, if necessary, in these languages for these areas.

Towns

This section gives writing conventions, where necessary, to allow settlement names to be given consistency in your database. Furthermore, corresponding town names are given both in the indigenous languages, where appropriate, and in other European languages. This is to ensure that the data from databases built outside the country concerned (and therefore perhaps containing the non-autochthonal settlement names) can be altered to give the autochthonal name and to aid database consistency, and to enable output to be made in the language of the recipient.

Administrative districts

Where these are used in address output, they are listed. In other countries they are also listed to allow their recognition and removal from addresses as required.

Telephone numbers

Where telephone numbers have a given format for the whole of a particular country, this information is provided to allow basic checking of accuracy within a database.

Although this information is, to the best of my knowledge, correct at the time of going to press, changes occur regularly and are inevitable. If you have any doubts about any of this information, it is best to check it.

Accents and ASCII codes

Not all the characters which can be represented on a personal computer are available on the keyboard, and this becomes more of a problem when non-English languages are being used. The ASCII (American Standard Code for Information Interchange) character set contains 256 characters, which are available by holding down the ALT key and typing a 1-, 2- or 3-number code on the key pad.

The problem with ASCII is expressed in its name – American. With only 256 characters it is unable to represent even the major languages of Europe.

A consortium of computer manufacturers is developing a new character set, Unicode, which will contain 65,536 characters. Until it becomes common, however, we have to live under the restrictions that ASCII imposes upon us.

Users of database systems running under Windows™ should know that Windows™ uses an ANSI character set rather than the ASCII character set, which means that more characters are available when printing. However, great care must be taken especially when the data is to be used under DOS-based systems, when the ANSI characters may not be translated into the correct ASCII equivalent.

Accents

All European languages (including English) contain accented letters and/or unique letters which are not available on the standard computer keyboard. Some of these accents are available by using ASCII codes, some are not. The tables below give the characters necessary for the language concerned, the alternative 'non-ASCII' equivalent where available, and the ASCII code of the accented letter itself.

Note that the ASCII codes given are those from the ASCII International Character Set, ASCII, page 850, which is that in use on most computers in Western Europe. Users of different ASCII pages will be able to produce different characters, sometimes using different number combinations, but no ASCII page can produce all of the characters needed for all European languages.

Whilst it is not always possible to type the correctly accented letter using ASCII, accented letters can be output on most printers using alternative ASCII codes. Thus, for example, typing the code to produce a + symbol would, by using an alternative font set, be output as an accented character. To do this, however, means that you have to maintain a consistent platform for your output devices and you will have to use a different printing set for each language to be printed as all European accents cannot be covered in a single set.

Albanian

Spoken by about 4 million people, in Albania, in the Serbian province of Kosovo, and smaller numbers in Italy and Greece.

Letter	ASCII code:
â	131
Â	na*
ç	135
Ç	128
ë	137
Ê	na

Basque

Basque is spoken by some 700,000 people in the Spanish regions of País-Vasco and Navarra, and in south-eastern France.

Letter	ASCII code
é	130
É	144
ŕ	na
Ŕ	na

Breton

Breton, a Celtic language, is spoken in the westernmost parts of Brittany, France, by some 600,000 people.

Apostrophes are used within words in Breton.

Letter	ASCII code
ñ	164
ù	151

Catalan

Catalan is spoken by some 6 million people in Spain, Andorra and south-eastern France.

Letter	ASCII code
à	133
À	na
ç	135
Ç	128
é	130
É	144
è	138
È	na
í	161
Í	na
ó	162

*na = not available as an ASCII code

Ó	na
ú	163
Ú	na

Czech

Czech is spoken by about 10 million people in the Czech Republic.

Letter	ASCII code
á	160
Á	na
č	na
Č	na
d'	na
D'	na
é	130
É	144
ě	na
Ě	na
í	161
Í	na
ň	na
Ň	na
ó	162
Ó	na
ř	na
Ř	na
š	na
Š	na
t'	na
T'	na
ú	163
Ú	na
ů	na
Ů	na
ý	na
Ý	na
ž	na
Ž	na

Danish

Danish is spoken by 5 million people in Denmark, as well as some inhabitants of the Faroe Islands, Greenland and northern Germany.

Letter	Alternative	ASCII code
å	ae	134
Å	AE	143
æ	ae	145
Æ	AE	146
ø	oe	na
Ø	OE	na

Dutch

Dutch is spoken by about 14 million people in The Netherlands and about 5 million Belgians. There is a small Dutch-speaking minority in northern France.

Letter	Alternative	ASCII code
æ	ae	145
Æ	AE	146
ë	e	137
Ë	E	na
é	e	130
É	E	144
è	e	138
È	E	na
ê	e	136
Ê	E	na
ö	o	148
Ö	O	153
ó	o	162
Ó	O	na
ò	o	149
Ò	O	na
ô	o	147
Ô	O	na
ij	y	152
IJ	IJ	na

NB Only ë and é and their upper case equivalents are *commonly* found in Dutch. Note that the letter ij is a single letter in the Dutch alphabet, coming between y and z, but it is *always*, without exception, typed as two letters – i and j – in normal usage, or it is written as a y. You should also do this. Note, however, that when these occur at the beginning of a real noun, both the I and the J must be in upper case, i.e. Krimpen aan de IJssel.

Faroese

Faroese is spoken by most of the 40,000 inhabitants of the Faroe Islands. It is related to Icelandic and resembles old Norse.

Letter	ASCII code
á	160
Á	na
æ	145
Æ	146
ð	na
Ð	na
í	161
Í	na
ó	162
Ó	na
ø	na
Ø	na

ú	163
ý	na
Ý	na

Finnish

Finnish is spoken by about 4.5 million people in Finland, and by about 50,000 people in Russia and 30,000 in northern Sweden.

Letter	Alternative	ASCII code
ä	a	132
Ä	A	142
å	a	134
Å	A	143
ö	o	148
Ö	O	153

French

French is spoken by about 56 million people in France, 4 million people in Belgium, 3 million people in Switzerland and about 300,000 people in Luxembourg.

Letter	Alternative	ASCII code
à	a	133
À	A	na
â	a	131
Â	A	na
ç	c	135
Ç	C	128
ë	e	137
Ë	E	na
é	e	130
É	E	144
è	e	138
È	E	na
î	i	140
Î	I	na
ï	i	139
Ï	I	na
ô	o	147
Ô	O	na
œ	oe	na
Œ	OE	na
ù	u	151
Ù	U	na
û	u	150
Û	U	na
ü	u	129
Ü	U	154

French-speakers rarely assign accents to capital letters. Some listings will simply omit accents in upper case letters, others will use the lower case accented equivalent even where the rest of the word is in upper case.

Friesian or Frisian

There are about 300,000 speakers of Friesian in the province of Friesland in the northern Netherlands.

Letter	ASCII code
â	131
ê	136
ô	147
û	150
ú	163

Gaelic

Gaelic is spoken in two distinct varieties in Scotland and Ireland. It has almost 20,000 speakers in the former and some 500,000 in the latter.

Gaelic words do not contain the letters j, k, q, v, w, x, y or z.

Letter	ASCII code
á	160
Á	na
é	130
É	144
í	161
Í	na
ó	162
Ó	na
ú	163
Ú	na

German

German is one of the most widely spread European languages, spoken by about 80 million people in Germany, 7.7 million people in Austria, 4.4 million people in Switzerland, 66,000 people in Belgium, 28,500 people in the South Tyrol region of Italy and 29,000 people in Liechtenstein, as well as by smaller minorities in southern Denmark, eastern France and Luxembourg.

Letter	Alternative	ASCII code
ä	ae	132
Ä	AE	142
ö	oe	148
Ö	OE	153
ü	ue	129
Ü	UE	154
ß	ss	225

The ß is used only in lower case. The upper case equivalent is SS.

Greek

Greek is spoken by about 10 million people in Greece and Cyprus. It has its own alphabet which has to be transliterated for use with databases containing Roman script. The table below gives the transliteration symbol of each Greek character:

Letters			*Transliteration symbol*
A	α	(álfa)	a
B	β	(víta)	v
Γ	γ	(gháma)	gh (y before an e sound)
Δ	δ	(thélta)	th
E	ε	(épsilon)	e
Z	ζ	(zíta)	z
H	η	(íta)	i
Θ	ϑ	(thíta)	th
I	ι	(yóta)	i
K	κ	(kápa)	k
Λ	λ	(lámtha)	l
M	μ	(mi)	m
N	ν	(ni)	n
Ξ	ξ	(ksi)	ks
O	o	(ómikron)	o
Π	π	(pi)	p
P	ρ	(ro)	r
Σ	σ ς	(sigma)	s
T	τ	(taf)	t
Y	υ	(ípsilon)	i
Φ	φ	(fi)	f
X	χ	(hi)	h
Ψ	ψ	(psi)	ps
Ω	ω	(omégha)	o

Note that the letter ς is only used at the end of a word.

Hungarian

Hungarian is spoken by about 10 million people in Hungary, 1.5 million people in Romania, and by minorities in Slovakia, Slovenia, Croatia and Serbia.

Letter	*ASCII code*
á	160
Á	na
é	130
É	144
í	161
Í	na
ó	162
Ó	na
ö	148
Ö	153
ő	na
Ő	na
ú	163
Ú	na
ü	129
Ü	154

| ű | na |
| Ű | na |

Icelandic

Icelandic is spoken by 250,000 people in Iceland.

Letter	*Alternative*	*ASCII code*
á	a	160
Á	A	na
æ	ae	145
Æ	AE	146
ð	d	na
Ð	D	na
é	e	130
É	E	144
í	i	161
Í	I	na
ó	o	162
Ó	O	na
ö	o	148
Ö	O	153
œ	oe	na
Œ	OE	na
þ	th	na
Þ	TH	na
ú	u	163
Ú	U	na
ý	y	na
Ý	Y	na

Italian

Italian is spoken by about 57 million people in Italy and about 500,000 people in Switzerland.

Letter	*Alternative*	*ASCII code*
à		133
À		na
é	e'	130
É	E'	144
í	i'	161
Í	I'	na
ì		141
Ì		na
î		140
Î		na
ó	o'	162
Ó	O'	na
ò		149
Ò		na
ú	u'	163
Ú	U'	na
ù		151
Ù		na

Lapp

Lapp is spoken in the north of Norway, Sweden, Finland and Russia by some 35,000 people.

Letter	ASCII code
č	na
š	na

Letzebuergesch

Letzebuergesch, a language related to German, is the official language of Luxembourg and is spoken by some 350,000 people.

Letter	ASCII code
â	131
ä	132
é	130
ë	137
ô	147
ü	129

Maltese

Maltese, an ancient arabic language with strong Romance influences, is spoken by about 400,000 people in Malta.

Letter	ASCII code
ċ	na
Ċ	na
ġ	na
Ġ	na
għ	na
Għ	na
ħ	na
Ħ	na
ż	na
Ż	na

Norwegian

Norwegian is spoken by about 4 million people in Norway.

Letter	Alternative	ASCII code
å	aa	134
Å	AA	143
æ	ae	145
Æ	AE	146
ø	oe	na
Ø	OE	na

Polish

Polish is spoken by about 35 million people in Poland.

Letter	ASCII code
ą	na
Ą	na
ć	na
Ć	na
ę	na
Ę	na
ł	na
Ł	na
ń	na
Ń	na
ó	162
Ó	na
ś	na
Ś	na
ź	na
Ź	na
ż	na
Ż	na

Portuguese

Portuguese is spoken by about 10 million people in Portugal.

Letter	ASCII code
á	160
Á	na
à	133
À	na
â	131
Â	na
ã	na
Ã	na
ç	135
Ç	128
é	130
É	144
è	138
È	na
ê	136
Ê	na
í	161
Í	na
ì	141
Ì	na
ó	162
Ó	na
ò	149
Ò	na

ô	147
Ô	na
õ	na
Õ	na
ú	163
Ú	na

Provençals

Provençals is a Romance language related to French and Catalan, found in south-eastern France. It has a number of dialects.

Letter	ASCII code
à	133
À	na
ç	135
Ç	128
é	130
É	144
è	138
È	na
ó	162
Ó	na

Rhaeto-Romanic

Dialects of Rhaeto-Romanic are spoken in Switzerland, western Austria and northern Italy by about 500,000 people.

Letter	ASCII code
è	138

Romanian

Romanian is spoken by about 20 million people in Romania. A similar language to Romanian, written using the Cyrillic alphabet, is spoken in Moldavia.

Letter	ASCII code
à	133
À	na
â	131
Â	na
ă	na
Ă	na
è	138
È	na
ì	141
Ì	na
î	140
Î	na
ş	na
Ş	na

ţ	na
Ţ	na
ù	151
Ù	na

Romany

Romany is the language of Europe's Gypsies, and knows many dialects and forms, each strongly influenced by the indigenous languages of the region which its speakers inhabit.

Apostrophes are used in Romany words.

Letter	ASCII code
č	na
š	na
ž	na

Serbo-Croat

Although Serbian and Croat are basically the same language, the former is written in Cyrillic script, the latter in Roman. This table, therefore, refers only to Croat, spoken by about 6 million people in Croatia, Slovenia, Bosnia-Herzegovina and Serbia.

Letter	ASCII code
č	na
Č	na
ć	na
Ć	na
đ	na
Đ	na
š	na
Š	na
ž	na
Ž	na

Slovenian

Slovenian is spoken by about 1.5 million people in Slovenia and small parts of Hungary and Italy.

Letter	ASCII code
č	na
š	na
ž	na

Sorbian

Sorbian is spoken by some 50,000 people in two distinct dialects in the south-easternmost part of the former East Germany. It is a Slavic language, and therefore difficult to reproduce using standard ASCII or ANSI character sets.

Letter	ASCII code
ć	na
Ć	na

ě	na
Ě	na
ł	na
Ł	na
ń	na
Ń	na
ó	162
Ó	na
ř	na
Ř	na
ś	na
Ś	na
š	na
Š	na

Spanish (Castilian)

Castilian Spanish is spoken by about 27.5 million people in Spain.

Letter	Alternative	ASCII code
á	a	160
Á	A	na
é	e	130
É	E	144
í	i	161
Í	I	na
ñ	n	164
Ñ	N	165
ó	o	162
Ó	O	na
ú	u	163
Ú	U	na
ü	u	129
Ü	U	154

Swedish

Swedish is spoken by about 8 million people in Sweden and about 300,000 people in western and southern Finland.

Letter	ASCII code
å	134
Å	143
ä	132
Ä	142
ö	148
Ö	153

Turkish

Turkish is spoken by about 57 million people in Turkey, and by minorities in Greece, Bulgaria and Cyprus.

Letter	ASCII code
â	131
Â	na
ç	135
Ç	128
ğ	na
Ğ	na
ı	na
î	140
Î	na
ö	148
Ö	153
ş	na
Ş	na
ü	129
Ü	154
û	150
Û	na
İ	na

Welsh

Welsh is spoken by about 600,000 people in Wales.

Letter	ASCII code
ä	132
Ä	142
â	131
Â	na
ë	137
Ë	na
ê	136
Ê	na
ï	139
Ï	na
î	140
Î	na
ö	148
Ö	153
ô	147
Ô	na
ŵ	na
Ŵ	na
v̈	na
V̈	na
v̂	na
V̂	na
ŷ	na
Ŷ	na

There are no accepted alternatives to accented characters in Welsh.

‖ Job titles

It is very important to code the job titles of contact names within the database because the number of job titles in circulation, with their appropriate abbreviations and acronyms, is surprisingly high. This means that only a certain proportion of programmatic coding is possible. Coding is needed to ensure that you can direct your mail within a company to the appropriate person. If you mail to specialized functions, you may have to look further than this table for correct translations, but this table gives the translations of the most commonly occurring job titles. You should note that job titles are often given in a language other than that of the country concerned – often German for Eastern Europe and English for Scandinavia – so you should take this into account when creating job-title look-up tables.

NB: For the German titles, -r indicates a man, -in indicates a woman. In Dutch, titles ending in -teur will usually end in -trice for females. The abbreviation (f) refers to females, (m) to males.

English	German	French	Spanish	Italian	Dutch	Portuguese
Accountant	–	(Agent) Comptable	–	Contabile Ragioniere	Accountant	Contabilista
Active Partner	Komplementär(in)	–		Socio Gerente	Vennoot (m)/Venote (f)	Sócio Activo
Administration Manager	Verwaltungsdirektor(in)	Directeur Administrati	Director Administrativo	Direttore Amministrativo	Administratie Manager	Director Administrativo Chefe de Pessoal Administrativo
Advertising Manager	Leiter(in) Werbung Werbungsleitung	Directeur Publicité	–	–	Manager Afdeling Advertenties	Gerente de Publicidade
Advisor	Betriebswirt(in)	Conseiller	–	Recercatore	Adviseur	Conselheiro
Area Manager	Gebietsleiter(in) Gebietsverkaufsleiter(in)	Chef de Secteur	–		Regio Manager Divisie Manager	Area da Gerencia
Art Director	Art Director	Directeur Artistique	–	Direttore Artistico Art Director	Art Director	Director Artistico
Assistant Director/ Assistant Manager	Assistent(in) der Geschäftsleitung Assistent(in) der Geschäftsleitung	Directeur Associé Sous-Directeur Adjoint Directeur Associé	Apoderado	Vice Direttore	Adjunct	Assistente do Director/ Assistente de Gerencio
Chairman	Vorsitzende(r)	Président	Presidente y Director General	Presidente	Voorzitter (m)/ Voorzitster (f)	Présidente
Chairman of the Board	Vorstandsvorsitzende(r)	Président du Conseil	–	Presidente del Consiglio	Voorzitter van de Direktie	Presidente do Conselho
Chairman of the Supervisory Board	Aufsichtsratvorsitzende(r)	Président du Comité de Surveillance	–	Presidente del Consiglio di Controllo Presidente del Consiglio di Sorveglianza	Algemene Direkteur Voorzitter van de Hoofddirektie	–
Chief Executive	Chief Executive Verleger(in)	Président Directeur Général	Presidente y Director General	Caro Esecutivo	Algemene Directeur	Chefe Executivo
Consultant	Fachberater(in)	Conseiller	–	Consigliere	Consultant	Consultor
Commercial Director	Direktor(in)	Directeur Commercial	Director Comercial	Direttore Commerciale Direttore Vendite	Commerceel Direkteur	Director Comercial
Company Management	Generaldirektor(in)	Administrateur Délégué	Administrador Gerente	Direttore Generale	Afgevaardigd Bestuurder Hoofddirektie	Gerencia do Empresa
Creative Director	Kreativ-Direktor(in)	Directeur de la Création Responsable Création	–	Direttore Creativo	Creative Director	Director Creativo
Deputy Chairman	Stellvertretende(r) Vorsitzende(r)	Vice Président Sous Directeur	–	Vice Presidente	Plaatsvervangend Voorzitter	–
Director	Direktor(in)	Directeur/Directrice Direction	Delegado a la Gerencia Delegado Director	Direttore	Direkteur/Direktrice	Director
Editor	Redakteur(in) Redaktion	Editeur Auteur	–	Editore Redattore	Redacteur	Editor

English	Deutsch	Français	Español	Italiano	Nederlands	Português
Editor-in-Chief	Chefredakteur(in)	–	–	Editore Capo Capo Redattore	Hoofd Redacteur	Editor-Chefe
EDP Director	EDV Direktor(in) EDV Leitung	–	Director de Informática Director de Proceso de Datos	Direttore EED (Elaborazione Elettronica dei Dati)	Hoofd Automatisering EDP Director	Director de EDP
Export Director	–	Directeur d'Exportation	–	–	Uitvoerdirekteur Export Directeur	Director de Exportacáo
Financial Director Financial Manager	Finanzleiter(in) Leiter(in) der Abteilung Finanzen	Directeur Financier Responsable Financier	Director Financiero –	Direttore Finanziario Direttore Finanziario	Financieel Direkteur Financieel Manager	Director Financeiro Gerente Financeiro
General Manager/ Managing Director	Betriebsleiter(in) Handlungsbevoll-mächtiger Leitende(r) Mitarbeiter(in) Bezirksdirektor(in) Stellvertretende(r) Direktor(in) Stellvertrentende(r) Geschäftsführer(in) Geschäftsführer(in) Geschäftsleitung	Directeur Général Gérant Administrateur	Administrador Consejero Gerente Director Generale Administrador Unico Administrador Gerente Administrador General Gerente	Direttore Generale Amministratore Delegate Amministratorer Aggiunto Direzione Generale	Algemeen Direkteur Zaakvoerder Bestuurder Bedrijfsleider Vestigingsleider Chef Hoofd	Director Geral Director do Gerencio
General Partner		–	–	Socio Accomandatario	–	–
Human Resources Manager	Personalleiter(in)	Directeur du Personnel	Director de Personal Director de Recursos Humanos	Direttore del Personale	Personeelsdirekteur Manager Personeelszaken	Gerente Recursos Humanos
Information Systems Director	Systemberater(in)	Directeur Informatique	Director de Informática	Direttore di Informatica Direzione di Informatica	Direkteur Rekencentrum Informaticadirekteur	Director Informatinos Sistemas
Joint Managing Director	–	Directeur Générale Adjoint	–	–	Algemeen Adjunct Direkteur	–
Limited Partner		–	–	Socio Accomandante	–	–
Manager	Manager(in)	Chef	–	Direttore Gestore Gerente Manager	Manager	Gerente
Marketing Manager	Marketingleiter(in) Marketingberater(in)	Directeur Marketing	Director de Marketing	–	Marketing Manager	Gerente de Marketing
Media Manager	Medialeitung	Directeur Communication	–	Direttore Media	Media Manager	–

English	German	French	Spanish	Italian	Dutch	Portuguese
Member of Co-operative	Genoss(e)(in)	Membre de la Coopérative	–	Membro di Cooperativa	Lid van Coöperatie	–
Member of the Board	Vorstandsmitglied Vorstände	Membre du Conseil	–	Membro del Consiglio	Lid van de Hoofddirektie	Membro do Conselho
Member of the Supervisory Board	Aufsichtsratmitglied	Membre de la Comité de Surveillance	–	Membro del Consiglio di Controllo Membro del Consiglio di Sorveglianza	Lid van de Hoofddirektie	Membro do Conselha do Super
Nominal Partner				Socio Nominale		
Partner	Gesellschafter(in) Prokurist(in)	Associé Partenaire	Socio	Socio Membro del Consiglio di Sorveglianza	Partner Mede-eigenaar	Sócio
President	Präsident(in)	Président Président Directeur Général Président Direction Général	Presidente Presidente y Director General	Presidente Vorstände	President Direkteur	Presidente
Production Director	Leiter(in) Produktion	Directeur de la Production Directeur de Fabrication Chef de Fabrication	Direccion de Produccion Jefe de Produccion Cap de Produccion	Direttore di Produzione Direttore di Stabilimento	Produktie direkteur	Director de Producós
Project Leader	Projektleiter(in)	Directeur des Projets	–	Direttore dei Progetti	Projektleider	Lider de Projecto
Proprietor	Inhaber(in)	Propriétaire	Proprietario Titular	Proprietario	Eigenaar	Proprietário
Public Relations Officer	Referent für öffentlichkeitsarbeit	Sécretaire aux Relations Publiques		Addetto alle Pubbliche Relazioni	PR-Medewerker	Relações Publicas
Publicity Director	Pressesprecher(in)	Directeur de la Publicité	–	–	Publiciteitsdirekteur	Director de Publicidade
Publisher	Herausgeber(in)	–	–	Editore	Uitgever	Publicador Editor
Purchasing Manager	Einkaufsleiter(in)	Directeur d'Achats	Director de Compras Director de Approvisionamientas	Procuratore	Inkoopdirecteur	Gerente de Compras
Salesperson	Verkäufer(in)	Commercial Vendeur	Proprietario	Venditore Commesso [in a shop]	Vertegenwoordiger Verkoper	Vendedor
Sales Manager	Verkaufsleiter(in)	Chefs des Ventes	Delegado de Ventas Director de Ventas	Capo Vendite	Hoofd Verkoop Verkoopsleider	Gerente di Vendas
Secretary	Sekretärin/Sekretär	Secrétaire	Secretario	Segretaria(f)/ Segretario(m)	Sekretaresse/Sekretaris	Secretária

English	German	French	Spanish	Italian	Dutch	Portuguese
Secret Partner Silent Partner	– Kommanditist(in)	– Commenditaire Bailleur	– –	Socio Occulto Socio Accomandante(	Stille Vennoot	– Sócio naõ Activo
System Manager Teacher	Systemberäter(in) Dozent(in) Fachlehrer(in) Lehrer(in) Professor(in)	Responsable Système Professeur Instituteur/Institutrice Enseignant/Enseignante	Director de Sistemas de Información	Docente Professore Insegnante	System Manager Docent	Gerente de Sistema Professor
Technical Director	Technische(r) Leiter(in) Technische(r) Direktor(in) Fertigungsleiter(in)	Directeur Technique Direction Technique Responsable Technique	Director Técnico Direccion Técnico	Direttore Tecnico Direzione Tecnica Responsabile Tecnico	Technische Direkteur	Director Técnico
Vice-President	Vizepräsident(in)	Vice President	Vicepresidente	Vice Presidente	Vice-voorzitter	Vice-Presidente

English	Norwegian	Finnish	Greek	Danish	Swedish
Accountant	Revisor	Tilintarkastaja	Logistis	Revisor	Revisor
Active Partner	Aktiv Kompanjong	Vastuullinen yhtiömies	Omorithmos Eteros	–	Aktiv Kompanjon
Administration Manager	Administrasjonssjef	Hallintopäällikkö	Dikitikos Diefthindis	Administrationschef	Administrationschef
Advertising Manager	Annonsesjef	Mainospäällikkö	Diefthindis Diafimisis	Annonce Chef	Annonschef
Advisor	Rådgiver	Neuvonantaja	Simvoulos	Rådgiver	Rådgivare
Area Manager	Distriktssjef	Aluepäällikkö	Diefthindis Periferias	Distrikts Chef	Distriktschef
Art Director	AD	AD	Kallithenikos Diefthindi	Kreativ Chef	Art Director
Assistant Director	Vise Direktør	Apulaisjohtaja	Ipodikitis	Vice-Direktør	Vice Direktör
Assistant Manager	Assisterende Leder	Apulaispäällikkö	Ipodiefthindis	Assisterende Leder	Vice Chef
Chairman	Formann Ordstyrer	Puheenjohtaja	Proedros	Formand	Ordförande
Chairman of the Board	Styreformann	Johtokunnan puheenjohtaja	Proedros Dikitikou	Bestyrelses Formand	Styrelseordförande
Chairman of the Supervisory Board	Styreformann	Johtokunnan puheenjohtaja	Proedros Epoptikou Simvouliou	–	Styrelseordförande
Chief Executive	Administrerende Direktør	Pääjohtaja	Stelehos	–	Verkstäande Chef
Consultant	Konsulent	Konsultti	Simvoulos	Konsulent	Konsult
Commercial Director	Økonomi Direktør	Kaupallinen johtaja	Emborikos Diefthindis	Økonomi Direktør	Ekonomidirektör
Company Management	Firma Ledelse	Yritysjohto	Diefthinsis Eterias	Firma Ledelse	Ledningsgrupp
Creative Director	Kreativ Leder	Taiteellinen johtaja	Diefthindis Dimiourgikou Tmimatos	Kreativ Leder	Art Director
Deputy Chairman	Vise Formann	Varapuheenjohtaja	Anaplirotis Proedros	Næstformand	Vice Ordförande
Director	Direktør	Johtaja	Dikitis	Direktør	Direktör
Editor	Redaktør	Toimittaja	Sindaktis	Redaktør	Redaktör
Editor-in-Chief	Sjefsredaktør	Päätoimittaja	Arhisindaktis	Chef-redaktør	Chefredaktör
EDP Director	EDB Sjef	ATK-johtaja	Diefthindis Piroforikis (Mihanografisis)	EDB Chef	EDB chef
Export Director	Eksportsjef	Vientijohtaja	Diefthindis Exagogon	Eksportchef	Exportchef
Financial Director	Økonomi Direktør	–	Ikonomikos Dikitis	Økonomi Direktør	Ekonomidirektör
Financial Manager	Økonomisjef	Talouspäällikkö	Ikonomikos Diefthindis	Økonomi Chef	Ekonomichef
General Manager	Daglig Leder	Pääjohtaja	Genikos Diefthindis	Daglig Leder	Direktör
Human Resources Manager	Personalsjef	Henkilöstöpäällikkö	Prosoparhis	Personale Chef	Personalchef
Information Systems Director	Informasjonssjef	Tiedotusjohtaja	Diefthindis Piroforiakon Sistimaton	–	Informationchef

English	Norwegian	Finnish	Greek	Danish	Swedish
Joint Managing Director	–	–	Kini Diahirisis Eterias Diefthindis	–	Koncernchef
Manager	Sjef, Leder	Päällikkö, Johtaja	Diefthindis	Chef, Leder	Chef
Managing Director	Direktør	Toimitisjohtaja (TJ)	Diefthinon Simvoulos	Direktør	Verkställande Direktor
Marketing Manager	Markedssjef	Markkinointipäällikkö	Diefthindis Marketing	Markeds Chef	Marknadschef
Media Manager	Pressesjef, Markedssjef	Lehdistöpäällikkö	Diefthindis Meson Enimerosis	Presse Chef	Presschef
Member of Co-operative	Medlem av Samvirke	Osuuskunnan jäsen	Melos Sineterismou	Medlem af Samvirke	Medlem av Kooperativ
Member of the Board	Styremedlem	Hallituksen jäsen	Melos Dikitikou Simvouliou	Bestyrelsesmedlem	Styrelseledamot
Member of the Supervisory Board	Styremedlem	Johtokunnan jäsen	Me.os Epoptikou Simvouliou	–	Styrelse Medlem
Partner	Kompanjong, Partner	Kumppani (Kni.), Osakas, Yhtiömies	Eteros	Partner	Kompanjon, Delägare
President	President, Formann	Presidentti, Johtaja	Proedros	–	President
Production Director	Produksjonssjef	Tuotantojohtaja	Diefthindis Paragogis	Produktions Chef	Produktionschef
Project Leader	Prosjektleder	Projektipäällikkö	Ipefthinos Schediasmou	Projekt Leder	Projektledare
Proprietor	Eier	Omistaja	Id.oktitis	Ejer	Ägare
Public Relations Officer	PR-Sjef	PR-päällikkö	Ipefthinos Dimosion Scheseon Diefthindi	PR Chef	PR chef
Publicity Director	–	Mainosjohtaja	Diefthindis Dimosion Scheseon	–	Press chef
Publisher	Forlegger	Kustantaja	Ekdotis	Forlægger	Förläggare
Purchasing Manager	Innkjøpssjef	Ostopäällikkö	Diefthindis Promithion	Indkøbs Chef	Inköpschef
Salesman	Selger, Salgskonsulent	Myyntimies	Politis	Sælger	Säljare
Sales Manager	Salgssjef	Myyntipäällikkö	Diefthindis Poliseon	Salgs chef	Säljchef
Secretary	Sekretær	Sihteeri	Grammatefs	Sekretær	Sekreterare
Silent Partner	Passiv Kompanjong	Äänetön yhtiömies	Eterorithmos Eteros	Interessent	Passiv Kompanjon
System Manager	Systemansvarlig	Systeemipäällikkö	Ipefthinos Sistimatos	–	System chef
Teacher	Lærer	Opettaja	Daskalos (Kathigitis)	Lærer	Lärare
Technical Director	Teknisk Direktør	Tekninen johtaja	Tehnikos Diefthindis	Teknisk Chef	Teknisk chef
Vice-President	Vise Formann	Varapresidentti, Varajohtaja	Andiproedros	–	Vice President

▊▊ Salutations

The salutations which are described here are those which are suitable for printing on an address label. Unlike English, some European languages use a different salutation in letter headings. This is a translation matter and therefore outside the scope of this book. For this reason also you should address the recipient in the letter in the language of the letter. E.g., Dhr. van den Broek in The Netherlands should be addressed as Mr. van den Broek in an English letter because 'Dear Dhr. van den Broek' would be incorrect.

English	French	German	Spanish[1]
Mr or M'r (Mister)	M (Monsieur)	Herr	S. (Señor), D. (Don), Señor Don
Mrs or M'r's (Missus or Missis)	Mme (Madame)	Frau	Sra. (Señora), D^a (Doña), Señora Doña
Miss (Miss)	Melle (Madamoiselle)	Fraulein (Frl.)[2]	Señorita
Dr (Doctor)	Dr (Docteur)	Dr.	Dr. (Doctor), Dra. (Doctora)
MS or Ms or m.s.[3]	–	–	–
Prof.	–	Prof.	–

[1] Don (male) and Doña (female) are used before first names only.
Señor (male) and Señora (female) are used before either surname only or first and surname.
Señor Don (male) and Señor Doña (female) are used before first name and surname only.
[2] It is better not to use the salutation Fraulein for unmarried women – use instead Frau.
[3] Ms is best used when the marital status of the (female) recipient is unknown.
Equally, there is a large and increasing number of married and unmarried women who prefer to be addressed as Ms in all cases. This should be noted in your database.

English	Italian	Dutch	Portuguese
Mr or M'r (Mister)	Sig. (Signor/Signore[1])	Mr./Dhr. (Mijnheer/Deheer)	senhor (sr.)
Mrs or M'r's (Missus or Missis)	Sig^{ra} (Signora)	Mevr. (Mevrouw)	dona, senhora[2] (D., sra.)
Miss (Miss)	Sig^{na} (Signorina)	Juff.[3] (Juffrouw)	menina
Dr (Doctor)	Dr. (Dottor/Dottore)	Dr. (Doktor)	Dr.
MS or Ms or m.s.[4]	–	–	–
Prof.	Prof. (Professore)	–	Prof.

[1] Signor is used when followed by the name. Signore simply means 'mister'.
[2] Senhora is mainly used in rural areas.
[3] It is advisable not to use this form, which is, to say the least, not well received. Used Mevr. for both married and unmarried women.

[4] Ms is best used when the marital status of the (female) recipient is unknown.

Equally, there is a large and increasing number of married and unmarried women who prefer to be addressed as Ms in all cases. This should be noted in your database.

NB: A fuller list of salutations for Dutch-speakers is given in the chapter on The Netherlands.

English	Greek	Hungarian	Norwegian [1]	Finnish
Mr or M'r (Mister)	K.	Ur	Hr.	Herra (Hra)[2]
Mrs or M'r's (Missus or Missis)	K.	Asszony	Fr.	Rouva (Rva)[2]
Miss (Miss)	K.	Kisasszony	Frk.	Neiti (Nti)[2]
Dr (Doctor)	K.	Dr	Dr. (medical only)	Tohtori (Tri)[2]
MS or Ms or m.s.[3]	–	–	–	–
Prof.	–	–	–	–

[1] The title is rarely used if the first name is used. Another preference is to use the job title of the person.

[2] It is very old fashioned to use titles, especially in the business world. Use only the name of the person, or the job title.

[3] Ms is best used when the marital status of the (female) recipients is unknown.

Equally, there is a large and increasing number of married and unmarried women who prefer to be addressed as Ms in all cases. This should be noted in your database.

Country information

When working with cross-border mailings, you will need to choose a way to code each country. The table overleaf provides some suggestions: by name, car registration letter, by telephone code and by international sorting code. Choose carefully – not all countries are represented on each list, which could cause inflexibility in the database depending on the method you choose.

International sort code	Phone	Car	Autochtone	English	French	German	Spanish	Italian	Dutch
		AL	Shqipëri	Albania	Albanie	Albanien	Albania	Albania	Albanië
	33628	AND	Andorra	Andorra	Andorre	Andorra	Andorra	Andorra	Andorra
A	43	A	Österreich	Austria	Autriche	–	Austria	Austria	Oostenrijk
B	32	B	België/Belgique/Belgien	Belgium	Belgique	Belgien	Bélgica	Belgio	België
		BH	Bosna i Hercegovina	Bosnia-Herzegowina	Bosnie-Herzégovine	Bosnien-Herzegowina	Bosnia-Herzegowina	Bosnia-Erzegovina	Bosnië Herzegowina
	359	BG	Balgarija	Bulgaria	Bulgarie	Bulgarien	Bulgaria	Bulgaria	Bulgarije
		CRO	Hrvatska	Croatia	Croatie	Kroatien	Croacia	Croazia	Kroatië
	42	CZ	Česky	The Czech Republic	République Tchèque	Tschechische Republik	República Checa	Repubblica Ceca	Tsjechië
DK	45	DK	Danmark	Denmark	Danemark	Dänemark	Dinamarca	Danimarca	Denemarken
		EE	Eesti	Estonia	Estonie	Estland	Estonia	Estonia	Estland
FR	298	FR	Føroyar (Færøerne)	Faroe Islands	Iles Féroé	Faröer	Islas Feroe	Faeroer	de Faeröer (isole)
SF	358	SF	Suomi	Finland	Finlande	Finland	Finlandia	Finlandia	Finland
F	33	F	France	France	France	Frankreich	Francia	Francia	Frankrijk
D	49	D	Deutschland	Germany	Allemagne	–	Alemania	Germania	Duitsland
	44	GB	Great Britain	–	Grande-Bretagne	Großbritannien	Gran Bretaña	Gran Bretagna	Groot-Brittanië
	30	GR	Hellas	Greece	Grèce	Griechenland	Grecia	Grecia	Griekenland
		DK	Grønland	Greenland	Groenland	Grönland	Groenlandia	Groenlandia	Groenland
H	36	H	Magyarország	Hungary	Hongrie	Ungarn	Hungría	Ungheria	Hongarije
IS	354	IS	Ísland	Iceland	Islande	Island	Islandia	Islanda	IJsland
	353	IRL	Ireland (Éire)	Ireland	Irlande	Irland	Irlanda	Irlanda	Ierland
I	39	I	Italia	Italy	Italie	Italien	Italia	–	Italië
		LV	Latvijas	Latvia	Lettonie	Lettland	Letonia	Lettonia	Letland
FL	4175	FL	Fürstentum Liechtenstein	Liechtenstein	Liechtenstein	Liechtenstein	Liechtenstein	Liechtenstein	Liechtenstein
		LT	Lietuvos	Lithuania	Lituanie	Litauen	Lituania	Lituania	Litouwen
L	52	L	Letzeberg	Luxembourg	Luxembourg	Luxemburg	Luxemburgo	Lussemburgo	Luxemburg
			Makedonien	Macedonia	Macédoine	Macedonia	Macedonia	Macedonia	Macedonië
	356	M	Malta	Malta	Malte	Malta	Malta	Malta	Malta
	3393	MC	Monaco	Monaco	Monaco	Monaco	Monaco	Monaco	Monaco
			Crna Gora	Montenegro	Monténégro	Montenegro	Montenegro	Montenegro	Montenegro
NL	31	NL	Nederland	The Netherlands	Pays-Bas	Niederlande	Países Bajos	Paesi Bassi	–
N	47	N	Norge	Norway	Norvège	Norwegen	Noruega	Norvegia	Noorwegen
PL	48	PL	Polska	Poland	Pologne	Polen	Polonia	Polonia	Polen
P	351	P	Portugal	Portugal	Portugal	Portugal	Portugal	Portogallo	Portugal
R	40	RO	România	Romania	Roumanie	Rumänien	Rumania	Romania	Roemenië
	39549	RSM	San Marino	San Marino	Saint-Marin	San Mar	San Marino	San Marino	San Marino
			Srbija	Serbia	Serbie	Serbien	Serbia	Serbia	Servië
		SO	Slovensko	Slovakia	Slovaquie	Slowakei	Eslovaquia	Slovacchia	* Slowakije/Slovakije
		SLO	Slovenija	Slovenia	Slovénie	Slowenien	Eslovenia	Slovenia	Slovenië
E	34	E	España	Spain	Espagne	Spanien	–	Spagna	Spanje
S	46	S	Sverige	Sweden	Suède	Schweden	Suecia	Svezia	Zweden

41	CH	Schweiz/Suisse/Svizzera	Switzerland	Suisse	Schweiz	Suiza	Svizzera	Zwitserland
90	TR	Türkiye	Turkey	Turquie	Türkei	Turquia	Turchia	Turkije
44	GB	United Kingdom of Great Britain and Northern Ireland	-	Royaume-Uni	Vereinigtes Königreich von Großbritannien und Nordirland	Reino Unido de Gran Bretañae Irlanda del Norte	Regno Unido di Gran Bretagna e Nordo di Irlanda	Verenigd Koninkrijk
(Italy)	V	Città del Vaticano	Vatican City	Cité du Vatican	Vatikanstadt	Ciudad del Vaticano	-	Vaticaanstad
38	YU	Jugoslavija	Yugoslavia	Yougoslavie	Jugoslawien	Yugoslavia	Jugoslavia	Joegoslavië

* Slowakije is used by Dutch speakers from The Netherlands, Slovakije by Dutch speakers from Belgium.

 # Andorra

Until the beginning of 1993, Andorra was ruled jointly by the Spanish Bishop of Urgel and the President of France, making the country a co-principality. At the beginning of 1993, Andorra became a sovereign nation, and as such, on 30 July 1993 became a member of the United Nations.

Area: 467 sq. km (180 sq. miles)

Population: 46,976 (1986 census) 50,887 (1990 estimate)

Population density: 100.6 per sq. km (1986), 109 per sq. km (1990)

Capital: Andorra la Vella (population 18,463 (1986), 19,003 (1989 estimate))

Currency: French franc and Spanish peseta

Languages

The official language of Andorra is Catalan, but it is spoken by only 28 per cent of the population. Castilian Spanish is spoken by 56 per cent of the population, whilst 8 per cent speak French and 8 per cent speak other languages.

Administrative districts

Andorra is divided into 7 parishes (*Parroquies*).

Telephone numbers

Andorra forms part of the French telephone system. There are no area codes. The 8-digit subscribers' numbers all begin with 628.

Austria
Österreich

Area: 83, 857 sq. km (32,377 sq. miles)

Population: 7, 711, 512 (1990 estimate)

Population density: 93.2 per sq. km

Capital: Vienna (Wien) (population 1,533,176 (1991))

Currency: 1 Schilling = 100 Groschen

Languages

German is the official language, spoken by 99 per cent of the population. There are also minorities speaking Slovenian and Croat near the borders of Slovenia and Hungary.

Company names

Where the *nature* of a company is mentioned in the company name this *precedes* the name of the company, thus:

Bäcker Schmidt

You will often, however, find these activity indications *after* the company name, thus:

Schmidt, Bäcker
Schmidt (Bäcker)

Austrian company names will also often contain the name of the *inhaber(in)* (owner), usually indicated by the abbreviation 'Inh.'.

Company types

The following company types may be found in Austrian company names:

GmbH (also written Gesellschaft mbH)
KG
GmbH & Co. KG

Contact names

The words *zu Händen*, abbreviated to z.H. or z.Hd. mean 'For the attention of'.

Addresses

In company addresses the name of the company precedes the name of the contact. The house number follows the street name. The salutation of the person or the type of company comes on the top line alone. Thus:

Herrn
Günther Meyer
Beethovengasse 25
1020 WIEN

or

Bäcker Meyer
Herrn Mirgel
Klagenfurter Strasse 10
1000 WIEN

The general rule is that the thoroughfare name and the thoroughfare type are written as one word, thus:

Hauptstrasse
Bahnhofstrasse

There are two important exceptions. If the thoroughfare name refers to the real name of a place (e.g. a town name, a castle name, a forest name, etc.) then there is a space between the thoroughfare name and the thoroughfare type, thus:

Wiener Strasse
Tyroler Allee

The second exception is where complete personal names are used. In these cases, each component of the name and each thoroughfare type are separated with hyphens. Note, however, that surnames only are not covered by this exception. Thus:

Kaiser-Wilhelm-Strasse
Albert-Einstein-Strasse

but

Beethovenstrasse
Einsteinstrasse

In streets beginning with prepositions or some adjectives ('Am', 'An', 'Alter', etc.) the preposition or adjective is followed by a space, thus:

Alter Marktstrasse

Thoroughfare types

Below is a list of the most commonly occurring thoroughfare types, with the abbreviated form(s) which you are most likely to find in address databases:

Allee	
Berg	
Boulevard	Bd
Bruch	
Bühl	
Chaussee	Ch
Damm	
Gasse	
Graben	
Hafen	
Hof	
Kamp	
Markt	
Platz	Pl
Ring	
Strasse	Str
Ufer	
Wall	
Weg	
Weide	

Other nouns, adjectives and prepositions commonly found in address databases

NB: German grammar rules governing articles, prepositions and adjectives are complex, and there is no need to explain them here. It is only necessary to be able to recognize them when and where they occur in addresses. For this reason a list without further explanation is provided. As a very general rule of thumb, the prepositions and adjectives listed may have one of the following endings added: nothing; e; er; em; en or es.

der/die/das/den/dem/des	= the
ein/eine/eines/einen/einem /einer	= a, an
und	= and
bis	= till, until, up to
für	= for
von	= of, from
zu, zu der (zur), zu dem (zum), nach	= to, towards
bei, bei der/den/dem (beim)	= near, at
an, an der/den/dem (am)	= at, by, towards
auf, auf der/den/dem	= on
in, in der/den/dem (im)	= in
gegenüber	= opposite, facing
nächst, neben, neben der/dem/den	= next to
hinter, hinter der/den/dem	= behind
vor, vor der/den/dem	= before, in front of
zwischen, zwischen der/den/dem	= between, amongst
über, über der/den/dem	= over, above, beyond
unter, unter der/dem/den	= under, beneath, below
mit	= with

neu/neue	= new
alt/alte	= old
kurz/kurze/kurzen/ kurzer/kurzem/kurzes (K.)	= short
lang/lange/langen/ langer/langem/langes (L./Lge.)	= long
gross/grosse/grossen/ grosser/grossem/grosses (G.)	= large
klein/kleine/kleinen/ kleiner/kleinem/kleines (K./Kl./Kle.)	= small
nord	= north
ost	= east
süd	= south
west	= west
Sankt (St.)	= saint
Industrieterrein, Industriegebiet	= industrial estate

Postbox

This is written as Postfach (PF).

Postcodes

The postcode is written on the same line, and before, the name of the town.

Austrian postcodes consist of 4 consecutive digits. These codes do not correspond well to administrative districts, as many towns have more than one code, and many codes refer to more than one municipality.

Towns

The following list gives foreign language equivalents of Austrian town names:

German	English	French	Spanish	Italian	Dutch
Salzburg		Salzbourg	Salzburgo	Salisburgo	
Wien	Vienna	Vienne	Viena	Vienna	Wenen

Administrative Districts

Austria has 9 states (*Bundesländer*):

Burgenland
Kärnten
Niederösterreich
Oberösterreich
Salzburg
Steiermark
Tirol
Vorarlberg
Wien

These provinces cannot be obviously identified by referring to a digit in the postcode. The name of the province is never used in addresses.

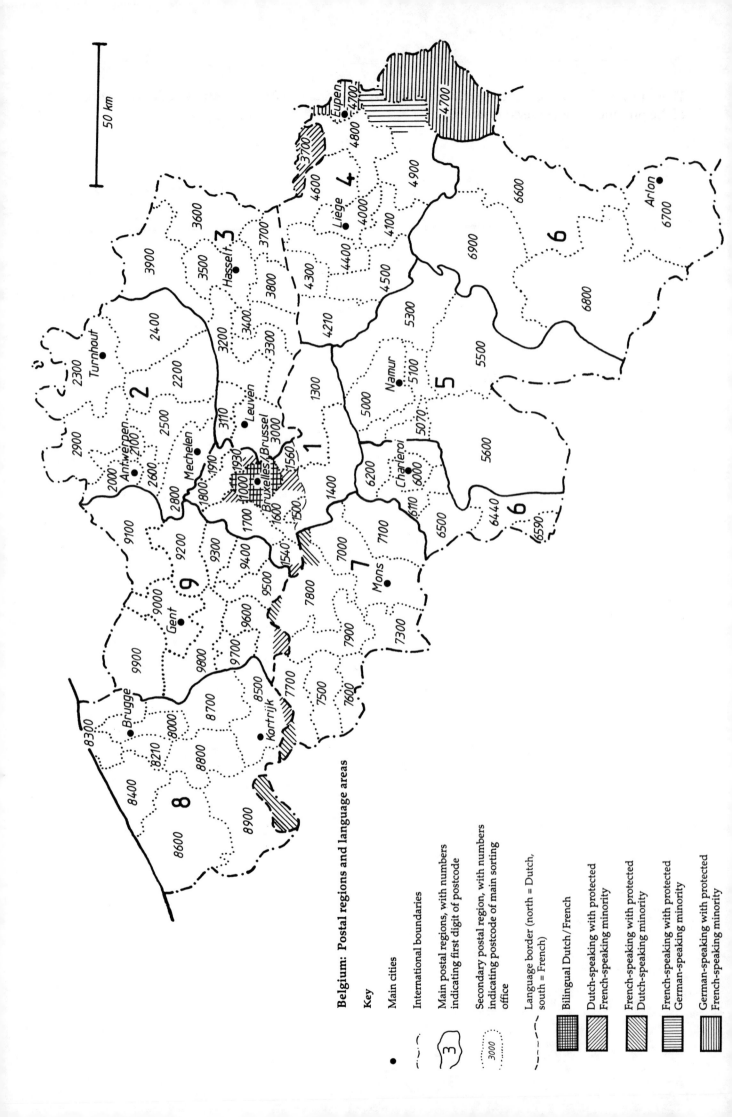

Belgium: Postal regions and language areas

Key

- Main cities

- International boundaries

- Main postal regions, with numbers indicating first digit of postcode

- Secondary postal region, with numbers indicating postcode of main sorting office

- Language border (north = Dutch, south = French)

- Bilingual Dutch/French

- Dutch-speaking with protected French-speaking minority

- French-speaking with protected Dutch-speaking minority

- French-speaking with protected German-speaking minority

- German-speaking with protected French-speaking minority

Belgium

**België/Belgique/
Belgien**

Area: 30,519 sq. km (11,783 sq. miles)

Population: (1991): 9,978,681

Population density: 330 per sq. km

Capital: Brussels (Bruxelles, Brussel) (population 960,324 (1990))

Currency: 1 Belgian franc/frank = 100 centimes

Languages

Belgium has three official languages, Dutch, French and German. The Dutch that Belgians speak is a distinctive dialect called Flemish, which is related to Dutch in the same way as British English and American English are related. Communications can be made in the Dutch of The Netherlands, but are much better received if in Flemish. Belgians are very language sensitive – you must bear this in mind always when communicating to or within Belgium.

The country has a federal structure, and the number of inhabitants in each area (1991) is as follows:

Flemish-speaking area	: 5,768,925 (57.8%)
French-speaking area (excluding German language area)	: 3,189,711 (32.0%)
German-speaking area	: 66,000 (0.7%)
Brussels	: 954,045 (9.6%)

Brussels is officially a bilingual Flemish-French area, but in fact approximately 80 per cent of the population speak French, 20 per cent Flemish.

Company names

In all three language areas, it is more correct, where the *nature* of a company is mentioned in its name, that this *precedes* the name of the company, thus:

Boulangerie Dupont
Bakkerij Janssens
Bäcker Schmidt

You will often, however, find these activity indications *after* the company name, thus:

Dupont, Boulangerie
Dupont (Boulangerie)
Janssens, Bakkerij
Janssens (Bakkerij)
Schmidt, Bäcker
Schmidt (Bäcker)

Company types

Company type indications will sometimes be present in both French and Flemish versions within the same name, thus:

Janssens NV/SA
or
NV Janssens SA

The following company types may be found in Belgian company names:

Flemish	*French*
BVBA	SPRL
CV	SC
CVA	SCA
GVC	SCS
NV	SA (the most common amongst businesses)
PVBA	SPRL
VOF	SNC
VZW	ASBL (indicates a charity)

Contact names

Belgian personal names often contain prepositions, especially 'van de/van der/de la/du' which mean, literally 'of the'. Unlike The Netherlands, there is no rule for the capitalization or writing of these prepositions. In the Flemish area, they are more often, though not exclusively, written with an upper case first letter. In some names these prepositions are written as one word with the rest of the surname, in others they are written as a separate word.

For Flemish speakers, the salutation which would be used on an address label is inappropriate for use within a letter.

Addresses

Structure:

Addresses will be written in French, Flemish or German, depending on the language of the region. In the bilingual regions, addresses may be written in either or both languages. Addresses should always be written in this format:

Recipient name
Street name [ ] number
postcode [ ] TOWN NAME

regardless of the language area. The order and format in which the thoroughfare name and thoroughfare type are written differ according to the language of the address. For example:

French language region

M. Emile Dubois
Rue du Diamant 215
4800 VERVIERS

Flemish language region

Dhr. Hugo Degroot
Kerkstraat 112
3000 LEUVEN

German language region

Herr Helmut Müller
Bergstrasse 23
4700 EUPEN

There should be nothing written or typed beneath the last line of the address.

Street address

In the Flemish areas, the thoroughfare type part of the address is suffixed to the rest of the street address without a space. An exception exists in the address 'Steenweg op [name of town]' or 'Steenweg naar [name of town]'. For example:

Groenmolenstraat 5
Bergensesteenweg 7
Steenweg op Leuven 19

In the French language addresses, the thoroughfare type part of the street address is prefixed, with spaces between the words. For example:

rue Monfort 8
rue d'Arlon 98
avenue de la Gare 4

In the German-speaking areas, the general rule is that the thoroughfare type part of the address is suffixed to the rest of the address, as in the Flemish areas. For example:

Hauptstrasse 3

However, there are two important exceptions. If the thoroughfare name refers to the real name of a place (e.g. a town name, a castle name, a forest name, etc.) then there is a space between the thoroughfare name and the thoroughfare type. The second exception is where complete personal names are used. In these cases, each component of the name and each part of the street address string are separated with hyphens. Surnames *only* are *not* covered by this exception. Thus:

Lüticher Strasse 9
Ludwig-von-Beethoven-Strasse 15
Beethovenstrasse 11

In streets beginning with prepositions or some adjectives ('Am', 'An', 'Alter' etc.), the preposition is followed by a space, thus:

Alter Marktstrasse 3

In the French language regions, thoroughfare types should correctly begin with a lower case letter. In all three regions, prepositions like 'de la' and 'op' should also be written without a capital letter.

In bilingual areas, street addresses might be written with both the French thoroughfare type as a prefix and the Flemish thoroughfare type as a suffix. For example:

Rue du Beethovenstraat 12

This is unnecessary, and one may be removed.

If the address has a box number, add this after the address so:

street name [ ] number [– bus] number (Flemish or German)

 or

street name [ ] number [– boite] number (French)

For example

Bergstraat 15 – bus 19
Rue d'Arlon 90 – boite 23

Thoroughfare types

Below is a list of the most commonly occurring thoroughfare types, with the abbreviated form(s) which you are most likely to find in address databases:

Flemish	Abbreviations	Flemish	Abbreviations
Allée		Markt	Mkt
Baan	Bn	Park	Pk
Berg	Bg	Plantsoen	
Centrum		Plein	Pl
Dal		Rui	
Dam		Singel	
Dijk		Square	Sq
Dreef	Dr	Steenweg	Stwg, Swg
Dwarsstraat		Straat	Str
Dwarsweg		Straatweg	
Gracht		Vaart	
Hof		Veld	
Kaai		Vest	
Kade		Vliet	
Kanaal		Weg	
Laan	Ln	Wijk	
Lei			

Flemish	Abbreviations	French	Abbreviations
allée		avenue	ave

boulevard	bd, bld	mont/	mt
canal		montagne	
centre		parc	
champ		place	pl
chaussée	ch, chee	quai	
chemin		quartier	qu
clos		route	rte
cour		Route	
digue		National	RN
impasse	imp	rue	r
marché		square	sq
		val/vallée	

German	Abbreviations	German	Abbreviations
Allee		Kamp	
Berg		Markt	
Boulevard	Bd	Platz	Pl
Bruch		Ring	
Chaussee	Ch	Strasse	Str
Damm		Ufer	
Gasse		Wall	
Hafen		Weg	
Hof		Weide	

Other nouns, adjectives and prepositions commonly found in address databases

Flemish

NB : The following abbreviations are used: (n) = neuter; (g) = gendered and plural. Abbreviated forms are given in brackets.

het (sometimes 't) (n), de (g)	= the
een	= a, an
en	= and
tot	= till, until, up to
voor	= for
van	= of, from
op, naar	= to, towards
bij	= near, by
aan	= on (sea, for example), at
aan de (a/d)	= on (a river)
op	= on
in	= in
tegenover	= opposite
naast	= next to
achter	= behind
vóór	= in front of
tussen	= between
over	= over
onder	= under
met	= with
nieuw (n) (nw.)/nieuwe (g) (nwe.)	= new

oud (n)/oude (g)	= old
kort (n) (K.)/korte (g) (Kte.)	= short
lang (n) (L.)/lange (g) (Lge.)	= long
groot (n) (G./Gt.)/	
grote (g) (G. or Gte.)	= large
klein (n) (K./Kl.)/	
kleine (g) (K. or Kle.)	= small
noord	= north
oost	= east
zuid	= south
west	= west
sint (St.)	= saint
Industriepark	= industrial estate

French

NB: The following abbreviations are used: (m) = masculine form; (f)= feminine form; (pl) = plural form. Except where specified, the plural form of adjectives is the correctly gendered singular form followed by an 's'.

le (m)/la (f)/les (pl)	= the
(NB : le and la are written l'	
before a vowel or an unaspirated h)	
un (m)/une (f)	= a, an
et	= and
à/au (m)/à la (f)/aux (pl)	= till, until, up to, to
pour	= for
de (before a proper noun)/du (m)/	
de la, de l' (f)/des (pl)	= of, from
à	= at
près de	= by, near to
sur	= on (a river, the sea)
dans	= in
en face de	= opposite
à côté de	= next to
derrière	= behind
devant	= in front
entre	= between
avec	= with
sous	= under
lès (occurs *only* in place names)	= near
nouveau (m)/nouvelle (f)/	
nouveaux (m.pl.)/nouvelles (f.pl.)/	
nouvel (m, before a vowel or unaspirated h)	= new
vieux (m, pl)/vieille (f)/vielles	
(f.pl.)/vieil (m, before	
a vowel or an unaspirated h)	= old
court (m) (Ct.)/courte (f) (Cte.)	= short
long (m) (Lg.)/longue (f) (Lgue.)	= long
grand (m) (Gr./Grd.)/grande (f) (Gr./Grde.)	= large
petit (m) (P./Pt.)/petite (f) (P./Pte.)	= small

nord	= north
est	= east
sud	= south
ouest	= west

saint (m) (St.)/sainte (f) (Ste.)	= saint

Parc Industriel	=industrial estate
Zone d'Activités (Z.A.C.)	
Zone Industrielle (Z.I.)	
Zone Artisanale (Z.A.)	

German

NB: German grammar rules governing articles, prepositions and adjectives are complex, and there is no need to explain them here. It is only necessary to be able to recognize them when and where they occur in addresses. For this reason a list without further explanation is provided. As a very general rule of thumb, prepositions and adjectives may have one of the following endings added: nothing; -e; -er; -em; -en; or -es.

der/die/das/den/dem/des	= the
ein/eine/eines/einen/einem/einer	= a, an
und	= and
bis	= till, until, up to
für	= for
von	= of, from
zu, zu der (zur), zu dem (zum), nach	= to, towards
bei, bei der/den/dem (beim)	= near, at
an, an der/den/dem (am)	= at, by, towards
auf, auf der/den/dem	= on
in, in der/den/dem (im)	= in
gegenüber	= opposite, facing
nächst, neben, neben der/dem/den	= next to
hinter, hinter der/den/dem	= behind
vor, vor der/den/dem	= before, in front of
zwischen, zwischen der/den/dem	= between, amongst
über, über der/den/dem	= over, above, beyond
unter, unter der/dem/den	= under, beneath, below
mit	= with
neu/neue	= new
alt/alte	= old
kurz/kurze/kurzen/ kurzer/kurzem/kurzes (K.)	= short
lang/lange/langen/langer/ langem/langes (L./Lge.)	= long
gross/grosse/grossen/ grosser/grossem/grosses (G.)	= large
klein/kleine/kleinen/ kleiner/kleinem/kleines (K./Kl./Kle.)	= small
nord	= north
ost	= east
süd	= south
west	= west
sankt (St.)	= saint
Industrieterrein, Industriegebiet	= industrial estate

Postbox

This is written as: Postbus (PB) in Flemish; Boite Postale (BP) in French; and Postfach (PF) in German.

Postcodes

All postcodes in Belgium have 4 consecutive numbers, the first digit being a number between 1 and 9. Not all numbers between 1000 and 9999 have been utilized for postcodes. No postcodes currently exist beginning with the digits 57, 58 or 59. The boundaries of the postcode regions correspond, in almost all cases, with the boundaries of the municipalities before fusion of some municipalities took place in 1975 and 1982. In a small number of cases, some streets in one municipality have the postcode of the neighbouring municipality. Even so, postcodes correspond well to language regions. Postcodes are written before, and on the same line as, the town, thus:

3000 LEUVEN

The municipality named should be that which applied prior to fusion in 1975 and 1982.

In the cases of certain cities a second part of the postcode, indicating a sorting office within the main postcode region is sometimes added after the town name. This is essential, especially in the case of postboxes, as without it delivery will be impossible. For example:

1080 Bruxelles 8

Regional language can be determined on the basis of postcodes as follows:

Dutch

1500–3999, 8000–9999

Note: Postcode areas 1547, 1640, 1780, 1950, 1970, 3717, 3790, 8587 and 9600 have facilities for French-speaking minorities.

French

1300–1499, 4000–4699, 4800–5699, 6000–7999

Note: Postcode areas 7700, 7780, 7850 and 7880 have facilities for Dutch-speaking minorities. Postcode areas 4950 and 4960 have facilities for German-speaking minorities.

German

4700–4799

Note: All of the German-language areas of Belgium have facilities for French-speaking minorities.

Brussels (Bilingual French-Dutch)

1000–1299

Towns

Towns are usually written in the address in capital letters.

Many towns in Belgium have more than one name – one Flemish, one French or one German and one French. Belgians are extremely language sensitive, and it is important to use the correct town name.

Town names consisting of more than one word are hyphenated with the exception of town names written in German in the German language area, and towns beginning with the words 'LE', 'LA', 'DE', 'HET', ' 'T' and ' 'S' where there is a space between this word and the next (other words in the same town name will be hyphenated). For example:

La Roche-en-Ardenne
Le Roux
's Gravenbrakel
De Panne
Sankt Vith
Saint-Vith

The following lists give the corresponding settlement names in the various languages. The first list gives the French equivalent for Flemish-speaking settlements; the second gives the Flemish and German equivalents for French-speaking settlements; the third gives the French equivalents for German-speaking settlements; and the fourth gives the alternatives for bilingual settlements. Finally, a list of corresponding town names in other European languages is given. Some of the names refer to bilingual municipalities, although in these municipalities one language is recognized as being dominant. A postcode following the autochthonal name indicates to which settlement the alternatives refer, when more than one settlement of the same name exists.

Name equivalents for Flemish-language settlements

Flemish	*French*
Aalst (9300)	Alost
Antwerpen	Anvers
Baarle-Hertog	Baerle-Duc
Beert	Brages
Bever	Biévène
Borgloon	Looz
Brugge	Bruges
Dendermonde	Termonde
De Panne	Le Panne
Diets-Heur	Heur-le-Tiexhe
Diksmuide	Dixmude
Drongen	Tonchiennes
Dworp	Tourneppe
Eeklo	Ecklo
Galmaarden	Gammerages
Gent	Gand
Geraardsbergen	Grammont
Goetsenhoven	Gossoncourt
Helkijn	Helchin
Herk-de-Stad	Herck-la-Ville
Ieper	Ypres
Jeuk	Goyer
Kelmis	La Calamine

Flemish	French
Kortrijk	Courtrai
Lauw	Lowaige
Leopoldsburg	Bourg-Léopold
Leuven	Louvain
Lier	Lierre
Mechelen	Malines
Mechelen-Bovelingen	Marlinne
Menen	Menin
Mesen	Messines
Moelingen	Mouland
Nieuwkerke	Neuve-Eglise
Nieuwpoort	Nieuport
Oostende	Ostende
Oudenaarde	Audenarde
Roeselare	Roulers
Ronse	Renaix
Rukkelingen-Loon	Roclenge-Looz
Rutten	Russon
Scherpenheuvel	Montaigu
's Gravenvoeren	Fouron-le-Comte
Sint-Genesius-Rode	Rhode-Saint-Genèse
Sint-Martens-Voeren	Fouron-Saint-Martin
Sint-Niklaas	Saint-Nicolas
Sint-Pieters-Kapelle	Saint-Pierre-Capelle
Sint-Pieters-Voeren	Fouron-Saint-Pierre
Sint-Stevens-Woluwe	Woluwe-Saint-Etienne
Sint-Truiden	Saint-Trond
Sluizen	Sluse (Limburg)
Spiere	Espierres
Spiere-Helkijn	Espierres-Helchin
Temse	Tamise
Tielt	Thielt
Tienen	Tirlemont
Tongeren	Tongres
Veulen	Fologne
Veurne	Furnes
Vilvoorde	Vilvorde
Vorsen	Fresin
Waasmont	Waasten
Walshoutem	Houtain-l'Evêque
Warneton	Waasten
Zoutleeuw	Léau

Name equivalents for French-language settlements

French	Flemish	German
Archennes	Eerken	
Arlon	Aarlen	
Ath	Aat	
Bassenge	Bitsingen	
Bassilly	Zullik	
Bastogne	Bastenaken	
Bas-Warneton	Neerwaasten	

French	Flemish	German
Beauverchain	Bevekom	
Bettincourt	Bettenhoven	
Bierghes	Bierk	
Bois-de-Lessines	Lessenbos	
Bombaye	Bolbeek	
Braine-l'Alleud	Eigenbrakel	
Braine-le-Château	Kasteelbrakel	
Braine-le-Comte	's Gravenbrakel	
Clabecq	Klabbeek	
Comines	Komen	
Deux-Acren	Twee Akren	
Dottignies	Dottenijs	
Ellezelles	Elzele	
Enghien	Edingen	
Flobecq	Vloesberg	
Genappe	Genepiën	
Ghislenghien	Gellingen	
Glons	Glaaien	
Grez-Doiceau	Graven	
Halle	Hal	
Hannut	Hannuit	
Henri-Chapelle	Hendrik-Kapelle	
Hombourg	Homburg	
Hoves	Hove (Hainault)	
Huy	Hoei	
Ittre	Itter	
Jauche	Geten	
Jodoigne	Geldenaken	
Jodoigne-Souveraine	Opgeldernaken	
Jurbise	Jurbeke	
La Hulpe	Terhulpen	
Lanaye	Ternaaien	
L'Ecluse	Sluizen (Brabant)	
Lessines	Lessen	
Liège	Luik	
Limbourg	Limburg	
Lincent	Lijsem	
Linsmeau	Linsmeel	
Lixhe	Lieze	
Marcq	Mark	
Mélin	Malen	
Mouscron	Moeskroen	
Namur	Namen	
Nivelles	Nijvel	
Oisquercq	Oostkerk	
Oleye	Liek	
Ollignies	Woelingen	
Oreye	Oerle	
Othée	Elch	
Otranges	Wouteringen	
Papignies	Papegem	
Pellaines	Pellen	

French	Flemish	German
Perwez	Perwijs	
Petit-Enghien	Lettelingen	
Piétrain	Petren	
Racour	Raatshoven	
Rebecq-Rognon	Roosbeek (Brabant)	
Roclenge-sur-Geer	Rukkelingen-aan-de-Jeker	
Rosoux-Crenwick	Roost-Krenwik	
Russeignies	Rozenaken	
Saintes	Sint-Renelde	
Saint-Jean-Geest	Sint-Jans-Geest	
Saint-Remy-Geest	Sint-Remigius-Geest	
Silly	Opzullik	
Soignies	Zinnik	
Steenkerque	Steenkerke	
Tourinnes-la-Grosse	Deurne (Brabant)	
Tournai	Doornik	
Trognée	Tubeke	
Visé	Wezet	
Waimes		Weismes
Waremme	Borgworm	
Warsage	Weerst	
Wauthier-Braine	Woutersbrakel	
Wavre	Waver	
Wihogne	Nudorp	
Zétrud-Lumay	Zittert-Lummen	

Name equivalents for German-language settlements

German	French
Amel	Amblève
Büllingen	Bullange
Bütchenbach	Butgenbach
Sankt Vith	Saint-Vith

Name equivalents for Bilingual settlements

French	Flemish
Bruxelles	Brussel

Name equivalents in other European languages

Autochthone	English	German	Spanish	Italian
Antwerpen	Antwerp		Amberes	Anversa
Arlon		Arel		
Bastogne		Bastenaken		
Brugge	Bruges	Brügge	Brujas	Bruges
Bruxelles , Brussel	Brussels	Brüssel	Bruselas	Brusselle
Gent	Ghent		Gante	Gand
Ieper	Ypres	Ypern	Ipres	

Kortrijk	Courtrai		Courtrai	
Leuven	Louvain	Löven	Lovaina	Lovagno
Liège		Lüttich	Lieja	Liegi
Mechelen	Malines		Malinas	Malines
Menen	Menin			
Oostende	Ostend	Ostende		Ostenda

The following municipalities (with their postcodes) are majority Flemish speaking with a protected French-speaking minority. Note that in this and the following lists the status of the municipalities are established by law and do not necessarily represent the true proportion of speakers within them.

1547 Bever
3717 Herstappe
1950 Kraainem
9600 Ronse
1640 Sint-Genesius-Rode
8587 Spiere-Helkijn (includes Spier and Helkijn)
3790 Voeren (includes Moelingen, 's-Gravenvoeren, Sint-Martens-Voeren, Sint-Pieters-Voeren, Remersdaal and Teuven)
1780 Wemmel
1970 Wezembeek-Oppem

The following municipalities are majority French speaking with a protected Flemish-speaking minority :

7780 Comines-Warneton (includes Ploegsteert, Warneton, Bas-Warneton, Comines and Houtem)
7850 Enghien (includes Petit-Enghien and Marcq)
7880 Flobecq
7700 Mouscron (includes Luingne, Herseaux and Dottignies)

The following municipalities are majority French speaking with a protected German-speaking minority:

4960 Malmedy (includes Beverc é, and Bellevaux-Ligneuville)
4950 Waimes (includes Faymonville and Robertville)

The following municipalities are majority German speaking with a protected French-speaking minority:

4770 Amel (includes Heppenbach and Meyerode)
4760 Büllingen (includes Rocherath and Manderfeld)
4790 Burg-Reuland (includes Thommen and Reuland)
4750 Bütgenbach (includes Elsenborn)
4700 Eupen (includes Kettenis)
4720 Kelmis (includes Hergenrath and Neu-Moresnet)
4710 Lontzen (includes Walhorn)
4730 Raeren (includes Hauset and Eynatten)
4780 Sankt-Vith (includes Recht, Crombach, Lommersweiler and Schoenberg)

Brussels

Brussels is a bilingual area, with some 80 per cent of the population speaking French, the rest having Flemish as a mother tongue. Virtually all of the Flemish-speaking minority speak French, but mailing indiscriminately in French is not well received. It is therefore essential that mailings are sent and other communications made in the language of the respondent, not the language of the area.

Bruxelles and Brussel are used interchangeably. In the interests of consistency, use either one or 'Brussels' within the database and output Bruxelles or Brussel according to the language of the recipient. Alternatively, using 'Brussels' is acceptable (and better received than either of the alternatives to a speaker of the 'other' language), especially in business-to-business mailings.

Brussels consists of 19 municipalities. Because addresses will often use the French or Flemish municipality name, or a version of the name 'Brussels', it is better, in the interests of consistency, to change these names to 'Brussels' or its equivalent in the database. The municipalities are, listed here with the French version first, for no particular reason, and with their postcodes:

1070	Anderlecht
1160	Auderghem/Oudergem
1080	Berchem-Sainte-Agathe/Sint-Agatha-Berchem
1000	Bruxelles/Brussel
1040	Etterbeek
1140	Evere
1190	Forest/Vorst
1080	Ganshoren
1050	Ixelles/Elsene
1090	Jette
1080	Koekelberg
1080	Molenbeek-Saint-Jean/Sint-Jans-Molenbeek
1060	Saint-Gilles/Sint-Gillis
1030	Saint-Josse-ten-Noode/Sint-Joost-ten-Node
1030	Schaerbeek/Schaarbeek
1180	Uccle/Ukkel
1170	Watermael-Boitsfort/Watermaal-Bosvoorde
1200	Woluwe-Saint-Lambert/Sint-Lambrechts-Woluwe
1150	Woluwe-Saint-Pierre/Sint-Pieters-Woluwe

Administrative districts

Belgium is a federal state with a bewildering number of administrative layers based on geographical area and language community. It has 10 provinces split into 41 *arrondissements*. Fortunately they should never be used in addresses. The provinces are all unilingual, although some will contain some municipalities where there are facilities for a language minority. The provinces with their abbreviations, languages and *arrondissements* are as follows:

Antwerpen (Antw.) (Flemish speaking. French name: Anvers)
    Antwerpen
    Mechelen
    Turnhout
Brabant Wallon* (Bt.W.) (French speaking. Flemish name: Waals Brabant)
    Nivelles
Hainault (Ht.) (French speaking. Flemish name: Henegouwen)
    Ath
    Charleroi

      Mons
      Soignes
      Thuin
      Tournai
Liège (Lg.) (French and German speaking. Flemish name: Luik;
  German name: Lüttich)
      Huy
      Liège
      Verviers
      Waremme
Limburg (Limb.) (Flemish speaking. French name: Limbourg)
      Hasselt
      Maaseik
      Tongeren
Luxembourg (Lux.) (French speaking. Flemish name: Luxemburg)
      Arlon
      Bastogne
      Marche-en-Famenne
      Neufchâteau
      Virton
Namur (Nam.) (French speaking. Flemish name: Namen)
      Dinant
      Namur
      Philippeville
Oost Vlaanderen (O.-Vl.) (Flemish speaking.
  French name: Flandre-Orientale)
      Aalst
      Dendermonde
      Eeklo
      Gent
      Oudenaarde
      Sint-Niklaas
Vlaams Brabant* (Vl-Bt.) (Flemish speaking.
  French name: Brabant-Flamand)
      Leuven
      Vilvoorde
West Vlaanderen (W.-Vl.) (Flemish speaking.
  French name: Flandre-Occidental)
      Brugge
      Diksmuide
      Ieper
      Kortrijk
      Oostende
      Roeselare
      Tielt
      Veurne

*The currenctly unified province of Brabant will officially be split into these two new provinces along the language border on 1 January 1995.

Bulgaria
Balgarija

Area: 110,994 sq. km (42,855 sq. miles)

Population: 8,989,165 (1990 estimate)

Population density: 81.0 per sq. km.

Capital: Sofia (Sofiya) (population 1,141,142 (1990))

Currency: 1 lev = 100 stotinki. The plural of lev is leva, the singular of stotinki is stotinka.

Languages

Bulgarian is the official language spoken by 85 per cent of the population. Turkish is spoken by 8 per cent of the population and Romany by 3 per cent. Macedonian is also spoken on the borders of Montenegro, Serbia and Greece.

Addresses

Addresses are written in the following format:

    Recipient name
    Street name[ ]number
    postcode[ ]TOWN NAME

For example:

    Dr Tzantcho Gantchev
    Dimo Hadjidimov 6
    1606 SOFIA

Postcodes

Postcodes have 4 consecutive digits and are written on the same line, and before, the town name.

Towns

Sofiya, the capital, is known as Sofia in English, Dutch and French, and Sofía in Spanish.

Administrative districts

Bulgaria has 9 *oblasts*:

Burgas
Lovech
Khaskovo
Mihailovgrad
Plovdiv
Razgrad
Sofiya – City
Sofiya – Province
Varna

 **Cyprus**

Cyprus has since the summer of 1974 been militarily divided between the Turkish and Greek Cypriot communities.

Area: 9,251 sq. km (3,572 sq. miles)

Population: 695,000 (1989 estimate for the whole island)

Population density: 75.1 per sq. km

Capital: Nicosia (population 162,500 (1986))

Currency: 1 Cyprus pound = 100 cents

Languages

Greek is spoken by 73 per cent of the population, Turkish by 23 per cent. There are small minorities speaking Arabic and Armenian. English is common. The Greek Cypriot dialect is different from that spoken in Greece itself.

Telephone numbers

The international country code for Cyprus is 357, but settlements in the Turkish controlled area are reached via Turkey, international code 90. In these latter cases, dial 90–5-area code (three digits) subscriber's number. In the Greek areas, the area code can have 3, 4 or 5 digits.

Denmark
Danmark

Area : 43,093 sq. km. (16,638 sq. miles)

Population: 5,146,469 (1991 estimate)

Population density: 119.4 per sq. km

Capital: Copenhagen (København), (population 464,773 (1991 estimate))

Currency: 1 krone = 100 øre

Languages

The official language, Danish, is spoken by 98 per cent of the population. Faroese is spoken in the Faroe Islands. English is widely spoken. German is spoken by a minority in Jutland; Inuit in Greenland.

Addresses

Addresses are written in this format:

    Recipient name
    Street name [ ]number
    postcode[ ]TOWN NAME{[ ]sorting code}

for example:

    Torben Raldorf
    Tietgensgade 137
    1004 KØBENHAVN V

The thoroughfare type is suffixed to the thoroughfare name without a space. As with other Scandinavian languages, the definite article does not appear as a separate word but as a suffix (–en) at the end of the word.

Thoroughfare types

The most commonly occuring thoroughfare types are listed below:

alle
banen
boulevard
buen
dammen
gaard
gade
gangen
havn
holmen
plads
stråde
toften
torv
varden
vej

Other nouns, adjectives and prepositions commonly found in address databases:

NB: the following abbreviations are used: g = gendered, n = neuter, s = singular, pl = plural.

den, det	= the (but only when followed by an adjective preceding a noun. Otherwise -en (gendered) or -et (neuter) is added to the end of the noun. So, for example, vej = road, den store vej = the big road, but . . . vejen)
en, et	= a, an
og	= and
til	= till, until, up to
for, til	= for
af	= of
fra	= from
mod, imod	= to, towards
i nærheden af	= near, by
på	= on
i	= in
overfor	= opposite
ved siden af	= next to
bagefter	= behind
foran	= in front of
mellem	= between
over	= over
under	= under
med	= with
ny (g s), nyt (n s), nye (pl)	= new
gammel (g s), gammelt (n s), gamle (pl)	= old
kort (s), korte (pl)	= short
lang (g s), langt (n s), lange (pl)	= long

stor (g s), stort (n s), store (pl)	= big
lille (s), små (pl)	= small
nord	= north
øst	= east
syd	= south
vest	= west

(NB: When used with nouns, the words for north, south, east and west are prefixed without a space to the noun to which they refer, e.g. Sydgade = South Street.)

Postbox

This is written as Postboks, abbreviated to PB.

Postcodes

Postcodes in Denmark and Greenland are composed of 4 consecutive digits. Some urban areas have a suffix to the town name to indicate the area of the town served or the region. The suffixes are as follows:

N	North
S	South
Ø	East
V	West
NV	North-West
NO	North-East
SV	South-West
SO	South-East
K	Central (København)
C	Central (Odense, Århus and Frederiksberg)

Postcodes for Greenland can be distinguished as they begin with the numbers 39. Postcodes for the Faroe Islands have 3 digits only, and should be preceded with the international sorting code FR.

Provincial communities usually have a single postcode for the whole borough. Smaller towns (Esbjerg, Odense, Ålborg, Århus, Vejle and København N, NV, S, SV and Ø) distinguish different areas by postcode, whilst København K and V, and Frederiksberg C have different postcodes for some streets.

Postbox numbers 1001–1029 in København are in area K, 1501–1529 in area V. In Odense C, postbox numbers have the postcode 5100 as opposed to 5000; in Ålborg postbox numbers have the postcode 9100 as opposed to 9000; and in Århus C postbox numbers have the postcode 8100 as opposed to 8000.

Towns

The following list gives foreign language equivalents of Danish town names:

Danish	English	French	German	Spanish	Italian	Dutch
Gråsten			Gravensfn.			
Høyer			Hoyer			
København	Copenhagen	Copenhague	Kopenhagen	Copenhague	Copenhagen	Kopenhagen
Tønder			Tondern			

Administrative districts

Denmark has 14 counties (*Amter*) and 2 municipalities (*Staden*).

Counties

Århus
Bornholm
Frederiksborg
Fyn
København
Nordjylland
Ribe
Ringkøbing
Roskilde
Sønderjylland
Storstrøm
Vejle
Vestsjælland
Viborg

Municipalities

København
Odense

Telephone numbers

Since 16 May 1989, Denmark has had no area codes. Each subscriber has a completely new 8 digit number. The numbers from each region can be identified by the initial digit(s) of this new number:

Copenhagen – city centre	3-
Copenhagen – rest	4-
Sealand, Lolland-Falster, Moen, Bornholm	5-
Funen	6-
South Jutland	74-
South and East Jutland	75-
East Jutland	86-
East and North Jutland	97-
North Jutland	98-

Finland
Suomi

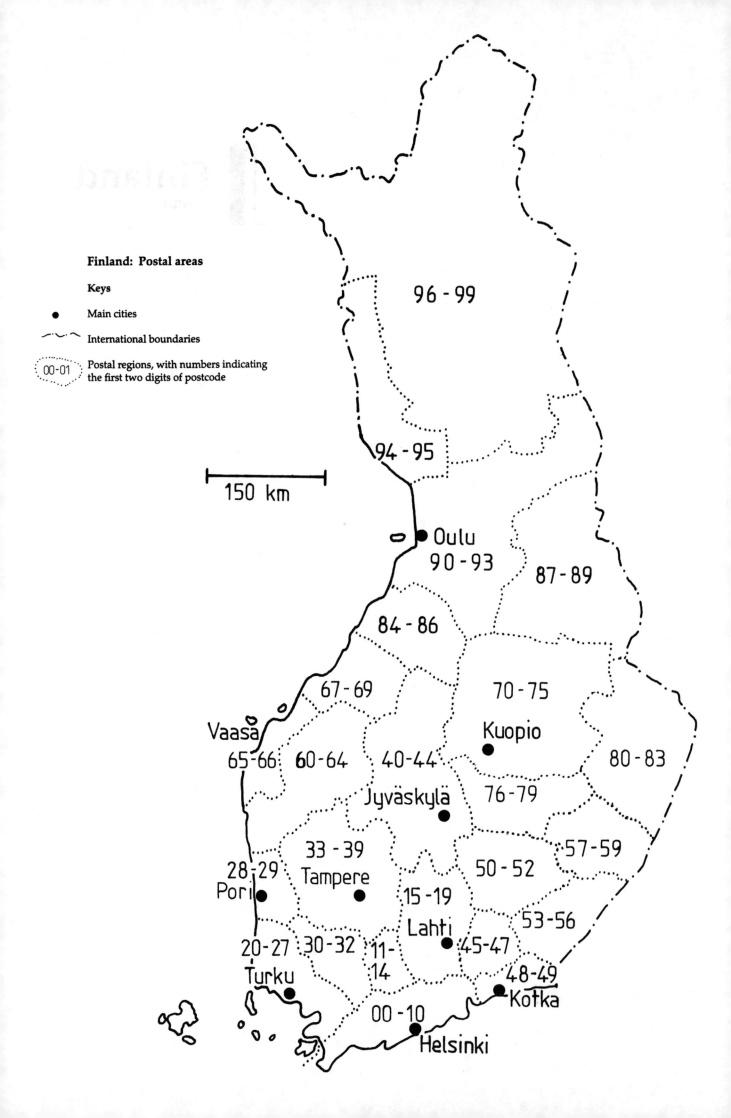

Finland: Postal areas

Keys

●   Main cities

⌁   International boundaries

(00-01)   Postal regions, with numbers indicating the first two digits of postcode

150 km

96 - 99

94 - 95

Oulu
90 - 93

87 - 89

84 - 86

67 - 69

70 - 75

Vaasa

Kuopio

65 - 66   60 - 64   40 - 44

80 - 83

Jyväskylä

76 - 79

33 - 39

57 - 59

28 - 29   Tampere

50 - 52

Pori

15 - 19

Lahti

53 - 56

20 - 27   30 - 32   11 - 14

45 - 47

48 - 49

Turku

Kotka

00 - 10

Helsinki

Finland
Suomi

Area: 338,145 sq. km (130,559 sq. miles)

Population: 4,974,383 (1989 estimate)

Population density: 14.7 per sq. km

Capital: Helsinki/Helsingfors (population 490,629 (1989))

Currency: 1 markka(finnmark) = 100 penniä

Languages

Finland has two official languages: Finnish, spoken by 94 per cent of the population; and Swedish, spoken by 6 per cent. Some 1,700 people (in the far north) speak Lapp. Some 22,900 of the Swedish speakers inhabit the Åland Islands, where they form 95 per cent of the population. The Swedish speakers are concentrated in two areas, along the southern coast between Helsinki and Hangö, and along the western coast between Pori and Jakobstad.

There are 24 municipalities that are unilingually Swedish, 17 with a Swedish majority and 23 where the minority is Swedish (in all cases, the municipality must contain at least 3000 people or 8 per cent of the population as Swedish speakers to be declared bilingual). The names of the relevant municipalities are listed in the towns section of this chapter.

Company types

The following company type indications will be identified in address databases:

KY (usually followed by the name of the owner)
OY
RY

Addresses

Finnish addresses are written in this format:

Recipient name
Streetname[ ]number
postcode[ ]TOWN NAME {[ ]sorting code}

for example:

Mikka Herttua
Haanvuorentie 34
49420 HAMINA 2

In multilingual areas street addresses can be given in either language.
Ja is the Finnish word for 'and'.

In Finnish, articles do not exist as separate words but are added as endings to the words to which they refer. There is no separate word for Saint in Finnish.

Thoroughfare types

Below is a list of the most commonly occurring thoroughfare types, with the abbreviated form(s) which you are most likely to find in address databases. Finnish, perhaps Europe's most complex language, has 16 cases, and appropriate declensions are added at the ends of words, including words indicating thoroughfare types.

Finnish	Abbreviation	Translation
Bulevardi, Bulevard		Avenue
Esplanadi		Esplanade
Gatan, Gate, Gata	Gt., G.	Street
Katu		Street
Kuja		Alley (cul-de-sac)
Portti		Gate
Rinne		Street
Tie		Street
Vägen, Väg	V.	Road

There is no rule governing hyphenation in street addresses.

Postbox

This is written as Posti Loaero (PL) in Finnish, Box in Swedish.

Postcodes

Postcodes are composed of 5 consecutive digits. These are written on the same line, and before, the town name. The first 2 digits of the postcode indicate the area of Finland covered (the sorting office). The next two digits indicate the area within this region (on the basis of municipality). The last digit of the postcode can be only 0 or 1. If it is 0 it refers to a street address. If it is 1 it refers to a postbox number.

In larger towns there is a sorting code following the town name. For example:

02361 ESPOO 36

This number is usually (but not always) the third, the fifth or the third and fourth digit of the postcode.

Some isolated areas do not have door-to-door postal deliveries, and these areas are served, especially for newspaper deliveries, by buses. These delivery lines have postcodes ending in 899 or 999.

In many towns in Finland, different streets, and different house numbers within those streets, belong to different postcode areas. These can be identified only by reference to the *Postinumero-luettelo* (Postcode book) under the heading 'Postiosoitehakemistot Kadunnimistöineen'.

Towns

As Finland is a bilingual country, many settlements have both a Finnish and a Swedish name. The following list gives the alternative names for these settlements:

Unilingually Swedish-speaking municipalities

Swedish	Finnish
Houtskär	Houtskari
Larsmo	Luoto
Malax	Maalahti
Mariehamn	Maarianhamina
Maxmo	Maksamaa
Närpes	Närpiö

Other unilingually Swedish-speaking municipalities are:

Brändö
Eckerö
Finström
Föglö
Geta
Hammarland
Iniö
Jomala
Kökar
Korsnäs
Kumlinge
Lemland
Lumparland
Saltvik
Sottunga
Sund
Vårdö
Västanfjärd

Municipalities with a Swedish-speaking majority

Swedish	Finnish
Ekenäs	Tammisaari
Ingå	Inkoo
Jakobstad	Pietersaari
Karis	Karjaa
Korpo	Korpoo
Korsholm	Mustasaari

Swedish	Finnish
Kronoby	Kruunupyy
Nagu	Nauvo
Oravais	Oravainen
Pargas	Parainen
Pernå	Pernaja
Sibbo	Sipoo
Tenala	Tenhola
Vörå	Vöyri

Other municipalities with a Swedish-speaking majority are:

Dragsfjärd
Kemiö
Liljendal

Municipalities with a Swedish-speaking minority

Finnish	Swedish
Espoo	Esbo
Hanko	Hangö
Helsinki	Helsingfors
Kaskinen	Kaskö
Kauniainen	Grankulla
Kirkkonummi	Kyrkslätt
Kokkola	Karleby
Kristiinankaupunki	Kristinestad
Lohja	Lojo
Loviisa	Lovisa
Myrskylä	Mörskom
Phytää	Pyttis
Porvoo	Borgå
Ruotsinpyhtää	Strömfors
Särkisalo	Finby
Siuntio	Sjundeå
Turku	Åbo
Uusikaarlepyy	Nykarleby
Vaasa	Vasa
Vantaa	Vanda

Other municipalities with a Swedish-speaking minority are:

Lapinjärvi
Pohja
Porvoon

Other settlements

Finnish	Swedish
Ähtäri	Etseri
Ähtävä	Esse
Ahvenkoski	Abborfors
Anttila	Andersböle

Artjärvi	Artsjö
Askainen	Villnäs
Degerby Ul	Nylands Degerby
Emäsalo	Emsalö
Enontekiö	Enontekis
Eurajoki	Euraåminne
Fiskari	Fiskars
Hailuoto	Karlö
Hamari	Hammars
Hämeenkyrö	Tavastkyro
Hämeenlinna	Tavastehus
Hamina	Fredrikshamn
Hangonkylä	Hangöby
Hanko Pohjoinen	Hangö Norra
Härkäpää	Härpe
Heikinkylä	Hindersby
Heinlahti	Heinlax
Hiittinen	Hitis
Hinthaara	Hindhår
Hyvinkää	Hyvinge
Iisalmi	Idensalmi
Ikaalinen	Ikalis
Ilola	Illby
Ilomantsi	Ilomants
Inari	Enare
Ingermaninkylä	Ingermansby
Isojoki	Storå
Isokyrö	Storkyro
Jakari	Jackarby
Järvenpää	Träskända
Jepua	Jeppo
Jokioinen	Jockis
Joroinen	Jorois
Kaarenkyla	Karsby
Kaarina	St. Karins
Kajaani	Kajana
Kalkiranta	Kalkstrand
Kälviä	Kelviå
Kankkila	Kanböle
Karijoki	Bötom
Karjalohja	Karislojo
Karkkila	Högfors
Kaunislahti	Grundsjö
Kaustinen	Kaustby
Kerava	Kervo
Kerkoo	Kerko
Kiila	Kila
Kimito	Kemiö
Kirkniemi	Gerknäs
Koivulahti	Kvevlax

Finnish	*Swedish*
Kokemäki	Kumo
Kolppi	Kållby
Koskenkylän Saha	Forsby Såg
Köyliö	Kjulo
Kujala	Gränden
Kulloo	Kullo
Kulloonkylä	Kulloby
Kuninkaankylä	Kungsböle
Kustavi	Gustavs
Lahti	Lahtis
Laihia	Laihela
Lapinkylä	Lappböle
Lappeenranta	Villmanstrand
Lappohja	Lappvik
Lappträsk	Lapinjärvi
Lapua	Lappo
Lapväärtti	Lappfjärd
Lielahti TL	Lielax
Lieto	Lundo
Liminka	Limingo
Lohtaja	Lochteå
Luoma	Bobäck
Martinkylä	Mårtensby
Masala	Masaby
Meltolan Sairaala	Mjölbolsta Sjukhus
Merikarvia	Sastmola
Metsälä	Ömossa
Mikkeli	St. Michel
Mustio	Svartå
Naantali	Nådendal
Nedervetil	Ala-Veteli
Nikkilän Sairaala	Nickby Sjukhus
Noormarkku	Norrmark
Nousiainen	Nousis
Oitmäki	Oitbacka
Oravaisten Tehdas	Oravais Fabrik
Oulu	Uleåborg
Paattinen	Patis
Paimio	Pemar
Paippinen	Paipis
Päivölä	Solberg
Pännäinen	Bennas
Pärnäinen	Pärnäs
Pellinki	Pellinge
Pernajan Vanhakylä	Gammelby
Perniö	Bjärnå
Piikiö	Pikis
Pikkala	Pickala
Pinjainen	Billnäs

Pirkkala	Birkala
Pohjankuru	Skuru
Pomarkku	Påmark
Pori	Björneborg
Porlammi	Porlom
Pornainen	Borgnäs
Pukaro	Pockar
Purola	Svartbäck
Raahe	Brahestad
Raippaluoto	Replot
Raisio	Reso
Rauma	Raumo
Ruotsinkylä	Svenskby
Rymättylä	Rimito
Sannainen	Sannäs
Sauvo	Sagu
Savonlinna	Nyslott
Siipyy	Sideby
Siltakylä	Broby
Sulva	Solf
Suurpellinki	Storpellinge
Tähtelä	Täkter
Taivassalo	Tövsala
Talma	Tallmo
Tampere	Tammerfors
Teerijärvi	Terjärv
Tesjoki	Tessjö
Teuva	Östermark
Tiukka	Tjöck
Tolkkinen	Tolkis
Tornio	Torneå
Tuusula	Tusby
Ulvila	Ulvsby
Upinniemi	Obbnäs
Uusikaupunki	Nystad
Vähäkyrö	Lillkyro
Valko	Valkom
Vehralahti	Veckelax
Veikkaala	Veikars
Veteli	Vetil
Vihti	Vichtis
Virkkala	Virkby
Virrat	Virdois
Voolahti	Vålax
Ylitornio	Överthorneå

The predominant language of the Åland islands (Ahvenanmaan lääni) is Swedish.

Finns often use abbreviations to indicate certain towns, such as HKI for Helsinki and MH for Mariehamn. If you find these in a database or directory, the equivalents are given in the *Postinumero-luettelo* under the heading *'Vahvistetut Nimilyhenteet'*.

Administrative districts

Finland has 12 provinces (*Lääni*). They are not used in addresses. They are as follows:

Åland (Ahvenanmaa)
Häme
Keski-Suomi
Kuopio
Kymi
Lappi
Mikkeli
Oulu
Pohjois-Karjala
Turku-Pori
Uusimaa
Vaasa

Telephone numbers

Area codes begin with a 9 in Finland. As the area code for Helsinki and surrounds is 90, callers from outside Finland will use '0' as the area code.

France

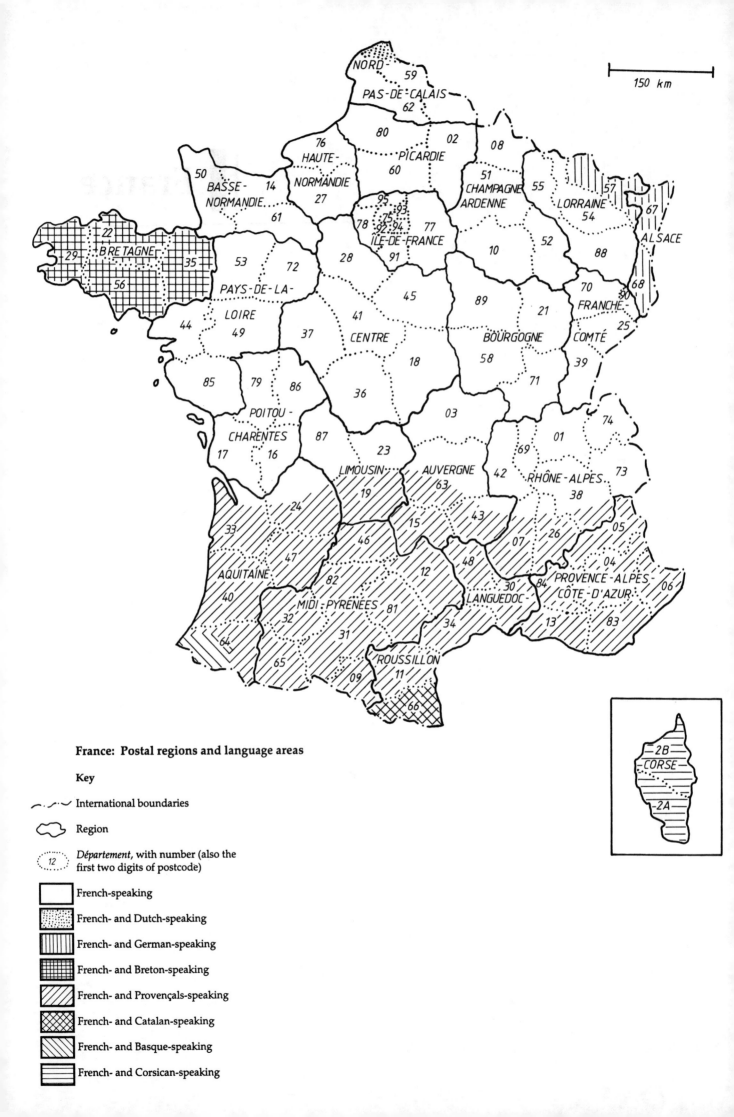

France: Postal regions and language areas

Key

⌁ International boundaries

◯ Region

⦂12⦂ *Département*, with number (also the first two digits of postcode)

☐ French-speaking

⦙ French- and Dutch-speaking

⦀ French- and German-speaking

▦ French- and Breton-speaking

▨ French- and Provençals-speaking

▩ French- and Catalan-speaking

▨ French- and Basque-speaking

☰ French- and Corsican-speaking

 **France**

Area: 543,965 sq. km. (210,026 sq. miles)

Population: 56,440,000 (1990 estimate)

Population density: 104.1 per sq. km

Capital: Paris (population 2,152,423 (1990))

Currency: 1 French franc = 100 centimes

Languages

French is the only official language of France. Few people do not speak French, but only 87 per cent of the population speak French as a mother tongue. Along France's borders a number of people speak other languages – German in Alsace-Lorraine on the border with Germany; Letzebuergesch on the border with Luxembourg; Flemish in the north on the Belgian border; Provençals (Occitan) in the south; Catalan in the south near the Spanish border; and Basque in the south-west on the Spanish border. Breton is still spoken in Brittany. In Corsica Corsican, a dialect of Italian, is spoken. There are significant numbers of people speaking these languages:

Basque	: 7%
Provençals	: 3%
German (Alsatian)	: 2%
Breton	: 1%

France is a highly unitary state, and these languages are rarely given more than a passing recognition that they exist. It is highly unusual (but not impossible) to come across addresses written in any language other than French.

Company names

It is more correct, where the *nature* of the company is mentioned in its name, that this *precedes* the name of the company, thus:

Boulangerie Lalosse et Cie.

135

You will often, however, find these activity indications *after* the company name, thus:

> Lalosse, Boulangerie
> Lalosse (Boulangerie)

Equally, articles are often put in brackets after the name of the company, so:

> Le Centre
> becomes
> Centre (Le)

This is also the case with initials. Thus:

> Boulangerie J. Dumalin
> becomes
> Dumalin (Boulangerie J.)

STE in a company name is an abbreviation of *Société* (company).

Company Types

The company types SARL and SA will often be found in address databases.

Addresses

Addresses are rarely written in any language other than French.
Addresses are usually written in this format:

> Recipient name
> number[ ]thoroughfare type[ ]Thoroughfare name
> postcode[ ]TOWN NAME{[ ]SORTING CODE}

> or

> Recipient name
> number[,]thoroughfare type[ ]Thoroughfare name
> postcode[ ]TOWN NAME{[ ]SORTING CODE}

For example

> Mme Marie Page
> 23 rue de Grenell
> 75700 PARIS CÉDEX

> or

> Mme Marie Page
> 23, rue de Grenell
> 75700 PARIS CÉDEX

If the address has a box number, add this after the number:

number[boite]number[,]thoroughfare type [ ] Thoroughfare name

You will also find indications of the staircase or building in which the inhabitant lives:

[Escalier No.]number

or

[Bâtiment]number

The number might also be followed by the word

bis

Numbers may be written as follows:

1–4
1/4
1 à 4 (1 to 4), or
1 et 4 (1 and 4)

The thoroughfare type part of the address is prefixed to the thoroughfare name with a space between the words. For example:

7, rue Amiens
123, avenue de la Gare

It is more accurate to write the thoroughfare types in lower case, as above.

Thoroughfare types

Below is a list of the most commonly occuring thoroughfare types, (with the abbreviated forms which you are most likely to find in address databases:

allée		mont/montagne	mt
avenue	av., ave.	parc	
boulevard	bld., bd.	place	pl.
centre		quai	
champ		quartier	qu.
chaussée	ch., chee.	route	rte.
chemin		Route Nationale	RN
clos		rue	r.
cour		square	sq.
impasse	imp.	val/vallée	
marché			

Other nouns, adjectives and prepositions commonly found in address databases:

NB: The following abbreviations are used (m) = masculine form; (f) = feminine form; (pl) = plural form. Except where specified, the plural form of adjectives is the correctly gendered singular form followed by an 's'.

le (m)/la (f)/les (pl)	= the
(NB : le and la are written l' before a vowel or an unaspirated h)	
un (m)/une (f)	= a, an
et	= and

à/au (m)/à la (f)/aux (pl)	= till, until, up to, to
pour	= for
de (before a proper noun)/du (m)/ de la, de l' (f)/des (pl)	= of, from
à	= at
près de	= by, near to
sur	= on (a river, the sea)
dans	= in
en face de	= opposite
à côté de	= next to
derrière	= behind
devant	= in front
entre	= between
avec	= with
sous	= under
lès (occurs *only* in place names)	= near
nouveau (m)/nouvelle (f)/nouveaux (m.pl.)/nouvelles (f.pl.) /nouvel (m, before a vowel or unaspirated h)	= new
vieux (m, pl)/vieille (f)/vielles (f.pl.)/vieil (m, before a vowel or an unaspirated h)	= old
court (m) (Ct.)/courte (f) (Cte.)	= short
long (m) (Lg.)/longue (f) (Lgue.)	= long
grand (m) (Gr./Grd.)/grande (f) (Gr./Grde.)	= large
petit (m) (P./Pt.)/petite (f) (P./Pte.)	= small
nord	= north
est	= east
sud	= south
ouest	= west
saint (m) (St.)/sainte (f) (Ste.)	= saint
Parc Industriel Zone d'Activités (Z.A.C.) Zone Industrielle (Z.I.) Zone Artisanale (Z.A.) Centre Commercial (C.C.)	= Industrial Estate

Note that prepositions are written in lower case in addresses.

Postbox

This is written as Boite Postale, shortened to BP.

Postcodes

Postcodes consist of 5 consecutive digits. They are always placed before and on the same line as the town name. The first two digits are the *département* number. Where the *département* number is less than 10 it is preceded by 0, for example 05100. *Département* 2A has postal codes beginning with 200 and 201, *département* 2B has postal codes beginning with 202 and 206. The *préfecture* (capital) of each *départment* has as its last three digits 000.

Most communes have their own unique postal code number. However, some scattered rural communities have more than one code. 32 cities have more than one distribution office and therefore more than one code. These, with their codes, are:

Aix-en-Provence	13090, 13100
Ajaccio	20000, 20090
Amiens	80000, 80080, 80090
Angers	49000, 49100
Bastia	20200, 20600
Bordeaux	33000, 33100, 33200, 33300, 33800
Cergy	95000, 95800
Clermont-Ferrand	63000, 63100
Dunkerque	59140, 59240, 59640
Fort-de-France	97200, 97234
Grenoble	38000, 38100
Le Havre	76600, 76610, 76620
Le Mans	72000, 72100
Lille	59000, 59800
Limoges	87000, 87100, 87280
Metz	57000, 57050, 57070
Montpellier	34000, 34070, 34080, 34090
Mulhouse	68100, 68200
Nancy	54000, 54100
Nantes	44000, 44100, 44200, 44300
Nice	06000, 06100, 06200, 06300
Nîmes	30000, 30900
Orléans	45000, 45100
Paris (16th arrondissement)	75016, 75116
Perpignan	66000, 66100
Rennes	35000, 35200, 35700
Rouen	76000, 76100
Saint-Étienne	42000, 42100
Strasbourg	67000, 67100, 67200
Toulon	83000, 83100, 83200
Toulouse	31000, 31100, 31200, 31300, 31400, 31500
Tours	37000, 37100, 37200

Five *communes* have two codes with different names for the same *commune*:

> Antibes : 06600 Antibes and 06160 Juan les Pins
> Cannes : 06400 Cannes and 06150 Cannes la Bocca
> Meudon : 92190 Meudon and 92360 Meudon la Forêt
> Saint-Denis : 93200 Saint-Denis and 93210 La Plaine-Saint-Denis
> Saint-Maurs-des-Fossés : 94100 Saint-Maur-des-Fosses and 94210
> La Varenne-Saint-Hilaire

Three cities (Paris with 20, Lyon with 9 and Marseille with 16) are split into *arrondissements*. These have their own postal codes, the number of the *arrondissement* being the last two digits of the postal code (with the exception of the Paris 16th *arrondissement*, with 2 codes – 75016 and 75116).

Large companies, town halls and so on can have their own unique postal code. In these cases the town name is followed by the word CÉDEX, thus :

75910 PARIS CÉDEX

Military bases need no street address, but the town name is followed by either AIR (air-force base), NAVAL (naval base) or ARMÉES (army base).

There are 6,000 main post offices serving the 36,000 *communes*. Before 1989, where the recipient did not live in the same *commune* as that in which the main post office was situated, both *communes* had to be named, thus:

Monsieur Durand
12, rue des Rossignols
Villemoisson-sur-Orge
91360 Epinay-sur-Orge

Since 1989 this is no longer necessary. Now the code is that of the main post office, but the *commune* is that of the recipient, so:

Monsieur Durand
12, rue des Rossignols
91360 Villemoisson-sur-Orge

Postcodes beginning with 97 belong to France's West Indian *départements*.
Postcodes beginning with 98 belong to the independent state of Monaco.

Towns

All town names consisting of more than one word are hyphenated, with the exception of those beginning with 'LE', 'LA' or 'LES', where there is a space between this word and the next. All other words within a town name beginning with one of these words will be hyphenated, for example:

La Ferté-Vidame
Le Château-d'Oléron

The following lists give corresponding settlement names in different languages. Although the French language names are usually used by the French Post Office, some of the regional languages have their own names for towns in their regions. They are used by the speakers of the appropriate regions and, therefore, can be used by you if so desired.

French	*Breton*
Auray	Alre
Bain-de-Bretagne	Baen
Baud	Baod
Belle-Isle-en-Terre	Berac'h
Blain	Blaen
Bourbriac	Boulvriag
Callac	Kallag
Cancale	Konkaver
Carhaix	Karaez
Châteaubourg	Kastell-Jiron
Châteaubriant	Kastell-Briant
Châteaulin	Kastellin
Cléguérec	Klegereg
Clisson	Klison
Concarneau	Konk-Kerne
Crozon	Kroazon
Fouesnant	Fouenan
Fougeray	Felgerieg
Fougères	Foujera
Gouarec	Gwareg

Guéméné-Penfao	Gwenvenez-Pennfao
Guéméné-sur-Scorff	Ar-Gemene
Guer	Gael
Guérande	Gwenrann
Guimiliau	Gwimilio
Guingamp	Gwengamp
Hennebont	An-Herbont
Huelgoat	An-Uhel-Goad
Josselin	Josilin
Jugon	Pl-Yugon
L'Aber-Wrec'h	An-Enez-Werc'h
La-Guerche-de-Bretagne	Ar C'herch
Lamballe	Lambal
Landerneau	Landerne
Lanmeur	Lanveur
Lannion	Lanuon
Le-Conquet	Konk-Leon
Le-Faou	Ar-Faou
Le-Faouët	Ar-Faoued
Le-Folgoët	Ar-Folgoad
Le-Mont-Saint-Michel	Menez-Mikael-Ar-Mor
Locronan	Lokorn
Lorient	An-Oriant
Loudéac	Loudieg
Louvigné	Louvigneg
Mallestroit	Malastreg
Martigné-Ferchaud	Marzineg
Maure-de-Bretagne	Maour
Montfort	Monforz
Morlaix	Montroulez
Nantes	Naoned
Paimpol	Pempoull
Painboeuf	Pembro
Penmarch	Penn-Marc'h
Perros-Guirec	Perroz
Pipriac	Prispinag
Plélan-le-Grand	Ploulan-Vraz
Plessé	Plousei
Pleyben	Pleiben
Plöermel	Plouarzel
Plouay	Pouskorv
Ploudalmézeau	Gwetalmeze
Plouescat	Ploueskad
Plougastel-Daoulas	Plougastell-Daoulas
Pontchâteau	Pont-ar-C'hastell
Pont-Croix	Pont-e-Kroaz
Pontivy	Pondivi
Pont-L'Abbé	Pont-n-Abad
Portsall	Porsall
Questembert	Kistreberzh
Quiberon	Kiberon
Quimper	Kemper
Quimperlé	Kemperle
Quintin	Kintin

French	Breton
Rennes	Roazon
Rohan	Roc'han
Roscoff	Rosgo
Saint-Aubin-d-Aubigné	Sant-Albin-an-Hiliber
Saint-Brieuc	Sant-Brieg
Sainte-Anne-d'Auray	Ker-Anna
Saint-Etienne-de-Montluc	Sant-Stevan
Saint-Guénole	Sant-Gwerole
Saint-Jean-Brévelay	Sant-Yec'han-Brevele
Saint-Malo	Sant-Malo
Saint-Nazaire	Sant-Nazer
Saint-Philbert-de-Grand-Lien	Sant-Filiber
Saint-Pol-de-Léon	Kastell-Paol
Saint-Quay-Portrieux	Plouc'ha-Sant-Ke
Saint-Thégonnec	Sant-Tegoneg
Scaër	Skaer
Trégastel	Tregastell
Tréguier	Langreger
Vannes	Gwened
Vitré	Ar C'hantreg

French	Basque
Bayonne	Baiona
Mauléon-Soule	Maule
Saint-Jean-Pied-de-Port	Don Garazi

French	Catalan
Collioure	Cotlliure
Perpignan	Perpiny

French	English	German	Spanish	Italian	Dutch
Aire-sur-la-Lys					Ariën aan de Leie
Arras					Atrecht
Avignon				Avignone	
Bailleul					Belle
Bergues					Sint-Winoksbergen
Boulogne					Bonen
Calais					Kales
Cambrai					Kamerrijk
Cassel					Kassel
Dijon				Digione	
Dunkerque	Dunkirk	Dünkirchen	Dunquerque		Duinkerke
Eperleques					Sperleke
Gravelines					Gravelingen
Halluin					Halewijn
Hazebrouck					Hazebroek
Lille				Lilla	Rijssel
Lyon				Lione	
Marseille				Marsiglia	
Menton				Mentone	
Merville					Mergem
Mulhouse		Mulhausen			
Narbonne				Narbona	
Nice		Nizza	Niza	Nizza	

Paris	Paris	Paris	Paris	Parigi	Parijs
Perpignan				Perpignano	
Saint-Omer					Sint Omaars
Strasbourg		Straßburg	Estrasburgo	Strasburgo	Straatsburg
Tarascon				Tarascona	
Toulouse				Tolosa	
Wissant					Witsant

Administrative districts

France is divided into 22 *régions*, 102 *départements* (6 of which are in her overseas territories) and around 36,000 communes (municipalities). The *départements* are numbered, and these numbers are important because they appear in the postal codes. Initially these numbers were assigned by alphabetical order, but since the first classification some changes have been made which have altered this order.

Départements

Département	*Region*
01 Ain	Rhône-Alpes
02 Aisne	Picardie
2A Corse-du-Sud	Corse
2B Haute-Corse	Corse
03 Allier	Auvergne
04 Alpes-Haute-Provence	Provence – Alpes – Côte-d'Azur
05 Hautes-Alpes	Provence – Alpes – Côte-d'Azur
06 Alpes-Maritimes	Provence – Alpes – Côte-d'Azur
07 Ardèche	Rhône-Alpes
08 Ardennes	Champagne-Ardennc
09 Ariège	Midi-Pyrénées
10 Aube	Champagne-Ardenne
11 Aude	Languedoc-Roussillon
12 Aveyron	Midi-Pyrénées
13 Bouches-du-Rhône	Provence – Alpes – Côte-d'Azur
14 Calvados	Basse-Normandie
15 Cantal	Auvergne
16 Charente	Poitou-Charentes
17 Charente Maritime	Poitou-Charentes
18 Cher	Centre
19 Corrèze	Limousin
20 (see 2A and 2B)	
21 Côte d'Or	Bourgogne
22 Côte d'Armor (previously Côte-du-Nord)	Bretagne
23 Creuse	Limousin
24 Dordogne	Aquitaine
25 Doubs	Franche-Comté
26 Drôme	Rhône-Alpes
27 Eure	Haute Normandie
28 Eure-et-Loire	Centre
29 Finistère	Bretagne
30 Gard	Languedoc-Roussillon
31 Haute Garonne	Midi-Pyrénées
32 Gers	Midi-Pyrénées
33 Gironde	Aquitaine
34 Hérault	Languedoc-Roussillon
35 Ille-et-Villaine	Bretagne

Département	*Region*
36 Indre	Centre
37 Indre-et-Loire	Centre
38 Isère	Rhône-Alpes
39 Jura	Franche-Comté
40 Landes	Aquitaine
41 Loir-et-Cher	Centre
42 Loire	Rhône-Alpes
43 Haute Loire	Auvergne
44 Loire-Atlantique	Pays de la Loire
45 Loiret	Centre
46 Lot	Midi-Pyrénées
47 Lot-et-Garonne	Aquitaine
48 Lozère	Languedoc-Roussillon
49 Maine-et-Loire	Pays de la Loire
50 Manche	Basse-Normandie
51 Marne	Champagne-Ardenne
52 Haute-Marne	Champagne-Ardenne
53 Mayenne	Pays de la Loire
54 Meurthe-et-Moselle	Lorraine
55 Meuse	Lorraine
56 Morbihan	Bretagne
57 Moselle	Lorraine
58 Nièvre	Bourgogne
59 Nord	Nord Pas-de-Calais
60 Oise	Picardie
61 Orne	Basse Normandie
62 Pas-de-Calais	Nord Pas-de-Calais
63 Puy-de-Dôme	Auvergne
64 Pyrénées Atlantiques	Aquitaine
65 Hautes Pyrénées	Midi-Pyrénées
66 Pyrénées-Orientales	Languedoc-Roussillon
67 Bas-Rhin	Alsace
68 Haut-Rhin	Alsace
69 Rhône	Rhône-Alpes
70 Haute Saône	Franche-Comté
71 Saône-et-Loire	Bourgogne
72 Sarthe	Pays de la Loire
73 Savoie	Rhône-Alpes
74 Haute Savoie	Rhône-Alpes
75 Paris	Ile-de-France
76 Seine-Maritime	Haute-Normandie
77 Seine-et-Marne	Ile-de-France
78 Yvelines	Ile-de-France
79 Deux-Sèvres	Poitou-Charentes
80 Somme	Picardie
81 Tarn	Midi-Pyrénées
82 Tarn-et-Garonne	Midi-Pyrénées
83 Var	Provence – Alpes – Côte-d'Azur
84 Vaucluse	Provence – Alpes – Côte-d'Azur
85 Vendée	Pays de la Loire
86 Vienne	Poitou-Charentes
87 Haute Vienne	Limousin
88 Vosges	Lorraine
89 Yonne	Bourgogne

90 Belfort		Franche-Comté	
91 Essonne		Ile-de-France	
92 Hauts-de-Seine		Ile-de-France	
93 Seine-Saint-Denis		Ile-de-France	
94 Val-de-Marne		Ile-de-France	
95 Val-d'Oise		Ile-de-France	

These départements are in the West Indies

97-1 Guadeloupe
97-2 Martinique
97-3 Guyane
97-4 Reunion
97-5 Saint-Pierre-et-Miquelon
97-6 Mayotte

Régions

Alsace	Ile-de-France
Aquitaine	Languedoc-Roussillon
Auvergne	Limousin
Basse-Normandie	Lorraine
Bourgogne	Midi-Pyrénées
Bretagne	Nord – Pas-de-Calais
Centre	Pays de la Loire
Champagne-Ardenne	Picardie
Corse	Poitou – Charentes
Franche-Comté	Provence – Alpes – Côte-d'Azur
Haute-Normandie	Rhône-Alpes

Telephone numbers

The zone Paris/Ile de France (*départements* 75-Paris, 77-Seine-et-Marne, 78-Yvelines, 91-Essonne, 92-Hauts-de-Seine, 93-Seine-Saint-Denis, 94-Val-de-Marne and 95-Val d'Oise) has the area code 1 (without a preceding 0 or 9) and an 8 digit subscriber's number beginning with the numbers 3, 4 or 6.

Zone Province (the rest of France and the independent state of Monaco) does not have an area code except when being called from Paris, when the area code is 16. The subscribers' numbers have 8 digits commencing with the digits which previously formed the area code (refer to the list below).

The independent state of Andorra has no area code, except when called from Paris, when the code is 16. The 8-digit subscriber's numbers all begin with 628.

The first two digits of the subscriber's number were originally the area code numbers and indicate the *départements*, though they are not the same as the *département* number. Some départements have shared numbers. The equivalents are as follows:

Départements	*Indicatifs* (first 2 digits)	*Départements*	*Indicatifs* (first 2 digits)
01	50, 71, 79	04	92
02	23	05	92
2A	95	06	93
2B	95	07	75
03	70	08	24

Départements	Indicatifs (first 2 digits)	Départements	Indicatifs (first 2 digits)
09	61	53	43
10	25	54	8
11	68	55	29
12	65	56	97
13	42, 90, 91	57	8
14	31	58	86
15	71	59	20, 27, 28
16	45	60	4
17	46	61	33
18	48	62	21
19	55	63	73
20 (see 2A and 2B)		64	59
21	80	65	62
22	96	66	68
23	55	67	88
24	53	68	89
25	81	69	7, 74
26	75	70	84
27	32	71	85
28	37	72	43
29	98	73	79
30	66	74	50
31	61	75	1
32	62	76	35
33	56	77	6
34	67	78	3
35	99	79	49
36	54	80	22
37	47	81	63
38	74, 76	82	63
39	84	83	94
40	58	84	90
41	54	85	51
42	77	86	49
43	71	87	55
44	40	88	29
45	38	89	86
46	65	90	84
47	53	91	6
48	66	92	1
49	41	93	1
50	33	94	1
51	26	95	3
52	25		

Germany
Deutschland

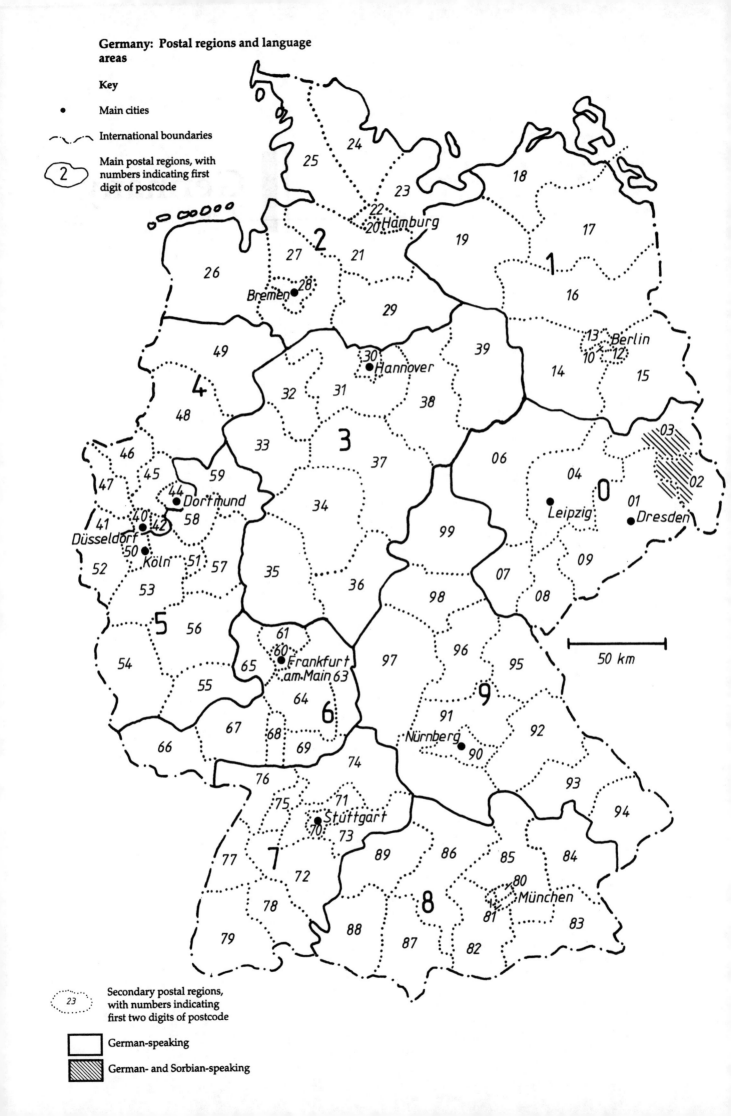

Germany: Postal regions and language areas

Key

- **•** Main cities

- **⌁** International boundaries

- ⌔2 Main postal regions, with numbers indicating first digit of postcode

⌜23⌝ Secondary postal regions, with numbers indicating first two digits of postcode

▢ German-speaking

▨ German- and Sorbian-speaking

50 km

Germany
Deutschland

Area: 356,945 sq. km. (137,817 sq. miles)

Population: 79,670,000 (1990 estimate)

Population density: 223.2 per sq. km

Capital: Berlin (population 3,410,000 (1989 estimate))

Currency : 1 Deutschmark = 100 Pfennig

Languages

German is the official language, spoken by 98 per cent of the population. Sorbian, also known as Wendish and Lusation, is a Slavic language spoken in Lusatia, which is a small area in the south-east of the former East Germany. There are some 50,000 speakers of two dialects: Upper Sorbian (around the city of Bautzen), resembling Czech; and Lower Sorbian, spoken around Cottbus, resembling Polish. Other minority languages include Danish in Jutland and Friesian in Jutland and Emden.

Company names

It is more correct to place the words indicating the *nature* of a company in front of the name of the company, thus:

Bäcker Klaus Schmidt

You will, however, often find these activity indications *after* the company name, thus:

Klaus Schmidt, Bäcker
Klaus Schmidt (Bäcker)

German company names will also often contain the name of the *inhaber(in)* (owner), usually indicated by the abbreviation 'Inh.'

Company Types

The following company types may be recognized in German company names:

AG
BGB Gesellschaft
Einzelfirma
Genossenschaft
GmbH (also often written Gesellschaft mbH)
GmbH & Co. KG
KG
KGAA
OHG
Stiftung

Contact names

The words *zu Händen*, abbreviated to z.H. or z.Hd. mean 'For the attention of'.

Addresses

In company addresses the name of the company precedes the name of the contact. The house number follows the street name. The salutation of the person or the type of company comes on the top line alone. Thus :

Herrn
Günther Meyer
Goethestrasse 25
20002 Hamburg

or

Bäcker Meyer
Herrn Mirgel
In der Raste 10
53001 Bonn

The general rule is that the thoroughfare name and the thoroughfare type are written as one word, thus:

Hauptstrasse
Bahnhofstrasse

There are two important exceptions. If the thoroughfare name refers to the real name of a place (e.g. a town name, a castle name, a forest name, etc.) then there is a space between the thoroughfare name and the thoroughfare type, thus:

Mainzer Strasse
Hamburger Allee

The second exception is where complete personal names are used. In these cases, each component of the street name is separated with a hyphen. Note, however, that surnames only are not covered by this exception. Thus:

Kaiser-Wilhelm-Strasse
Albert-Einstein-Strasse

but

Beethovenstrasse
Einsteinstrasse

In street names beginning with prepositions or some adjectives ('Am', 'An', 'Alter', etc.) the preposition or adjective is followed by a space, thus:

Alter Marktstrasse

Thoroughfare types

Below is a list of the most commonly occurring thoroughfare types, with the abbreviated form(s) which you are most likely to find in address databases:

Allee		Hof	
Berg		Kamp	
Boulevard	Bd	Markt	
		Platz	Pl
Bruch		Ring	
Bühl		Strasse	Str
Chaussee	Ch	Ufer	
Damm		Wall	
Gasse			
Graben		Weg	
Hafen		Weide	

Other nouns, adjectives and prepositions commonly found in address databases

NB: German grammar rules governing articles, prepositions and adjectives are complex, and there is no need to explain them here. It is only necessary to be able to recognize them when and where they occur in addresses. For this reason a list without further explanation is provided. As a very general rule of thumb, the prepositions and adjectives listed may have one of the following endings added: nothing; -e; -er; -em; -en or -es.

der/die/das/den/dem/des	= the
ein/eine/eines/einen/einem/einer	= a, an
und	= and
bis	= till, until, up to
für	= for
von	= of, from
zu, zu der (zur), zu dem (zum), nach	= to, towards
bei, bei der/den/dem (beim)	= near, at
an, an der/den/dem (am)	= at, by, towards
auf, auf der/den/dem	= on
in, in der/den/dem (im)	= in
gegenüber	= opposite, facing
nächst, neben, neben der/dem/den	= next to
hinter, hinter der/den/dem	= behind
vor, vor der/den/dem	= before, in front of
zwischen, zwischen der/den/dem	= between, amongst
über, über der/den/dem	= over, above, beyond
unter, unter der/dem/den	= under, beneath, below

mit	= with
neu/neue	= new
alt/alte	= old
kurz/kurze/kurzen/kurzer/ kurzem/kurzes (K.)	= short
lang/lange/langen/langer/ langem/langes (L./Lge.)	= long
gross/grosse/grossen/ grosser/grossem/grosses (G.)	= large
klein/kleine/kleinen/ kleiner/kleinem/kleines (K./Kl./Kle.)	= small
nord	= north
ost	= east
süd	= south
west	= west
sankt (St.)	= saint
Industrieterrein, Industriegebiet	= industrial estate

Postbox

This is written as Postfach followed by a number of digits in this pattern:

Postfach XX XX XX

Postboxes have their own postcodes, referring to the location of the post office where the box is situated, not of the company itself.

Postcodes

The postcode is written on the same line, and before, the name of the town.

The 4-digit postcode, valid since 1961, was changed on 1 July 1993. The old 4-digit postcode correspondend to a municipality.

The new postcodes contain 5 digits, and begin with any digit between 0 and 9. The first digit indicates the area of Germany in which the address is situated :

0 = Dresden/Leipzig
1 = Berlin
2 = Hamburg
3 = Hannover
4 = Düsseldorf/Essen
5 = Köln/Bonn
6 = Frankfurt
7 = Stuttgart
8 = München
9 = Nürnberg/Erfurt

The second digit indicates a smaller region within this area.

The third digit indicates a city, a part of a city, or a municipality.

The last two digits are split into three categories, each indicating (a) postboxes; (b) large users (receiving on average more than 2,000 letters per working day); and (c) groups of residences/businesses.

So, for example, a postcode may be built up as follows:

39	Region
390	Musterhausen
39001-39058	Post boxes
39060-39078	Large users
39080-39097	Deliveries (residences/businesses)
391	Bischofstadt
etc.	

Postbox users now have two postcodes, one referring to their post box (for letters), the other referring to their street address (for packages etc.).

The international sorting codes W- and O- (indicating respectively West and East Germany) have been replaced by the single international sorting code D-.

The delivery office number (the number which followed the town name, e.g. 2000 Hamburg 46) is no longer used.

Sorbian, a Slavic language, will be encountered in the following postcode areas:

01916, 01917, 01920, 02625, 02627, 02633, 02692, 02694, 02699, 02906, 02943, 02957, 02959, 02977, 02979, 02991, 02997, 02999, 03042–03055, 03042, 03044, 03058, 03096, 03099, 03130, 03139, 03149, 03172, 03185, 03197, 03205, 03222, 03226, 15907, 15913.

Towns

In the Sorbian-speaking area in the south-eastern part of the former East Germany, most towns and villages have both a German and a Sorbian name. The following list shows the corresponding names with their postcode areas:

German	Sorbian	Postcode
Arnsdorf	Warnoćicy	02633
Auritz	Wuricy	02627
Babow	Bobow	03099
Bärenbrück	Barbuk	03185
Baruth	Bart	02627
Bärwalde	Bjerwald	02999
Basabkwitz	Bozankecy	02625
Baschütz	Bošecy	02627
Bautzen	Budyšin	02625
Belgern	Běla Hora	02627
Belten	Bełośin	03226
Binnewitz	Bónjecy	02627
Birkau	Brěza	02633
Bloaschütz	Błohašecy	02627
Blösa	Brězow	02627
Bluno	Bluń	02979
Bocka	Bokowc	01920
Bolbritz	Bolborcy	02627
Bornitz	Boranecy	02627
Boxberg	Hamor	02943
Brahmow	Brama	03096

Brehmen	Brěmjo	02694
Brieschko	Brěžki	02997
Briesen	Brjazyna	03096
Briesing	Brězynka	02694
Brießnitz	Brězecy	02627
Brohna	Bronjo	02627
Brösa	Brězyna	02694
Brösang	Brězynka	02633
Bröthen	Brětnja	02979
Buchwalde	Bukonjna	02694
Burg	Bórk	02979
Burg	Borkowy	03096
Burghammer	Bórkhamor	02979
Burgneudorf	Nowa Wjes	02979
Buscheritz	Bóšericy	02633
Byhleguhre	Běla Gora	15913
Byhlen	Bělin	15913
Calau	Kalawa	03205
Camina	Kamjenej	02627
Caminau	Kamjenej	02699
Canitz-Christina	Konjecy	02627
Cannewitz	Kanecy	01920
Cannewitz	Skanecy	02627
Caseritz	Kozarcy	01920
Caßlau	Koslow	02699
Coblenz	Koblicy	02633
Cölln	Chelno	02627
Commerau	Komorow	02694
Commerau bei Königswartha	Komorow p Rakec	02699
Cortnitz	Chortnica	02627
Cosul	Kózły	02692
Cottbus	Chośebuz	03042–03055
Crosta	Chróst	02694
Crostwitz	Chróścicy	01920
Cunnewitz	Konjecy	01920
Dahlitz	Dalic	03099
Dahlowitz	Dalicy	02694
Dahren	Darin	02633
Daranitz	Torońca	02627
Dauban	Dubo	02906
Denkwitz	Dženikecy	02692
Diehmen	Demjany	02633
Dissen	Dešno	03096
Döberkitz	Debrikecy	02627
Doberschau	Dobruša	02692
Doberschütz	Dobrošecy	02694
Doberschütz bei Neschwitz	Dobrošicy p Njeswačidło	02699
Dobranitz	Dobranecy	02633
Döbschke	Debiškow	02633
Döhlen	Delany	02627
Dörgenhausen	Němcy	02979
Drachhausen	Hochoza	03185
Drauschkowitz	Družkecy	02633

Drehna	Tranje	02999
Drehnow	Drjenow	03185
Drehsa	Droždźij	02627
Dreikretscham	Haslow	02633
Dreistern	Tři Hwězdy	02633
Dreiweibern	Tři Žony	02999
Dretschen	Drječin	02633
Drewitz	Drjejce	03197
Driewitz	Drěwcy	02999
Droben	Droby	02699
Dubrauke	Dubrawka	02627
Dubring	Dubrjenk	02997
Dürrbach	Dyrbach	02906
Dürrwicknitz	Wěteńca	01920
Ebendörfel	Bělšecy	02692
Eichow	Dubje	03099
Entenschenke	Kača Korčma	02699
Eulowitz	Jiłocy	02692
Eutrich	Jitk	02699
Fehrow	Prjawoz	03096
Fleißdorf	Ługi	03226
Forst	Baršć	03149
Förstgen	Dołha Boršć	02906
Friedersdorf	Bjedrichecy	02999
Gablenz	Jabłońk	02953
Gaußig	Huska	02633
Gebelzip	Hbjelsk	02627
Geierswalde	Lejno	02991
Geißlitz	Kislica	02694
Glaubnitz	Hłupońca	01920
Gleina	Hlina	02694
Glinzig	Glinsk	03099
Gnaschwitz	Hnašecy	02692
Göbeln	Kobjelń	02694
Göda	Hodźij	02633
Golenz	Holca	02633
Gränze	Hrańca	01920
Gröditz	Hrodźišćo	02627
Großbrösern	Přezdřeń	02627
Großdönschütz	Debsecy	02692
Groß Düben	Dźěwin	02959
Großdubrau	Wulka Dubrawa	02694
Großkunitz	Chójnica	02692
Groß Neida	Wulka Nydej	02979
Großpostwitz	Budestecy	02692
Groß Särchen	Wulke Ždźary	02999
Groß Saubernitz	Zubornica	02627
Großwelka	Wulki Wjelkow	02627
Grötsch	Groźišćo	03185
Grubditz	Hrubośicy	02627
Grubschütz	Hrubjelčicy	02692
Grünbusch	Haj	02627

Guben	Gubin	03172
Guhra	Hora	02699
Guhrow	Gory	03096
Gulben	Gołbin	03099
Günthersdorf	Hunćericy	02633
Guttau	Hučina	02694
Haasow	Hažow	03058
Haide	Hola	02957
Halbendorf	Brežowka	02959
Halbendorf, Spree	Połpica, Sprjewa	02694
Heinersbrück	Most	03185
Hermsdorf	Hermanecy	02999
Hochkirch	Bukecy	02627
Höflein	Wudwor	01920
Holscha	Holešow	02699
Holschdubrau	Holešowska Dubrawka	02699
Horka	Hórki	01920
Hornow	Lěśće	03130
Horscha	Hóršow	02906
Hoske	Hózk	02997
Hoyerswerda	Wojerecy	02977
Jannowitz	Janecy	02633
Jänschwalde	Janšojce	03197
Jänschwalde Ost	Janšojce podzajtšo	03197
Jauer	Jawora	01920
Jauernick	Jawornik	02627
Jenkwitz	Jenkecy	02627
Jeschütz	Ješicy	02694
Jeßnitz bei Puschwitz	Jaseńca p Bóšicy	02699
Jeßnitz, Gebirge	Jaseńca, Horiny	02627
Jetscheba	Jatřob	02694
Johannisbad	Janska kupjel	01920
Johnsdorf	Jeńšecy	02699
Kamenz	Kamjenc	01917
Kaschel	Košla	02906
Kaschwitz	Kašecy	01920
Katschwitz	Koćica	02633
Kaupen	Kupy	02957
Kauppa	Kupoj	02694
Keula	Kulowc	02997
Kleinbautzen	Budyšink	02627
Kleinbrösern	Přezdrěńk	02627
Kleindöbschütz	Małe Debsecy	02692
Kleinförstchen	Mała Boršć	02633
Kleingaußig	Mała Huska	02633
Kleinhänchen	Mały Wosyk	01920
Kleinholscha	Mały Holešow	02699
Kleinkunitz	Chójnička	02692
Klein Loitz	Łojojc	03130
Klein Oelsa	Wolešnica	02906
Klein Partwitz	Bjezdowy	02979
Kleinpraga	Mała Praha	02633

Klein Radisch	Radšowk	02906
Kleinsaubernitz	Zubornička	02694
Kleinseidau	Zajdow	02627
Kleinseitschen	Žičeńk	02633
Kleinwelka	Mały Wjelkow	02627
Klitten	Klětno	02906
Klix	Klukš	02694
Knappenrode	Hórnikecy	02979
Koblenz	Koblicy	02999
Kohlwesa	Kolwaz	02627
Kolkwitz	Gołkojce	03099
Königswartha	Rakecy	02699
Kopschin	Kopšin	01920
Kotitz	Kotecy	02627
Kotten	Koćina	02997
Kreba	Chrjebja	02906
Kreckwitz	Krakecy	02627
Kringelsdorf	Krynhelecy	02943
Krimnitz	Kśimnice	03222
Krinitz	Krójca	02699
Kronförstchen	Křiwa Boršš	02627
Kubschütz	Kubšicy	02627
Kumschütz	Kumšicy	02627
Kunersdorf	Kosobuz	03099
Kuppritz	Koporcy	02627
Laske	Łask	01920
Lauske	Łusč	02627
Lehde	Lědy	03222
Lehn	Lejno	02627
Lehndorf	Lejno	01920
Leipe	Lipje	03226
Leutwitz	Lutyjecy	02633
Liebegast	Lubhozdź	02997
Liebon	Liboń	02633
Lieske	Lěskej	02694
Limberg	Limbark	03099
Lippen	Lipiny	02999
Lippitsch	Lipič	02699
Lissahora	Liša Hora	02699
Litschen	Złyčin	02999
Litten	Lětoń	02627
Lobendorf	Łobožice	03226
Loga	Łahow	02633
Lohsa	Łaz	02999
Lömischau	Lemišow	02694
Lomsche bei Luppa	Łomsk p Łupoj	02694
Lomske	Łomsk	02699
Löschau	Lešawa	02627
Lubachau	Lubochow	02627
Lübben	Lubin	15907
Lübbenau	Lubnjow	03222
Luga	Łuh	02699
Luppa	Łupoj	02694

Luppedubrau	Łupjanska Dubrawka	02694
Luttowitz	Lutobč	02627
Malschwitz	Malešecy	02694
Maltitz	Malećicy	02627
Margarethenhütte	Margarećina Heta	02694
Märkischheide	Wusoka	03226
Maukendorf	Mučow	02979
Maust	Hus	03185
Mehltheuer	Lubjenc	02627
Merzdorf	Žylowk	03042
Meschwitz	Mječicy	02627
Milkel	Minakał	02699
Milkersdorf	Gornej	03099
Milkwitz	Miłkecy	02627
Miltitz	Miłoćicy	01920
Mönau	Manjow	02999
Mortka	Mortkow	02999
Mücka	Mikow	02906
Mühlrose	Miłoraz	02959
Mulkwitz	Mułkecy	02959
Muschelwitz	Myšecy	02633
Müschen	Myšyn	03096
Nardt	Narć	02979
Naundorf	Njabožkojce	03226
Naußlitz	Nowoslicy	01920
Nebelschütz	Njebjelčicy	01920
Nechern	Njechorń	02627
Nedaschütz	Njezdašecy	02633
Neschwitz	Njeswačidło	02699
Neubloaschütz	Nowe Błohašecy	02633
Neubornitz	Nowe Boranecy	02627
Neu Brohna	Nowe Bronjo	02627
Neu Buchwalde	Nowa Bukojna	02999
Neudiehmen	Nowe Dejany	02633
Neudorf	Nowa Wjes	02906
Neudorf	Nowa Wjes	02997
Neudorf bei Königswartha	Nowa Wjes p Rakecy	02699
Neudorf bei Neschwitz	Nowa Wjes p Njeswačidło	02699
Neudörfel	Nowa Wjeska	01920
Neudörfel	Nowa Wjeska	02694
Neudorf, Spree	Nowa Wjes, Sprjewja	02694
Neuendorf	Nowa Wjas	03185
Neuhof	Nowy Dwór	01920
Neujeßnitz	Nowa Jaseńca	02699
Neukuppritz	Nowe Koporcy	02627
Neulauske	Nowy Łusč	02699
Neumalsitz	Nowe Małsecy	02625
Neupurschwitz	Nowe Poršicy	02627
Neupuschwitz	Nowe Bóšicy	02699
Neusärchen	Nowe Zdźarki	02694
Neustadt	Nowe Město	02979
Neustädtel	Nowe Město	01920
Neuwiese	Nowa Łuka	02979

Niedergurig	Delnja Hórka	02694
Niederkaina	Delnja Kina	02625
Niederuhna	Delni Wunjow	02627
Niesky	Niska	02906
Niethen	Nećin	02627
Nochten	Wochozy	02943
Nostitz	Nosaćicy	02627
Nucknitz	Nuknica	01920
Oberförstchen	Hornja Boršć	02633
Obergurig	Hornja Hórka	02692
Ober Prauske	Hornje Brusy	02906
Oberuhna	Horni Wunjow	02627
Oehna	Wownjow	02625
Oppitz	Psowje	02699
Ostro	Wotrow	01920
Pannewitz, Taucher	Banecy, Tuchor	01916
Panschwitz-Kuckau	Pančicy-Kukow	01920
Papitz	Popojce	03099
Paßditz	Pozdecy	02633
Peitz	Picnjo	03185
Petershain	Hóznica	02906
Pielitz	Splósk	02627
Pietzschwitz	Běčicy	02633
Piskowitz	Pěskecy	01920
Pließkowitz	Plusnikecy	02694
Plotzen	Błócany	02627
Pommritz	Pomorcy	02627
Prautitz	Prawoćicy	01920
Preilack	Pśiłuk	03185
Preititz	Přiwćicy	02627
Preske	Praskow	02633
Preuschwitz	Přišecy	02692
Prischwitz	Přěčecy	02633
Purschwitz	Poršicy	02627
Puschwitz	Bóšicy	02699
Quartitz	Chwaćicy	02694
Quoos	Chasow	02699
Rabitz	Rabocy	02627
Rachlau	Rachlow	02627
Rachlau	Rachlow	02997
Rackel	Rakojdy	02627
Räckelwitz	Worklecy	01920
Raddusch	Raduš	03226
Radewiese	Radowiza	03185
Radibor	Radwor	02627
Ralbitz	Ralbicy	01920
Rattwitz	Ratarjecy	02625
Rauden	Rudej	02999
Reichwalde	Rychwałd	02943
Reuthen	Ruśi	03130
Riegel	Roholń	02999
Rieschen	Zrěšin	02627

Rodewitz	Rodecy	02627
Rohne	Rowno	02959
Rosenthal	Różant	01920
Ruben	Rubyn	03096
Ruhethal	Wotpočink	02694
Saalau	Salow	02997
Sabrodt	Zabrod	02979
Saccassne	Zakaznja	03096
Sagar	Zagor	02957
Salga	Załhow	02694
Salzenforst	Słona Boršc	02627
Sandförstgen	Borštka	02627
Särchen	Zdźar	02694
Saritsch	Zarěč	02633
Särka	Žarki	02627
Saspow	Zaspy	03044
Säuritz	Žricy	01920
Scheckwitz	Šekecy	02627
Schleife	Slepo	02959
Schlungwitz	Słónkecy	02692
Schmeckwitz	Smječkecy	01920
Schmerlitz	Smjerdźaca	01920
Schmochtitz	Smochćicy	02627
Schmogrow	Smogorjow	03096
Schönau	Corny	01920
Schönhöhe	Šejnejda	03185
Schwarzadler	Čorny Hodler	02627
Schwarzaußlitz	Čorne Noslicy	02692
Schwarze Pumpe	Carna Plumpa	03139
Schwarzkolim	Čorny Chołmc	02991
Schweinerden	Swinjarnja	01920
Sdier	Zdźěr	02694
See	Jězor	02906
Seidewinkel	Židźino	02979
Seitschen	Žičeń	02633
Semmichau	Semichow	02633
Siebitz	Zejicy	01920
Siebitz	Dźiwoćicy	02633
Singwitz	Dźěžnikecy	02692
Soculahora	Sokolca	02627
Sollschwitz	Sulšecy	02633
Sollschwitz	Sulšecy	02997
Soritz	Sowrjecy	02627
Sornßig	Žornosyki	02627
Spittel	Špikały	02627
Spittwitz	Spytecy	02633
Spohla	Spale	02979
Spreetal	Sprjewiny Doł	02979
Spreewiese	Lichań	02694
Spreewitz	Šprjejcy	02979
Spremberg	Grodk	03130
Sprey	Sprjowje	02943
Steindörfel	Trjebjenća	02627

Steinitz	Šćeńca	02999
Stiebitz	Sćijecy	02625
Storcha	Baćoń	02633
Stradow	Tšadow	03226
Straupitz	Pšupc	15913
Striesow	Strjažow	03096
Strohschütz	Stróžišćo	02627
Suschow	Zušow	03226
Tätzschwitz	Ptačecy	02991
Tauer	Turjej	03185
Techritz	Ćěchorjecy	02692
Teichhäuser	Haty	01920
Temritz	Ćěmjercy	02627
Terpe	Terpje	03139
Tiegling	Tyhelk	02999
Trebendorf	Trjebin	02959
Truppen	Trupin	02699
Tschaschwitz	Casecy	01920
Übigau	Wbohow	02699
Uhyst	Delni Wujězd	02999
Vetschau	Wětošow	03226
Wadelsdorf	Zakrjejc	03130
Waditz	Wadecy	02627
Wartha	Stróža	02694
Wartha	Stróža	02999
Wawitz	Wawicy	02627
Weicha	Wichowy	02627
Weidlitz	Wutołčicy	02633
Weigersdorf	Wukrančicy	02906
Weißenberg	Wóspork	02627
Weißig	Wysoka	02627
Weißkeißel	Wuskidź	02957
Weißkollm	Běly Chołmc	02999
Weißnaußlitz	Běłe Noslicy	02633
Weißwasser	Běła Woda	02943
Wendischbaselitz	Serbske Pazlicy	01920
Werben	Wjerbno	03096
Weskow	Wjaska	03130
Wessel	Wjesel	02699
Wetro	Wětrow	02699
Wittichenau	Kulow	02997
Wolfshain	Šisej	03130
Wuischke bei Hochkirch	Wuježk p Bukecy	02627
Wuischke bei Weißenberg	Wuježk p Wóspork	02627
Wurschen	Worcyn	02627
Zahsow	Cazow	03099
Zeißig	Ćisk	02979
Zerkwitz	Cerkwica	03222
Zerna	Sernjany	01920
Zerre	Drětwa	02979
Zescha	Šěšow	02699

Zieschütz	Cyžecy	02627
Zimpel-Tauer	CympłTurjo	02906
Zischkowitz	Čéškecy	02633
Zockau	Cokow	02633
Zscharnitz	Čornecy	02633
Zschillichau	Čelchow	02694
Zschorna	Čornjow	02627

The following list gives foreign language equivalents of German city names.

NB: Towns ending in -burg in German are usually written ending in -bourg or -burgo in French and Italian respectively.

German	English	French	Spanish	Italian	Dutch
Aachen	Aix-la-Chappelle	Aix-la-Chapelle	Aquisgrán	Aquisgrana	Aken
Berlin			Berlín	Berlino	Berlijn
Braunschweig	Brunswick				
Breisach		Brisach			
Bremen				Brema	
Dresden		Drèsde		Dresda	
Frankfurt am Main	Frankfurt	Francfort		Francoforte	Frankfort aan de Main
Freiburg		Fribourg		Friburgo	
Hamburg	Hamburg	Hambourg	Hamburgo	Amburgo	
Kleve	Cleves				
Koblenz	Coblenz	Coblence	Coblenza		
Köln	Cologne	Cologne	Colonia	Colonia	Keulen
Konstanz	Constance	Constance		Constanza	
Leipzig				Lipsia	
Lübeck				Lubecca	
Mainz		Mayence	Maguncia		
München	Munich	Munich	Munich	Monaco (di Baviera)	
Nürnberg	Nuremberg			Norimberga	Neurenberg
Stuttgart				Stoccarda	
Trier			Tréveris		

Settlement names in Germany will ofter contain a suffix indicating geographical position such as *am Rhein* or *bei Kamenz*. The new postcodes incorporate this information and the Bundepost prefers that such suffixes are not used in addresses except where two settlements of the same name have the same postcode. The *Postleitzahlenbuch*, published by the Bundespost, gives the correct written form for each settlement.

Administrative districts

Germany has 16 states (*Bundesländer*) split into 36 regions (*Regierungsbezirke*). These names are not used in addresses. In the following list, the English translations are given in brackets:

State	Region
Baden-Württemberg	Freiburg
	Karlsruhe
	Stuttgart
	Tubingen
Bayern (Bavaria)	Mittelfranken
	Niederbayern
	Oberbayern
	Oberfranken

State	Region
	Oberpfalz
	Schwaben
	Unterfranken
Berlin	
Brandenburg	
Bremen	
Hamburg	
Hessen (Hesse)	Darmstadt Giessen Kassel
Mecklenburg-Vorpommern (Mecheleberg Pomerania)	
Niedersachsen (Lower Saxony)	Braunschweig Lüneburg Hannover Weser-Ems
Nordrhein-Westfalen (North Rhine-Westphalia)	Arnsberg Detmold Düsseldorf Köln Münster
Rheinland-Pfalz (Rhineland-Palatinate)	Koblenz Pfalz Trier
Saarland	
Sachsen (Saxony)	
Sachsen-Anhalt (Saxony-Anhalt)	
Schleswig-Holstein	
Thüringen (Thuringia)	

Greece
Hellas

Area: 131,957 sq. km. (50,949 sq. miles)

Population: 10,020,000 (1989 estimate)

Population density : 77.8 per sq. km

Capital: Athens (Athínai) (Population 885,737 (1981))

Currency: 1 drachma = 100 leptae

Languages

Greek (*Demotiki*) is the official language, spoken by 95 per cent of the population. Other languages spoken are Macedonian (2 per cent), Turkish (1 per cent) and Albanian (1 per cent).

Addresses

Addresses have the following structure:

    Contact name or Business name
    Street name[ ]number
    postcode[ ]TOWN NAME

For example:

    George Larsis
    Alkamenou 37
    11780 ATHÍNAI

Postcodes

Postcodes consist of 5 consecutive digits. They are written on the same line (the last line) and before the town name in the following format:

999[ ]99

for example:

145 63 Athens
546 45 Thessaloniki

Towns

The following list gives foreign language equivalents of Greek town names:

Greek	English	German	Spanish	Italian	Dutch
Athínai	Athens	Athen	Atenas	Atene	Athene
Patrai		Patras		Patrasso	
Pireus		Piräus	Pireo	Pireo	Piraeus
Ródos		Rhodos	Rodas	Rodi	Rhodos
Thessaloniki	Thessalonika	Salonika	Tesalónica	Salonicco	Thessalonica

Administrative districts

Greece has 9 regions (*Dhiamerisma*) plus Greater Athens and 52 departments (*Nomoi*). They are not used in addresses and are listed below with the English translation in backets:

Region	Department
Aegean Islands	Khíos
	Kikládhes
	Lésvos
	Sámos
	Sporádhes
Athinai (Athens)	
Ióníoi Nísoi	Kefalliniá
	Kérkira (Corfu)
	Levkás
	Zákinthos
Ípiros (Epirus)	Árta
	Ioánnina
	Préveza
	Thesprotia
Kríti (Crete)	Iráklion
	Khaniá
	Lasíthi
	Réthimnon
Makedhonía (Macedonia)	Dráma
	Flórina
	Grevená
	Imathía

	Kastoría
	Kaválla
	Khalkidhíki
	Kilkís
	Kozáni
	Pangaíon óros
	Pélla
	Piería
	Sérrai
	Thessaloníki
Pelopónnisos (Peloponnes)	Akhaïa
	Argolís
	Arkadhía
	Ilía
	Kórinthos
	Lakonía
	Messinía
Sterea Ellás-Évvoia	Aitolía-Akarnania
	Attiki
	Evritanía
	Évvoia
	Fokís
	Fthiótis
	Voíotía
Thessalía (Thessaly)	Kardhítsa
	Lárisa
	Magnisía
	Tríkkala
Thráki (Thrace)	Évros
	Rodhópi
	Xánthi

Greenland
Grønland

Greenland is a self-governing Island Region of Denmark but relies on Denmark for its foreign affairs.

Area: 2,175,600 sq. km (840,000 sq. miles)

Population: 55,533 (1991 estimate)

Population density: 0.026 per sq. km

Capital: Nuuk (previously called Godthåb) (population 12,181 (1991))

Currency : 1 Danish krone = 100 øre

Languages

The official languages are Danish and Greenlandic, an Inuit (Eskimo) language.

Postcodes

Greenland belongs to the Danish postal system and, like Denmark, all its postcodes consist of 4 consecutive digits placed before and on the same line as the settlement name. All Greenland postcodes begin with the number 39.

Towns

The following list gives corresponding settlement names in Greenland's two languages:

Inuit	*Danish*
Nuuk	Godthåb
Qeqertarsuaq	Godhavn
Kangerlussuaq	Søndre Strømfjord
Paamiut	Frederikshåb

Telephone numbers

The international dialling code is 299. There are no area codes.

Guernsey

Guernsey consists of the Channel Islands of Guernsey, Alderney, Sark and Herm. It is a Crown Dependency, and therefore not part of the United Kingdom of Great Britain and Northern Ireland. Except in matters of foreign affairs and defence, it is effectively an independent nation, and its inhabitants are fiercely proud of their status. The words 'United Kingdom', 'Great Britain' or 'England' should not be used in addresses - it is better to use 'Channel Islands'.

Area: Guernsey : 65 sq. km (25 sq. miles)
Alderney : 7.9 sq. km (3 sq. miles)
Sark: 5.5 sq. km (2.1 sq. miles)
Herm: 2 sq. km. (0.8 sq. miles)

Population: Guernsey : 55,482 (1986)
Alderney : 2,000 (1985 estimate)
Sark: 420 (1984)
Herm with
Jethou : 107 (1971)

Population density: Guernsey : 853.5 per sq. km
Alderney : 264.6 per sq. km.
Sark: 76.4 per sq. km.
Herm: 53.5 per sq. km

Capital: Guernsey: St. Peter Port (population 18,000)
Alderney : St. Anne's (population 1,000

Currency: 1 Pound Sterling = 100 pence.

Languages

English is the official language. A Norman patois, which has no written form, is spoken in some parishes.

Company names, contact names, addresses, postbox

The same rules and formats apply as in the United Kingdom.

Postcodes

A postcode system was introduced into Guernsey only in June 1993. It follows the same structure and format as United Kingdom postcodes. Each postcode begins with the letters GY.

Telephone numbers

Guernsey forms part of the United Kingdom telephone system. The international dialling code is 44, and the area code for the whole dependency is 0481.

Hungary
Magyarország

Area: 93,031 sq. km (35,919 sq. miles)

Population: 10,355,000 (1991 estimate)

Population density: 111.3 per sq. km

Capital: Budapest (population 2,016,132 (1990))

Currency: 1 forint = 100 fillér .

Languages

Hungarian is the official language, spoken by 97 per cent of the population. Romany (1 per cent), German (1 per cent) and Slovak (1 per cent) are also spoken.

Company names

A word indicating the *nature* of the company always follows the name of the company. The indication of legal company status follows this. So, for example:

Kovács Pékség Kft.

meaning Smith's Bakers Ltd. The main legal types found are Kft. (or KFT.) and BT.

Contact names

Contact names are always written with the surname first followed by the first name, without a comma separating them.

Addresses

Addresses may be written in one of the following formats, both of which are in common use and both of which are correct:

173

Recipient name
postcode[ ]TOWN NAME
Thoroughfare name[ ]thoroughfare type[ ]number

For example:

Nagy Sándor
1022 BUDAPEST
Hermann Ottó út 2

The alternative form is:

Recipient name
TOWN NAME
Thoroughfare name[ ]thoroughfare type[ ]number
postcode

For example:

Industrila Developments AB
BUDAPEST
Kavics utca 13
1025

When the address is split into more than one apartment, this can be indicated by showing the floor number in roman numerals, followed by a slash and then the apartment number in this way:

Kavics utca 13 II /3

The slash can be replaced by the word *em*, meaning floor, and the apartment number can be followed by the word *ajtó*, meaning door, in this way:

Kavios utca 13 II em 3 ajtó

Thoroughfare types

The thoroughfare type should always be written starting with a lower case letter, and it is written after and separately from the street name. The most commonly occurring thoroughfare types, with their abbreviated forms, are:

árok	mező
dűlő	park
fasor	rakpart (rpt.)
kert	sétány
körönd	sor
körút (krt.)	sugárúk (sgt.)
köz	tér
lejtő	tere
lépcső	út
liget	utca (u.)
	útja

The genitive forms tere and útja occur where the street name is in the plural, such as Roses Street (útja) or Heroes Square (tere). The types árok, dűlő, kert, lejtő, lépcső, liget, mező, park and sor can also be street names, as in the English Park Lane or Court Street, but their position in the address will always make clear whether it is a thoroughfare name (with a capital letter) or a thoroughfare type (without a capital letter).

Postbox

Postbox is written Postafiók, usually shortened to p.f., P.f., Pf. or pf.

Nouns and prepositions commonly found in address databases

In Hungarian, adjectives are added as suffixes to nouns and can therefore not be identified as separate words.

a (before a consonant), az (before a vowel)	= the
egy	= a, an
és	= and
új	= new
öreg/regi	= old
észak	= north
kelet	= east
dél	= south
nyugat	= west
Szent (Szt.)	= Saint (St.)

Postcodes

Postcodes consist of 4 consecutive numbers, written either before the town name or on their own on the last line of the address. They are sometimes written with spaces between each number.

Postcodes for Budapest always begin with a 1. The second and third digits indicate the district, whilst the last digit is determined by the post office.

Towns

Budapest is often abbreviated to Bp. in addresses.

Administrative districts

Hungary has 20 counties (*Megye*). They are not used in addresses. They are listed below:

Bács-Kiskun	Jász-Nagykun-Szolnok
Baranya	Komárom-Esztergom
Békés	Nógrád
Borsod-Abaúj-Zemplén	Pest
Budapest	Somogy
Csongrád	Szabolcs-Szatmár-Bereg
Fejér	Tolna
Györ-Moson-Sopron	Vas
Hajdú-Bihar	Veszprém
Heves	Zala

Iceland
Ísland

Area: 103,000 sq. km (39,769 sq. miles)

Population: 253,500 (1989 estimate)

Population density: 2.5 per sq. km

Capital: Reykjavik (Reykjavík) population 96,708 (1989 estimate))

Currency: 1 Icelandic krona = 100 aurar

Languages

Icelandic is spoken by 100 per cent of the population.

Contact names

Care must be taken when addressing Icelanders as members of the same family will have different surnames. Surnames are still formed from the name of the father followed by *dottír* for females and *son* for males. Thus Eirík and Rutar, son and daughter respectively of Magnus Jonsson will be Eirík Magnusson and Rutar Magnusdottír. For this reason, Icelandic telephone directories are ordered on the basis of first names.

Addresses

Addresses are written in the following format:

    Contact name
    Street name[ ]number
    postcode[ ]TOWN NAME

For example:

    Jon Jonsson
    Einimel 80
    107 REYKJAVIK

The thoroughfare type is suffixed to the thoroughfare name without a space, as in, for example:

Holtagata 5

Below is a list of the most commonly occurring thoroughfare types:

barð	melur
borg	múli
braut	nes
byggð	sel
fell	sendi
gata	siða
gerði	strætii
götu	tangitún
grund	teigur
hagi	torg
háls	tún
hjalli	vangur
hlíð	vegi
holt	vegur
land	vellir
lundur	

Postbox

This is written as Póshólf.

Towns

The capital of Iceland, *Reykjavík* is generally known as *Reykjavik* (without the accent on the final i) in most other European languages. It is known as *Reikiavik* in Spanish.

Administrative districts

Iceland has 8 regions:

Asturlandskjördæmi
Midvesturlandskjördæmi
Nordurlandskjördæmi eystra
Nordurlandskjördæmi vestra
Reykjaneskjördæmi
Reykjavík
Sudurlandskjördæmi
Vestfjardakjördæmi

They are not used in addresses.

Telephone numbers

Area codes in Iceland have 2 digits only.

Republic of Ireland

Éire

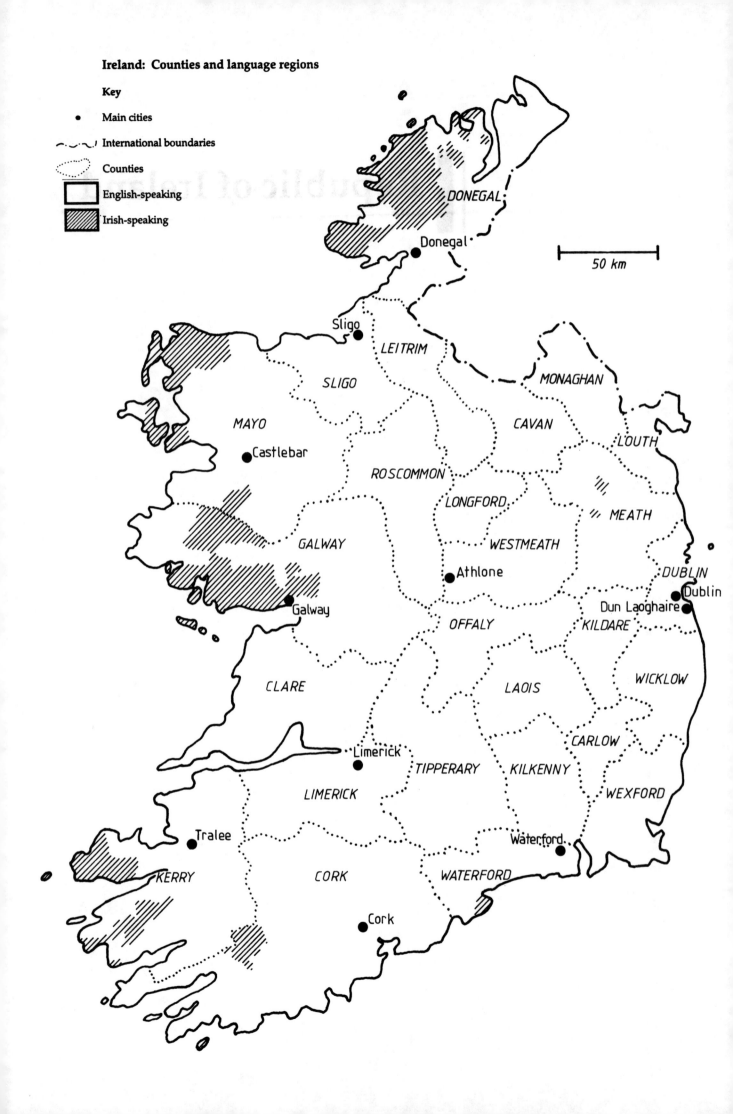

Ireland: Counties and language regions

Key

- **•** Main cities
- ·-··-··- International boundaries
- ⬭ Counties
- ⬜ English-speaking
- ▨ Irish-speaking

50 km

DONEGAL

● Donegal

● Sligo   LEITRIM

SLIGO   MONAGHAN

MAYO   CAVAN   LOUTH

● Castlebar   ROSCOMMON   LONGFORD   MEATH

WESTMEATH   DUBLIN

GALWAY   ● Athlone   ● Dublin

● Galway   OFFALY   Dun Laoghaire   KILDARE

CLARE   WICKLOW

LAOIS

CARLOW

● Limerick   TIPPERARY   KILKENNY   WEXFORD

LIMERICK

● Tralee   WATERFORD

KERRY   CORK   WATERFORD   ● Waterford

● Cork

Republic of Ireland
Éire

Area: 70,283 sq. km (27,136 sq. miles)

Population: 3,503,000 (1990 estimate)

Population density : 49.8 per sq. km.

Capital: Dublin (population 920,956 (1986))

Currency : Irish pound/punt = 100 pence

Languages

Ireland has two official languages: English, spoken by 95 per cent of the population, and Irish (Gaelic) spoken by the remaining 5 per cent. The Irish speakers are mainly to be found in 'An Ghaeltacht', areas to the west and south-west of the country.

Company names

Words indicating the *nature* of a company, when forming part of the company name, will always follow the name of the company, either after a comma or in brackets, thus:

John Smith, Bakers
John Smith (Bakers)

Company types

The following company types will be identified in Irish address databases:

Ltd
PLC

Addresses

Addresses are written in the following formats:

Recipient name
number[ ]Street name
TOWN NAME{[ ]sorting code}

or

Recipient name
number[,]Street name
TOWN NAME{[ ]sorting code}

For example:

Mr Gerard Carey
45 O'Connell Street
DUBLIN 1

The thoroughfare type is written after and separately from the thoroughfare name.

Thoroughfare types

Below is a list of commonly occurring thoroughfare types, with the abbreviated form(s), which you are most likely to find in address databases.

Alley		Hill	
Avenue	Ave.	Lane	
Boulevard	Bd.	Market	Mkt.
Centre	Ctr.	Mews	
Chambers		Parade	
Circus		Park	
Close		Place	Pl.
Court	Ct.	Quay	
Crescent	Cr.	Road	Rd.
Drive		Route	Rte.
Drove		Row	
Estate		Square	Sq.
Field		Street	St.
Gardens		Terrace	
Gate		Way	
Grove		Yard	

NB : The abbreviation for Saint is the same as that commonly used for Street, 'St.'.

Postbox

This is written as P.O. Box, Post Office Box, PO Box, or Postbox.

Postcodes

Ireland has no postcode system. Dublin addresses, however, will often contain a numeric sorting code, written after and on the same line as the town name.

Towns

Town names may be found in Gaelic, although they will more often be in English. The list below gives corresponding settlement names in English and Irish. The towns marked with an asterisk in the first list are in An Ghaeltacht, and their Irish names should therefore be used as preference. As Ireland has no postcodes, and the county is usually given in the address, the county in which the settlement is located is given.

English	Gaelic	County
Abbeyfeale	Mainistil na Féile	Limerick
Abbeyleix	Mainistir Laoise	Laois
* Achill Sound	Gob an Choire	Mayo
* Annagry	Anagaire	Donegal
Ardmore	Aird Mhór	Waterford
Arklow	An tInbhear Mór	Wicklow
Askeaton	Eas Géitine	Limerick
Athenry	Baile Átha an Ri	Galway
Athlone	Átha Luain	Westmeath
Athy	Baile Átha Í	Kildare
Balbriggan	Baile Brigín	Dublin
Ballaghaderreen	Bealach an Doírín	Roscommon
Ballina	Béal an Átha	Mayo
Ballinasloe	Beal Átha na Sluaighe	Galway
* Ballingeary	Béal Átha an Ghaorthaidh	Cork
Ballinrobe	Baile an Róba	Mayo
* Ballinskelligs	Baile an Sceilg	Kerry
* Ballydavid	Baile na nGall	Kerry
* Ballyferriter	Baile an Fheirtéaraigh	Kerry
Ballyhaunis	Béal Átha hAmhnais	Mayo
* Ballymakeera	Baile Mhic Ire	Cork
Ballymote	Baile an Mhotá	Sligo
Ballyshannon	Béal Átha Seanaidh	Donegal
* Ballyvourney	Baile Bhuirne	Cork
Baltinglass	Bealach Conglais	Wicklow
Bantry	Beanntraí	Cork
* Barna	Bearna	Galway
* Belmullet	Béal an Mhuirthead	Mayo
Belturbet	Béal Tairbirt	Cavan
* Binghamstown	An Geata Mór	Mayo
Birr	Biorra	Offaly
Blarney	An Bhlarna	Cork
Borris	An Buiríos	Carlow
Boyle	Mainastir na Búille	Roscommon
Bray	Bré	Wicklow
* Bunbeg	An Bun Beag	Donegal
Bunclody	Bun Clóidí	Wexford
Buncrana	Bun Chranncha	Donegal
Bundoran	Bun Dobhráin	Donegal
* Burtonport	Ailt an Chorráin	Donegal
Cahir	An Chathair	Tipperary

Cahirsiveen	Cathair Saidhbhín	Kerry
Callan	Callainn	Kilkenny
Cappoquin	Ceapach Choinn	Waterford
Carlow	Ceatharlach	Carlow
* Carna	Cárna	Galway
Carndonagh	Carn Domhnach	Donegal
* Carraroe	An Cheathrú Rua	Galway
* Carrick	An Charraig	Donegal
Carrickmacross	Carraig Mhachaire Rois	Monaghan
* Carrigart	Carraig Airt	Donegal
Cashel	Caiseal	Tipperary
Castlebar	Caisleán an Bharraigh	Mayo
Castlecomer	Caisleán an Chomair	Kilkenny
Castleisland	Oileán Chiarraí	Kerry
Castkerea	An Caisleán Riabhach	Roscommon
Cavan	An Cabhán	Cavan
Clara	Clóirtheach	Offaly
Claremorris	Clár Chlainne Mhuiris	Mayo
* Cloghan	An Clochán	Donegal
Clonakilty	Cloich na Coillte	Cork
* Clonbur	An Fhairche	Galway
Clones	Cluian Eios	Monaghan
Clonmel	Cluain Meala	Tipperary
Cóbh	An Cóbh	Cork
* Coelea	Cuil Aodha	Cork
Cong	Conga	Mayo
Cork	Corcaigh	Cork
* Costelloe	Casla	Galway
* Crolly	Croithli	Donegal
Croom	Cromadh	Limerick
Crosmolina	Crois Mhaoilíona	Mayo
Crosshaven	Bun an Tábhairne	Cork
* Dingle	An Daingean	Kerry
Donegal	Dún na nGall	Donegal
* Doochary	An Duchcharaid	Donegal
* Dooega	Dumha Éige	Mayo
* Downings	Dúnaibh	Donegal
Drogheda	Droichead Átha	Louth
Dublin	Baile Átha Cliath	Dublin
Dundalk	Dún Dealgan	Louth
Dungarvan	Dún Garbhan	Waterford
* Dungloe	An Clochán Liath	Donegal
Dunleer	Dún Léire	Louth
Dunmanway	Dún Mánmhaí	Cork
Dunmore	Dún Mór	Galway
* Dunquin	Dún Chaoin	Kerry
Edenderry	Éadan Doire	Offaly
Ennis	Inis	Clare
Enniscorthy	Inis Córthaidh	Wexford
Ennistimon	Inis Díomáin	Clare
* Falcarragh	An Fál Carrach	Donegal
Fermoy	Mainistir Fhear Maí	Cork
Fethard	Fiodh Ard	Tipperary

* Fintown	Baile na Finne	Donegal
Foynes	Faing	Limerick
Galway	An Ghaillimh	Galway
* Geesala	Gaoth Sáile	Mayo
* Glenamoy	Gleann na Muaidhe	Mayo
* Glencolumbkille	Gleann Cholm Cille	Donegal
Glengarriff	An Gleann Garbh	Cork
* Glinsk	Glinsce	Galway
Gorey	Guaire	Wexford
Gort	An Gort	Galway
* Gortahork	Gort an Choirce	Donegal
* Gortmore	An Gort Mór	Galway
* Gowla	Gabhla	Galway
Graiguenamanagh	Gráig na Manach	Kilkenny
Granard	Gránard	Longford
Greystones	Na Clocha Liatha	Wickford
* Gweedore	Gaoth Dobhair	Donegal
Headford	Áth Cinn	Galway
Hospital	An tOspigéal	Limerick
Inishcrone	Inis Crabhann	Sligo
* Inverin	Indreabhán	Galway
Julianstown	Baile Iúiliáin	Meath
Kanturk	Ceann Toirc	Cork
Kells	Ceanannus Mór	Meath
* Kilcar	Cill Charthaigh	Donegal
Kildare	Cill Dara	Kildare
Kilkee	Cill Chaoi	Clare
Kilkenny	Cill Chainnigh	Kilkenny
* Kilkieran	Cill Ciaráin	Galway
Killala	Cill Ala	Mayo
Killaloe	Cill Dalua	Clare
Killarney	Cill Áirne	Kerry
Killorglin	Cill Orglan	Kerry
Killybegs	Na Cealla Beaga	Donegal
Kilmallock	Cill Mocheallog	Limerick
Kilrush	Cill Rois	Clare
Kingscourt	Coill an Chollaigh	Cavan
Kinsale	Cionn tSáile	Cork
Leenan	An Líonan	Mayo
Letterkenny	Leitir Ceanainn	Donegal
Limerick	Luimneach	Limerick
Lisdoonvarna	Lios Dúin Bhearna	Clare
Lismore	Lios Mór	Waterford
Listowel	Lios Tuathail	Kerry
Longford	An Longfort	Longford
Loughrea	Baile Locha Riach	Galway
* Maam	Mám	Galway
Macroom	Maigh Chromtha	Cork
Malahide	Mullach Íde	Dublin
Mallow	Mala	Cork
Manorhamilton	Cluainín	Leitrim

Maynooth	Maigh Nua	Kildare
Millstreet	Sráid an Mhuilinn	Cork
Milltown Malbay	Sráid na Cathrach	Clare
Mitchelstown	Baile Mhisteála	Cork
Moate	An Móta	Westmeath
Mohill	Maothail	Leitrim
Monaghan	Muineachán	Monaghan
Mountmellick	Móinteach Mílic	Laois
Mountrath	Maighean Rátha	Laois
* Moycullen	Maigh Cuilinn	Galway
Mullingar	An Muileann gCearr	Westmeath
Naas	An Náa	Kildare
Navan	An Uaimh	Meath
Nenagh	An tAonach	Tipperary
Newcastle West	An Caisleán Nua	Limerick
Newmarket	Áth Trasna	Cork
New Ross	Ros Mhic Thriúin	Wexford
Oldcastle	An Seanchaisleán	Meath
Oughterard	Uachtar Ard	Galway
Portlaoise	Port Laoise	Laois
Portumna	Port Omma	Galway
Raphoe	Ráth Bhoth	Donegal
Rathdrum	Ráth Droma	Wicklow
Rathkeale	Ráth Caola	Limerick
Ráth Luire	An Ráth	Cork
Rathmelton	Ráth Mealtain	Donegal
Rathnew	Ráth Naoi	Wicklow
* Reananaree	Re na nDoiri	Cork
* Recess	Straith Salach	Galway
* Ring	An Rinn	Waterford
Roscrea	Ros Cré	Tipperary
Roscommon	Ros Comáin	Roscommon
* Rosmuck	Ros Muc	Galway
* Rossaveal	Ros an Mhil	Galway
Rosslare	Calafort Ros Láir	Wexford
* Screeb	Scriob	Galway
Skerries	Na Sceirí	Dublin
Skibereen	An Sciobairín	Cork
Sligo	Sligeach	Galway
Swords	Sord	Dublin
Tarbert	Tairbeart	Kerry
Templemore	An Teampall Mór	Tipperary
Thomastown	Baile Mhic Andáin	Kilkenny
Thurles	Durlas	Tipperary
Tipperary	Tiobraid Árann	Tipperary
Tralee	Trá Lí	Kerry
Tramore	Trá Mhór	Waterford
Trim	Baille Átha Troim	Meath
Tuam	Tuaim	Galway
Tubbercurry	Tobar an Choire	Sligo
Tulla	An Tulach	Clare

Tullamore	Túlach Mhór	Offaly
Tullow	An Tulach	Carlow
* Ventry	Ceann Tra	Kerry
Waterford	Port Láirge	Waterford
Westport	Cathair na Mart	Mayo
Wexford	Loch Garman	Wexford
Wicklow	Cill Mhantáin	Wicklow
Youghal	Eochaill	Cork

Dublin is known as Dublino in Italian.

Administrative districts

Ireland has 4 provinces and 26 counties. Note that only part of the province of Ulster is within the Irish Republic. Counties are usually mentioned in the address, preceded by the abbreviation 'Co.', meaning 'County', as Ireland has no postcodes.

Province	*County*
Connaught	Galway
	Leitrim
	Mayo
	Roscommon
	Sligo
Leinster	Carlow
	Dublin
	Kildare
	Kilkenny
	Laois
	Longford
	Louth
	Meath
	Offaly
	Westmeath
	Wexford
	Wicklow
Munster	Clare
	Cork
	Kerry
	Limerick
	Tipperary
	Waterford
Ulster	Cavan
	Donegal
	Monaghan

The remaining 6 counties of Ulster (Antrim, Armagh, Down, Fermanagh, Londonderry and Tyrone) form Northern Ireland, a constituent region of the United Kingdom.

 # Isle of Man

The Isle of Man is a Crown Dependency within the British Commonwealth. It is not part of the United Kingdom of Great Britain and Northern Ireland. Except in matters of foreign affairs and defence, it is effectively an independent nation, and its inhabitants are fiercely proud of their status. Do not use the words 'United Kingdom', 'Great Britain' or 'England' in the address.

Area: 572 sq. km (221 sq. miles)

Population: 64,282 (1986 census)

Population density: 112.4 per sq. km

Capital: Douglas (population 20,368 (1986))

Currency: Manx pound (equivalent of Pound Sterling) = 100 pence

Languages

English is spoken. Manx, a Celtic language, is still spoken by 50 people.

Company names, contact names, addresses, postbox

The same rules and formats apply as in the United Kingdom.

Postcodes

A postcode system was introduced into the Isle of Man only in early 1994. It follows the same structure and format as United Kingdom postcodes. Each postcode begins with the letters IM.

Telephone numbers

The Isle of Man forms part of the United Kingdom telephone system. The international dialling code is 44, the area code for the whole island is 0624.

Italy: Postal regions and language areas

Key

● Main cities

⌁⌒⌁ International boundaries

⟨01⟩ Postal region, with numbers indicating first two digits of postcode

☐ Italian-speaking

▨ Italian-, German- and Rhaetian-speaking

☰ Italian-, Friulian- and Slovenian-speaking

▨ Italian- and Sard-speaking

▨ Italian-, Sard- and Catalan-speaking

Italy
Italia

Area: 301,277 sq. km (116, 324 sq. miles)

Population: 57,576,429 (1989 estimate)

Population density: 191.1 per sq. km

Capital: Rome (Roma) (population 2,803,931 (1989))

Currency: Italian lira

Languages

Italian, the official language, is spoken by 94 per cent of the population. Other languages are Sard (2 per cent spoken in Sardinia), Rhaetian (or Ladin, spoken by about 10,000 people, mainly in South Tyrol), German (also spoken in South Tyrol), French (spoken in Piedmont), Friulian (a Rhaetian dialect, spoken in Friuli-Venezia-Giulia), Catalan (in Sardinia), Slovene (in Trieste and Friuli-Venezia-Giulia), Croat, Greek and Albanian (all mainly spoken in southern Italy). There are fewer than 2,000 speakers of Walser, a dialect of German, in the Piedmont mountain villages of Alagna, Pedemonte and Rimella.

The South Tyrol, Südtirol in German, Alto Adige or Bolzano in Italian (postcode area 39) has a population of 433,229 (1981), of which 66 per cent are German speakers, 30 per cent Italian speakers, 4 per cent Ladins (Rhaeto-Romanche).

Company names

In Italy it is more correct, where the *nature* of a company is mentioned in its name, that this *precedes* the name of the company, thus:

Fornaio Luigi

Company types

The following company types may be recognized in Italian company names:

SA (Societá Anonima)

SnC (Societá in nome Collettivo)
SpA (Societá per Azioni)
SrL (Societá a responsabilitá Limitata)

Addresses

Italian addresses are written in this format:

> Recipient name
> thoroughfare type[ ]thoroughfare name[ ]number
> postcode[ ]TOWN[(]PROVINCE[)]

or

> Recipient name
> thoroughfare type[ ]Thoroughfare name[,]number
> postcode[ ]TOWN[(]PROVINCE[)]

For example:

> Sig. Giovanni Masci
> via Garibaldi 27
> 47037 RIMINI (FORLI)

or

> Sig. Giovanni Masci
> via Garibaldi, 27
> 47037 RIMINI (FORLI)

The thoroughfare type is written before and separately from the thoroughfare name. The thoroughfare type should be written with the first letter in lower case.

Italian addresses may give the kilometre number of a house or company on long or inter-city routes rather than house numbers.

Thoroughfare types

Below is a list of the most commonly occurring thoroughfare types, with the abbreviated form(s) which you are most likely to find in address databases:

borgo	
contrada	c.^{da}
corso	c, cso, c.so
frazione	fraz, fr
largo	
lgo lungofiume (fiume can be replaced with the name of a river)	
lungolago (lago can be replaced with the name of a lake)	
lungomare (mare can be replaced with the name of a sea)	
piazza	p, pza
piazzale	p.^{le}
Strada Statale, Superstrada	SS (national route with km number)
strada	
traversa	
via	v
viale	vle, vl
vicolo	

Other nouns, adjectives and prepositions commonly found in address databases

NB: The form which certain common words take in Italian depends on a number of factors such as the gender of the following word, whether the next word is the definite article, whether the first letter of the next word is a vowel or a consonant, and whether that consonant is a z, ps or an s+ consonant. As this is rather complex, no explanation is given for each form but, where more than one form exists, each form is given.

il /i /l'/gli/lo/la/le	= the
un/uno/una/un'	= a, an
e	= and
fino a, sino a	= till, until
per	= for
di	= of
del/dei/dell'/ degli /dello /della/delle	= of the
verso, a, in	= to, towards
al, allo, alla, ai, agli, alle	= towards the
presso, vicino a, accanto a	= near, by, next to
su	= on (sea, a river), over
sul, sulla, sullo, sulle, sella	= on the
in	= in
nel, nello, nella, a	= in the
in faccia a, di fronte (a), dirimpetto (a)	= opposite
dietro, dopo, addietro, didietro	= behind
davanti a, dinanzi a	= in front of
fra, tra	= between
sotto	= under
sopra	= over
con	= with
nuovo, nuova, nuovi, nuove	= new
vecchio, vecchie, vecchia, vecchi	= old
corto, corta, corte, corti	= short
lungo, lunga, lunghi, lunghe	= long
grande, grandi	= large
piccolo, piccola, piccoli, piccole	= small
nord, del nord, settentrionale	= north
est, dell'est, orientale	= east
ovest, dell'ovest, occidentale,	= west
sud, del sud, meridionale	= south
Sann (masculine), Santa (feminine), Sant' (before a vowel), Santo (before a name beginning with a z, ps or s+ consonant; e.g. Santo Stefano) (abbreviated to S., St., Sta.)	= Saint
Zona Industriale	= industrial estate

Postbox

This is written as Casella Postale, abbreviated to CP.

Postcodes

Postcodes (*il Codice di Avviamento Postale* (C.A.P.)) consist of 5 consecutive digits, and are highly correlated with administrative districts.

The first number indicates one of 10 large postal zones. These do not correspond to Italy's provinces but the borders of the postal zones do follow the borders of the regions.

The first two numbers indicate the postal province. Italy has 95 administrative provinces and 91 postal provinces. The 9 number strings which are *not* found at the beginning of postcodes are as follows:

49, 59, 68, 69, 76, 77, 78, 79, 99

In three cases, two provinces share the same first two digits:

09 – Cagliari and Oristano
33 – Pordenone and Udine
86 – Campo-Basso and Isernia.

Where the third, fourth and fifth numbers are 100, this indicates the capital of the province, which always has the same name as the province. In the cases of the provinces which share a postcode, this number is attributed to Cagliari, Udine and Campo-Basso. The third digit of the postcode can only be 1 or 0. In one case, postcode 30170, the third digit is a one and it does not refer to a regional capital. In all other cases, a 1 indicates the regional capital.

Some of these capital cities, and a single non-capital city (Mestre) are exceptions in as much as they themselves are split into boroughs with postcodes where the last three digits fall between 101 and 199. These cities are as follows:

00100 Roma
10100 Torino
16100 Genova
20100 Milano
25100 Brescia
30100 Venezia
30170 Mestre
34100 Trieste
35100 Padova
37100 Verona
40100 Bologna
50100 Firenze
60100 Ancona
70100 Bari
80100 Napoli
90100 Palermo
95100 Catania

Other cities, municipalities and large villages are indicated with the last three digits of the postcode falling between 001 and 099.

The independent state of San Marino, region code SM, has the postcode 47031.

The independent state of Vatican City, has the postcode 00120.

Towns

The following list gives alternative town names. Note that it is important to use the correct version especially in the South Tyrol region, where you should use the German place names for German speakers. The towns in this region are marked with an asterisk.

Italian	English	French	German	Spanish	Dutch
Bologna	Bologne	Bologne		Bolonia	
* Bolzano			Bozen		
* Bressanone			Brixen		
* Brunico			Bruneck		
* Dobiacco			Tablach		
Firenze	Florence	Florence	Florenz	Florencia	Florence
Genova	Genoa	Gênes	Genua	Génova	Genua
Mantova	Mantua	Mantove	Mantua	Mantua	
* Merano			Meran		
Milano	Milan	Milan	Mailand	Milán	Milaan
Nápoli	Naples	Naples	Neapel		Napels
Padova	Padua	Padove	Padua	Padua	
Roma	Rome	Rome	Rom	Roma	Rome
Siena	Sienna	Sienne	Siena	Siena	
Torino	Turin	Turin	Turin	Turin	Turijn
Trento		Trente	Trient	Trento	
Venezia	Venice	Venise	Venedig	Venecia	Venetië
* Vipiteno			Sterzing		

Administrative districts

The correct abbreviation for the province in which an address is located should be included in brackets after and on the same line as the town name.

Italy has 95 provinces (*Provincie*) in 20 regions (*Regioni*). Every province is named after its capital city. In the three cases where two provinces share the same first two postcode digits, these are marked with an asterisk. The provinces and regions are listed below with the English translation in brackets:

Region	Province	Postcode	Postal abbreviation
Abruzzo	L'Aquila	67	(AQ)
	Chieti	66	(CH)
	Pescara	65	(PE)
	Teramo	64	(TE)
Basilicata	Matera	75	(MT)
	Potenza	85	(PZ)
Calabria	Catanzaro	88	(CZ)
	Cosenza	87	(CS)
	Reggio (di) Calabria	89	(RC)
Campania	Avellino	83	(AV)
	Benevento	82	(BN)
	Caserta	81	(CE)
	Napoli	80	(NA)
	Salerno	84	(SA)
Emilia-Romagna	Bologna	40	(BO)
	Ferrara	44	(FE)
	Forlì	47	(FO)
	Modena	41	(MO)
	Parma	43	(PR)
	Piacenza	29	(PC)
	Ravenna	48	(RA)
	Reggio (nell')Emilia	42	(RE)

Region	Province	Postcode	Postal abbreviation
Friuli-Venezia Giulia	Gorizia	* 34	(GO)
		34071	
		34073	
		34074	
		34077	
		34170	
	Pordenone	* 33	(PN)
		33072	
		33077	
		33078	
		33081	
		33082	
		33084	
		33085	
		33097	
		33170	
	Trieste	* 34	(TS)
		34011	
		34015	
		34018	
		34100	
	Udine	* 33	(UD)
		33010	
		33013	
		33028	
		33031	
		33033	
		33043	
		33052	
		33054	
		33057	
		33100	
Lazio	Frosinone	03	(FR)
	Latina	04	(LT)
	Rieti	02	(RI)
	Roma	00	(RM)
	Viterbo	01	(VT)
Liguria	Genova	16	(GE)
	Imperia	18	(IM)
	La Spezia	19	(SP)
	Savona	17	(SV)
Lombardia (Lombardy)	Bergamo	24	(BG)
	Brescia	25	(BS)
	Como	22	(CO)
	Cremona	26	(CR)
	Mantova	46	(MN)
	Milano	20	(MI)
	Pavia	27	(PV)
	Sondrio	23	(SO)
	Varese	21	(VA)

Marche	Ancona	60	(AN)
	Ascoli Piceno	63	(AP)
	Macerata	62	(MC)
	Pesaro e Urbino	61	(PS)
Molise	Campo-Basso	* 86	(CB)
		86016	
		86029	
		86034	
		86035	
		86036	
		86039	
		86047	
		86100	
	Isernia	* 86	(IS)
		86079	
		86081	
		86170	
Piemonte (Piedmont)	Alessandria	15	(AL)
	Asti	14	(AT)
	Cuneo	12	(CN)
	Novara	28	(NO)
	Vercelli	13	(VC)
	Torino	10	(TO)
Puglia	Bari	70	(BA)
	Brindisi	72	(BR)
	Foggia	71	(FG)
	Lecce	73	(LE)
	Taranto	74	(TA)
Sardegna (Sardinia)	Cagliari	* 09	(CA)
		09010	
		09012	
		09013	
		09014	
		09015	
		09016	
		09017	
		09019	
		09032	
		09036	
		09037	
		09038	
		09039	
		09041	
		09045	
		09047	
		09048	
		09055	
		09100	
	Nuoro	08	(NU)

Region	Province	Postcode	Postal abbreviation
	Oristano	* 09	(OR)
		09098	
		09170	
	Sassari	07	(SS)
Sicilia (Sicily)	Agrigento	92	(AG)
	Caltanissetta	93	(CL)
	Catania	95	(CT)
	Enna	94	(EN)
	Messina	98	(ME)
	Palermo	90	(PA)
	Ragusa	97	(RG)
	Siracusa	96	(SR)
	Trapani	91	(TP)
Toscana (Toscany)	Arezzo	52	(AR)
	Firenze	50	(FI)
	Grosseto	58	(GR)
	Livorno	57	(LI)
	Lucca	55	(LU)
	Massa-Carrara	54	(MS)
	Pisa	56	(PI)
	Pistoia	51	(PT)
	Siena	53	(SI)
Trentino-Alto Adige	Bolzano-Bozen	39	(BZ)
	Trento	38	(TN)
Umbria	Perugia	06	(PG)
	Terni	05	(TR)
Valle D'Aosta	Aosta	11	(AO)
Veneto	Belluno	32	(BL)
	Padova	35	(PD)
	Rovigo	45	(RO)
	Treviso	31	(TV)
	Venezia	30	(VE)
	Verona	37	(VR)
	Vicenza	36	(VI)

 **Jersey**

Jersey is a British Crown Dependency and therefore is not part of the United Kingdom of Great Britain and Northern Ireland. Except in matters of foreign affairs and defence, it is effectively an independent nation, and its inhabitants are fiercely proud of their status. The words 'United Kingdom', 'Great Britain' or 'England' should not be used in addresses; it is better to use 'Channel Islands'.

Area: 116.2 sq. km (44.8 sq. miles)

Population: 82,809 (1989)

Population density: 712.6 per sq. km

Capital: St. Helier (population 28,123 (1991))

Currency: 1 Pound Sterling = 100 pence

Languages

The official language of Jersey is English. A dialect of Norman-French is still spoken by some people. This patois has no written form.

Company names, contact names, addresses, postbox

The same rules and formats apply as in the United Kingdom.

Postcodes

A postcode system was introduced into Jersey only in June 1993. It follows the same structure and format as United Kingdom postcodes. Each postcode begins with the letters JE.

Telephone numbers

Jersey forms part of the United Kingdom telephone system. The international dialling code is 44, and the area code for the whole dependency is 0534.

Liechtenstein

Liechtenstein is a small German-speaking country sandwiched between Switzerland and Austria. As with many small European countries, Liechtenstein tends more towards one of its neighbours, Switzerland, than any other. Addresses for Liechtenstein will usually be found mixed into lists for Switzerland. They can be recognized by their postcodes.

Area: 160 sq. km (61.8 sq. miles)

Population: 29,000 (1989 estimate)

Population density: 180.5 per sq. km

Capital: Vaduz (population 5,000 (1990))

Currency: 1 Swiss franc = 100 centimes. (The principality belongs to the Swiss economic area).

Languages

German is spoken by 93 per cent of the population. A dialect of Alemannish is widely spoken.

Company names, contact names, street addresses, postbox

The same rules and formats apply as in Germany, Austria and German-speaking Switzerland.

Postcodes

Postcodes consists of 4 consecutive numbers. Liechtenstein forms part of the postal system of Switzerland. The towns with their postcodes are listed below:

Balzers	9496
Bendern	–under 9487 Gamprin-Bendern
Eschen	9492
Gamprin-Bendern	9487
Mäls	– under 9496 Balzers
Mauren FL	9493

Nendeln	9485
Planken	- under 9494 Schaan
Ruggell	9491
Schaan	9494
Schaanwald	9486
Schellenberg	9488
Triesen	9495
Triesenberg	9497
Vaduz	9490

Administrative districts

Liechtenstein is composed of 11 communes.

Telephone numbers

The country code is 41 75. No area code is required.

Luxembourg
Letzeburg

Area: 2,586 sq. km. (999 sq. miles)

Population: 378,400 (1989 estimate)

Population density: 146.3 per sq. km

Capital: Luxembourg (population 74,400 (1989 estimate))

Currency: 1 Luxembourg franc = 100 centimes (equal to the Belgian franc). Luxembourg forms part of the Belgian economic area.

Languages

The official language is Letzebuergesch, a German-Moselle-Frankish dialect which should be regarded as a distinct language related to German. French and German are widely spoken and understood.

Addresses

Street names can either be in French or Letzebuergesch. Increasingly, especially in the capital, street names are given in both languages. As Letzebuergesch itself has a number of dialects and therefore a number of different spellings for thoroughfare types depending on the region, a list of the thoroughfare types in Letzebuergesch cannot be given here.

The structure of the address is slightly different according to the language of the address inasmuch as in a French address, the thoroughfare type is prefixed to the thoroughfare name with spaces between the words, whereas addresses in Letzebuergesch have the thoroughfare type suffixed to the thoroughfare name without a space. Otherwise, addresses are structured thus:

Recipient name
number[ ]Street name
postcode[ ]TOWN NAME

or

Recipient name
number[,]Street name
postcode[ ]TOWN NAME

203

For example:

M Jacques Muller
71 route de Longway
4750 PETANGE

Thoroughfare types given in French should be written with the first letter in lower case.

Thoroughfare types

Please refer to the chapters on France and Belgium for lists of commonly occurring thoroughfare types and abbreviations.

Postcodes

Postcodes in Luxembourg have 4 consecutive numbers, beginning with a number between 1 and 9, and they are written on the last line of the address preceding the town name. Postcodes beginning with the following numbers are currently not used:

28, 29, 30, 31, 50, 51, 60, 70, 71, 78, 79, 89

Towns

The capital, Letzebuerg, is known as Luxembourg in English and French, Luxemburg in German and Dutch, Lussemburgo in Italian and Luxemburgo in Spanish.
   Many settlements have both a local Letzebuergesch name and a French name.

Administrative districts

Luxembourg has 3 districts and 12 cantons:

District	Canton
Diekirch	Clervaux
	Diekirch
	Redange
	Vianden
	Wiltz
Grevenmacher	Etternach
	Grevenmacher
	Remich
Luxembourg	Capellen
	Esch-sur-Alzette
	Luxembourg
	Mersch

Telephone numbers

The country code for Luxembourg is 352. There are no area codes.

 # Malta

Area: 316 sq. km (122 sq. miles)

Population: 349,014 (1988 estimate)

Population density: 1,105 per sq. km

Capital: Valetta (population 9,210 (1988 estimate))

Currency: Maltese pound/lira matija = 100 cents = 100 mils

Languages

Malta has two official languages: Maltese, spoken by 96 per cent of the population and English, spoken by 2 per cent. Italian is spoken by 2 per cent of the population.

Addresses

Addresses are written using the following structure:

    number[,] Street name
    TOWN [ ] POSTCODE
    {Island name}

Street names are usually written in Maltese, but some may be found translated into English. The name of the island is optional when the address is on the island of Malta, but is usually stated when the address is on Gozo (Għawdex) or Comina.

Postcodes

Malta introduced its postcode system only in 1993, and it is still not widely used. The postcode consists of three capital letters, indicating the delivery office, followed by two numbers on the island of Malta, and three numbers on the island of Gozo indicating the postperson's beat. The letters and numbers have a space between them, as for example:

VCT[ ]101

It is added after, and on the same line as, the settlement name. Government departments and ministries have the postcode CMR 0Z.

Towns

The following list gives a list of Maltese town names with their English equivalents:

Maltese	*English*
Birgu	Vittoriosa
Bormla	Cospicua
Għagn Sielem	Kemmuna
Rabat	Victoria
Raħal Ġdid	Paolo
San Pawl Il-Baħar	St Paul's Bay
Wied Il-Għajn	Marsascala

Telephone numbers

Malta has no area codes, the subscriber's number is dialled directly after the international code, which is 356.

 # Monaco

Monaco is a tiny but completely independent country entirely surrounded on its landward borders by France. For most rules and formats relating to this principality, refer to the chapter on France.

Area: 1.95 sq. km (0.75 sq. miles)

Population: 29,876 (1990 census)

Population density: 15,321 per sq. km

Capital: Monaco

Currency: 1 French franc = 100 centimes

Languages

The official language is French. Other languages spoken include Italian, Monegasque (a French dialect, a mixture of Provençals and Ligurian), Provençals and English.

Company names, contact names, addresses, postbox

The same rules and formats are used as in France. Please refer to the chapter on France.

Postcodes

Monaco forms part of the French postal system, and its addresses will usually be found mixed up with French addresses in databases. They can be identified by their postcodes, all of which begin with the number 98.

Telephone numbers

Monaco forms part of the French telephone system. The international dialling code is 33. Monaco has no area code except when calling from Paris, when the subscriber's number must be preceded by 16. All subscribers' numbers have 8 digits.

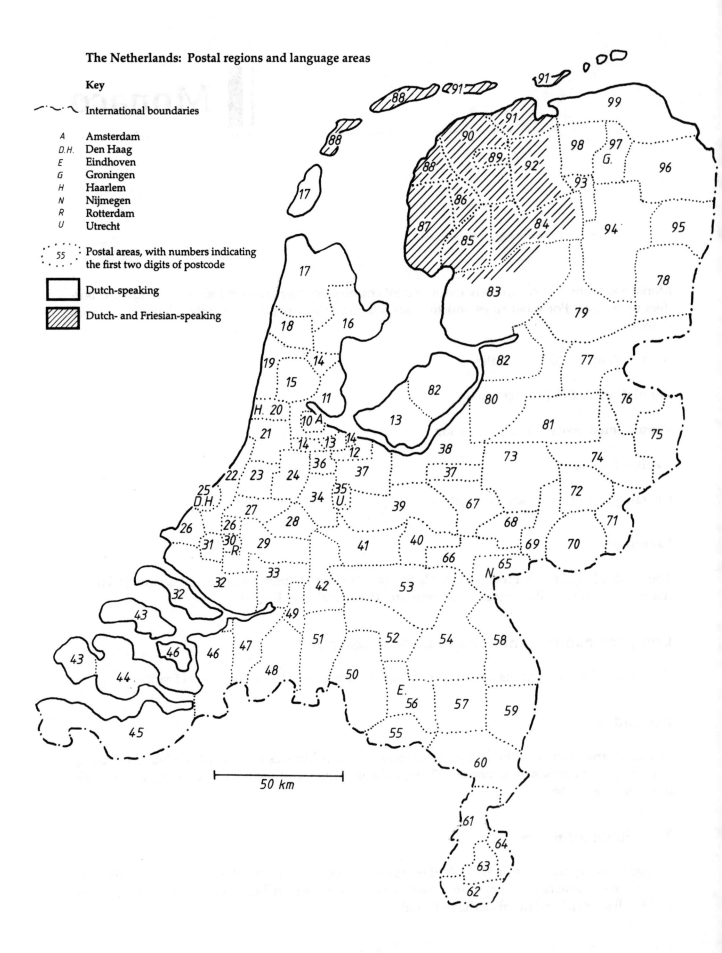

The Netherlands: Postal regions and language areas

Key

~~~ International boundaries

A   Amsterdam
D.H.   Den Haag
E   Eindhoven
G   Groningen
H   Haarlem
N   Nijmegen
R   Rotterdam
U   Utrecht

55   Postal areas, with numbers indicating
the first two digits of postcode

Dutch-speaking

Dutch- and Friesian-speaking

The Netherlands
Nederland

Holland comprises two provinces in the west of the country and no more. You should therefore refrain from addressing mail to 'Holland' and use the correct term – 'The Netherlands'.

Area: 33,938 sq. km (13,104 sq. miles)

Population: 14,943,486 (1990 estimate)

Population density: 440 per sq. km

Capital: Amsterdam (population 695,162 (1990))

Currency: 1 guilder = 100 cents

Languages

Dutch, spoken by 93 per cent of the population, is the official language. Friesian, spoken in Friesland, a province in the northern part of the country, is spoken by 5 per cent of the population.

Company names

It is more correct, where the *nature* of a company is mentioned in its name, that this *precedes* the name of the company, thus:

Bakkerij Janssens

You will often, however, find these activity indications *after* the company name, thus:

Janssens, Bakkerij
Janssens (Bakkerij)

Company types

The following company types may be found in Dutch company names:

BV
Coöperatie
CV
Maatschappij
NV
Stichting
VOF

Contact names

Dutch personal names often contain prepositions, especially 'van de' and 'van der' which mean, literally, 'of the'. As a rule, these parts of the persons name are written in lower case, thus:

Hans van de Duinen

Most Dutch people have two names – their official name and their day-to-day name. Thus a person with the official name J.C.M.P. (Johannes Cornelis Maria Pieter) van Agt may be known as Hans or Cees, for example. On mailings, one should avoid using either the day-to-day name or the official name – the abbreviation of the official name should be used. It is virtually impossible to match the official and day-to-day names of individuals on the basis of name only. In Dutch databases, therefore, two fields are best reserved for the first name – one containing the initials of the official first name, the other containing the day-to-day first name for recognition purposes.

The salutation which would be used on an address label is inappropriate for use within a letter.

Married Dutch women may take their husband's name but retain their own as a second surname in this way:

Marijke van den Broek marries Jan Nijpels

and becomes

Marijke Nijpels-van den Broek

Other married women retain their maiden names, though any children take the father's surname.

For written communications to people within companies, the abbreviation T.a.v., short for *Ter Attentie van* or *Ten aanzien van* and meaning 'For the attention of' often precedes the person's name in this way:

Bakkerij Janssens
T.a.v. Dhr. A. Janssens

Addresses

Structure

There are three official formats for Dutch addresses. The first, the 'official' form, is as follows:

- Street address with maximum 43 characters in capital and small letters
- The town with maximum 24 characters in capitals
- The IJ written as IJ (see section on Dutch in the chapter on accents)

For example:

Burgemeester de Cock van Opijnstraat 1
4001 VL TIEL

The second format is used by the Ministry of Internal Affairs for its address databases:

- Street address with maximum 24 characters in capitals and small letters
- The town with maximum 24 characters in capitals
- The IJ written as IJ

For example:
Burg d Cock v Opijnenstr 1
4001 VL TIEL

The third format is used by the post office:

- Street address with maximum 17 letters in capitals
- The town with maximum 18 letters in capitals
- The IJ written as Y

For example:

DE C V OPYNENSTR 1
4001 VL TIEL

In terms of database management, it is preferable to use a mixture of all three systems, thus:

- Street address, complete in capitals and small letters
- Town name, complete in capitals
- The IJ as IJ

For example:

Burgemeester de Cock van Opijnstraat 1
4001 VL TIEL

In some databases, you may find that prepositions, titles, initials and articles are put behind the rest of the thoroughfare type, thus:

Koningin Julianastraat becomes Julianastr., kon.;

and

Meester P. Troelstralaan becomes Troelstraln., mr. p.

but this system should *not* be used when addressing envelopes.

Some streets in The Netherlands are themselves numbered. Thus the figures 1e, 2e etc. in front of the street name indicate the number of the *street*, not of the habitation. These mean 1st, 2nd etc.

If you can choose between a street address and a postbox number for mailings, always use the postbox number with its postcode.

If you wish to add codes or messages to the label, these should always be placed above and to the left of the address.

Houseboats without a house number should have the house number replaced with the letters 'AB' (*aan boord* = on board) and the name of the boat.

Caravans without a house number should have the number replaced by the letters 'WW' (*woonwagen* = caravan).

The PTT (the Dutch Post Office) prefers addresses to have only 3 lines:

1. The name of the person or company.
2. The street name and housenumber; or the word 'Postbus' with a postbox number.
3. The postcode and the town.

For example:

   Dhr. J. van Dieten
   Morsstraat 111
   2312 BK LEIDEN
or
   Dhr. J. van Dieten
   Postbus 12
   2310 AA LEIDEN

Street addresses should be written :

   Street name[ ]number.

The last line should always consist of the postcode followed by the town name.
   If an address has a box number ('bus') this should be added after the address so:

   Street name[ ]number[bus]number

The thoroughfare type is suffixed to the thoroughfare name without a space. For example:

   Haarlemmerdijk 23
   Boslaan 98
   Groenweg 2

The street name may also consist of different components separated with a space thus:

   Eerste Anjeliers Dwaasstraat

This is usually the case when the street name begins with an adjective such as 'first', 'long' etc.
   The abbreviation 't/m' between numbers in an address is an abbreviation for *tot en me*t meaning 'up to and including'.

Thoroughfare types

Below is a list of the most commonly occurring thoroughfare types, with the abbreviated form(s) which you are most likely to find in address databases:

Baan		Laan,Leane, Loane	Ln
Berg		Markt	
Boulevard	Bd, Bld, Boulev	Park	Pk
Dijk	Dk	Plantsoen	Plnts
Donk		Plein	Pln
Dwarsstraat	Dwstr	Singel	Sngl
Dwarsweg	Dwwg	Straat, Strjitte	Str
Gracht	Gr	Straatweg	Strwg
Kade	Kd	Wal	
Kanaal	Kan	Weg	Wg

Other common nouns, adjectives and prepositions commonly found in address databases:

Dutch

Neuter	Abbrev.	Gendered and Plural (where different from neuter form)	Abbrev.	Translation
het (sometimes 't)		de		the
een				a, an
en				and
tot				till, until, up to
voor				for
van				of, from
op, naar				to, towards
bij				near, by
aan				on (sea, for example), at
aan de	a/d			on (a river)
op				on
in				in
tegenover				opposite
naast				next to
achter				behind
vóór				in front of
tussen				between
over				over
onder				under
met				with
nieuw	nw.	nieuwe	nwe.	new
oud		oude		old
kort	k.	korte	kte.	short
lang	l.	lange	lge.	long
hoog	hg.	hoge	hg.	high
laag	lg.	lage	lg.	low
groot	g./gt.	grote	g./gte.	large
klein	k./kl.	kleine	k./kle.	small
		gedempte	ged.	filled-in (of a canal)
		heilige	h.	holy
		kromme	kr.	crooked, curved
		verlengde	verl.	extended
noord	n.			north
		noordzijde	nz.	north side
oost	o.			east
		oostzijde	oz.	east side
zuid	z.			south
		zuidzijde	zz.	south side
west	w.			west
		westzijde	wz.	west side
kasteel	kast.			castle
sint	st.			saint
Industriepark				industrial estate

Friesian

Neuter	Abbrev.	Gendered and Plural (where different from neuter form)	Abbrev.	Translation
it (sometimes 't)		de (sometimes 'e)		the
in				a, an
en				and
oant, oan, ta				till, until, up to
foar				for
fan				of, from
nei				to, towards
by				near, by, close to
op				on
yn				in, into
foaroer				opposite
nêst, njonken				next to
efter				behind
foar				in front of
tusken				between
oer				over
ûnder				under
boppe				above
mei				with
nij		nije		new
âld		âlde		old
koart	kt.	koarte	kte.	short
lang	l.	lange	lge.	long
heeg	hg.	hege	hg.	high
leeg	lg.	lege	lg.	low
great	g./gt.	greate	g./gte.	large
lyts		lytse		small
noard	n.			north
east	e.			east
súd	s.			south
west	w.			west
sint	st.			saint

Addresses will also often contain the names of people with their titles or salutations. These titles are, and can be abbreviated as follows:

Title	*Abbreviation*	*Translation*
Aalmoezenier	Aalm	Chaplin
Admiraal	Adm	Admiral
Baron	Bar	Baron
Baronesse	Bsse	Baroness
Bisschop	Biss	Bishop
Burgemeester	Burg	Mayor
Commissaris	Comm	Commissioner

Deken	Dkn	Deacon
doctorandus	drs	academic grade masters degree, no translation
Dokter, Doctor	Dr	Doctor
Dominee	Ds	Minister, Vicar, Padre
Douairière	Dre	Dowager
Gebroeders	Gebr	Brothers
Generaal	Gen	General
Graaf	Gr	Earl
Gravin	Gr	Duchess
Hertog	Htg	Duke
Ingenieur	Ir	Engineer
Jonkheer	Jhr	Esquire
Kanunnik	Kan	Canon
Kapelaan	Kap	Curate, Chaplain
Kapitein	Kapt	Captain
Kardinaal	Kard	Cardinal
Keizer	Kzr	Emperor
Kolonel	Kol	Colonel
Koning	Kon	King
Koningin	Kon	Queen
Luitenant-Generaal	Lt Gen	Lieutenant-General
Majoor	Maj	Major
meester	Mr	Mister (academic grade)
Minister	Min	Minister (political)
Monseigneur	Mgr	Monseigneur
Notaris	Not	Notary
Pastoor	Past	Pastor
Pater	Ptr	Father (religious)
Paters	Ptrs	Fathers (religious)
President	Pres	President
Prins	Pr	Prince
Princes	Pr	Princess
Professor	Prof	Professor
Rector	Rect	Rector
Ridder	Rdr	Knight
Secretaris	Secr	Secretary
Sinjeur	Sinj	Cleric
Sint	St	Saint
Wethouder	Weth	Alderman
Zuster	Zr	Sister (religious)
Zusters	Zrs	Sisters (religious)

Thoroughfares in Friesland

In Friesland, in the north of The Netherlands, Friesian is spoken. It is very rare to come across a street name in Friesian in address databases, although Friesian-speakers themselves use them. Thoroughfares are only given a single name (although they are easily translated by users), in Dutch or in Friesian, and this is the one to be used by preference.

Postbox

This is written Postbus, abbreviated to PB.

Postboxes have their own postcodes. The PTT prefers the use of the postbox number to the street address. Do not use both the street address and the postbox address. If you do this, the PTT will attempt to deliver the package only to the postbox number. If the postcode for this postbox is incorrect (i.e. it refers to the street address), then the package will be returned as undeliverable.

Postcodes

There are more than 575,000 postcodes in The Netherlands, and around 30,000 are changed each year as new streets are created and old destroyed. Postcodes have 4 digits and two letters, the digits starting with a number between 1 and 9 (not 0). The layout is as follows:

9999[ ]AA

The postcode is written before, and on the same line as, the town name. There is no number after the town name to indicate the sorting office.

The digits indicate the town or district, the letters a group of some 25 habitations, offices, factories or postboxes. There is no correlation between codes and administrative districts. The main post offices always have the letters AA.

There should be no punctuation anywhere within the postcode, and there should be nothing written underneath the postcode.

The PTT produces software and look-up tables to aid users in keeping their databases up to date.

Towns

St., the abbreviation for Sint (Saint), can in all cases be used in town names except for the settlement of 'Sintjohannesga'.

Town names consisting of more than one word are not usually hyphenated.

Town names can begin with an apostophe, followed by an 's' or a 't'. Some of these names have alternative spellings which are perfectly acceptable to use, i.e.:

's-Hertogenbosch = Den Bosch
's-Gravenhage = Den Haag

Town names sometimes include the link 'aan' or 'aan de', meaning 'on' or 'on the'. 'Aan de' is often abbreviated to 'a/d'.

The following list gives foreign language equivalents of Dutch town names:

Dutch	*English*	*French*	*German*	*Spanish*	*Italian*
Arnhem			Arnherm		
Den Haag/'s-Gravenhage	The Hague	La Haye		La Haya	L'Aia
Hoek van Holland	The Hook of Holland				
Utrecht			Ütrecht		
Vlissingen	Flushing	Fléssingue		Flesingue	Flessinga

Town names in Friesland

In Friesland, in the north of The Netherlands, Friesian is spoken. Where a municipality (*gemeente*) recognizes both a Friesian and a Dutch name for the municipality, the PTT prefers that the Dutch name is used. Where the municipality uses a unilingular Friesian name, the PTT prefers that this name is used.

The following list is of settlements in Friesland which have both Dutch and Friesian names:

Dutch	*Friesian*
Aalsum	Ealsum
Abbega	Abbegea
Aegum	Eagum
Akmarijp	Eagmaryp
Anjum	Eanjum
Appelscha	Appelskea
Augsbuurt	Lytsewâld
Augustinusga	Stynsgea
Baaiduinen	Baaidunen
Baijum	Baaium
Bakhuizen	Bakhuzen
Bakkeveen	Bakkefean
Bantega	Bantegea
Beers	Bears
Beetgum	Bitgum
Beetgumermolen	Bitgummole
Beetsterzwaag	Beetstersweach
Bergum	Burgum
Berlikum	Berltsum
Birdaard	Burdaard
Blauwhuis	Blauhús
Blesdijke	Blesdike
Blija	Blije
Boelenslaan	Boelensloane
Bolsward	Boalsert
Boornbergum	Boarnburgum
Boornzwaag	Boarnsweach
Bornwird	Boarnwert
Bozum	Boazum
Britswerd	Britswert
Broeksterwoude	Broeksterwâld
Buitenpost	Bûtenpost
Burgwerd	Burchwert
Burum	Boerum
Cornjum	Koarnjum
Cornwerd	Koarnwert
Damwoude	Damwâld
Dedgum	Dedzjum
Deersum	Dearsum
Delfstrahuizen	Dolsterhuzen
De Veenhoop	De Feanhoop

De Wilgen	De Wylgen
Dijken	Diken
Dongjum	Doanjum
Doniaga	Dunegea
Drachtster Compagnie	Drachtster Kompenije
Driesum	Driezum
Drogeham	Droegeham
Dronrijp	Dronryp
Echten	Ychten
Echtenerbrug	Ychtenbrêge
Edens	Iens
Ee	Ie
Eernewoude	Earnewâld
Eesterga	Jistergea
Eestrum	Jistrum
Elahuizen	Ealahuzen
Elsloo	Elslo
Engelum	Ingelum
Engwierrum	Ingwierrum
Exmorra	Eksmoarre
Ferwerd	Ferwert
Ferwoude	Ferwâlde
Finksum	Feinsum
Firdgum	Furdgum
Fochteloo	Fochtel
Follega	Follegea
Folsgare	Folsgeare
Formerum	Formearum
Franeker	Frjentsjer
Frieschepalen	Fryske Peallen
Gaastmeer	Gaastmar
Garijp	Garyp
Gauw	Gau
Genum	Ginnum
Gerkesklooster	Gerkeskleaster
Gersloot	Gersleat
Giekerk	Gytsjerk
Goënga	Goaiïngea
Goëngahuizen	Goaiïngahuzen
Goëngarijp	Goaiïngaryp
Gorredijk	Gordyk
Grouw	Grou
Hantumeruitburen	Hantumerútbuorren
Hantumhuizen	Hantumhuzen
Hardegarijp	Hurdegaryp
Harlingen	Harns
Hartwerd	Hartwert
Haskerdijken	Haskerdiken
Haskerhorne	Haskerhoarne
Haulerwijk	Haulerwyk
Heeg	Heech
Heerenveen	It Hearrenfean

Hemelum	Himmelum
Hempens	Himpens
Hemrik	Himrik
Hennaard	Hinnaard
Herbaijum	Hjerbeam
Hiaure	Lyste Jouwer
Hijlaard	Hilaard
Hindeloopen	Hylpen
Hitzum	Hitsum
Hogebeintum	Hegebeintum
Holwerd	Holwert
Hoorn	Hoarne
Hoornsterzwaag	Hoarnstersweach
Huins	Húns
Idskenhuizen	Jiskenhuzen
Idzega	Idzegea
Idzegahuizum	Skuzum
IJlst	Drylts
IJsbrechtum	Ysbrechtum
Indijk	Yndyk
Irnsum	Jirnsum
Janum	Jannum
Jorwerd	Jorwert
Joure	Jouwer
Jubbega	Jobbegea
Jutrijp	Jutryp
Katlijk	Ketlik
Kimswerd	Kimswert
Kinnum	Kinum
Koefurderrige	Kûfurderrige
Kolderwolde	Kolderwâlde
Kollumerzwaag	Kollumersweach
Kootstertille	Koatstertille
Kornwerderzand	Koarnwertersân
Kortehemmen	Koartehimmen
Kubaard	Kûbaard
Langedijke	Langedike
Langezwaag	Langsweagen
Langweer	Langwar
Leeuwarden	Ljouwert
Legemeer	Legemar
Lioessens	Ljussens
Lions	Leons
Lippenhuizen	Lippenhuzen
Loënga	Loaïngea
Longerhouw	Longerhou
Luinjeberd	Lûnbert
Lutkewierum	Lytsewierrum
Luxwoude	Lúkswâld
Makkinga	Makkingea
Marssum	Marsum
Menaldum	Menaam

Metslawier	Mitselwier
Midlum	Mullum
Midsland	Midslân
Minnertsga	Minnertsgea
Mirns	Murns
Molenend	Mûnein
Molkwerum	Molkwar
Morra	Moarre
Munnikeburen	Munnekebuorren
Munnikezijl	Muntsjesyl
Niawier	Nijewier
Nieuwehorne	Nijhoarne
Nieuweschoot	Nijskoat
Nijeberkoop	Nijeberkeap
Nijega	Nyegea
Nijeholtpade	Nijeholtpea
Nijeholtwolde	Nijeholtwâlde
Nijelamer	Nijelemmer
Nijemirdum	Nijemardum
Nijetrine	Nijetrine
Nijhuizum	Nijhuzum
Nijland	Nijlân
Noordbergum	Noardburgum
Noordwolde	Noardwâlde
Oenkerk	Oentsjerk
Offingawier	Offenwier
Oldeberkoop	Aldeberkeap
Oldeboorn	Aldeboarn
Oldeholtpade	Aldeholtpea
Oldeholtwolde	Aldeholtwâlde
Oldelamer	Aldlemmer
Oldeouwer	Alde Ouwer
Oldetrijne	Aldetrine
Oosterbierum	Easterbierrum
Oosterend	Easterein (in the municipality of Littenseradiel)
Oosterend	Aasterein (on the island of Terschelling)
Oosterlittens	Easterlittens
Oostermeer	Eastermar
Oosternijkerk	Easternijtsjerk
Oosterwierum	Easterwierrum
Oosterwolde	Easterwâlde
Oosterzee	Eastersee
Oosthem	Easthim
Oostrum	Eastrum
Oost-Vlieland	East-Flylân
Opeinde	Pein
Oppenhuizen	Toppenhuzen
Oranjewoud	Oranjewâld
Oude Bildtzijl	Aldebiltsyl
Oudega	Aldegea (applies to all three settlements with this name in Friesland)
Oudehaske	Aldehaske
Oudehorne	Aldhoarne

Oude Leije	Aldeleie
Oudemirdum	Aldemardum
Oudeschoot	Aldskoat
Oudkerk	Aldtsjerk
Oudwoude	Aldwâld
Ouwsterhaule	Ousterhaule
Ouwster-Nijega	Ousternijegea
Paesens	Peazens
Parrega	Parregea
Peperga	Pepergea
Pietersbierum	Pitersbierrum
Pingjum	Penjum
Poppingawier	Poppenwier
Rauwerd	Raard
Ravenswoud	Ravenswâld
Ried	Rie
Rijperkerk	Ryptsjerk
Rijs	Riis
Rinsumageest	Rinsumageast
Rohel	Reahel
Roodhuis	Reahûs
Roodkerk	Readtsjerk
Roordahuizum	Roardhuzum
Rottevalle	Rottefalle
Ruigahuizen	Rûgehuzen
Sandfirden	Sânfurd
Schalsum	Skalsum
Scharnegoutum	Skearnegoutum
Scharsterbrug	Skarsterbrêge
Scherpenzeel	Skerpenseel
Schettens	Skettens
Schiermonnikoog	Skiermûntseach
Schingen	Skingen
Schraard	Skraard
Seerijp	Stryp
Sexbierum	Seisbierrum
Siegerswoude	Sigerswâld
Sijbrandaburen	Sibrandabuorren
Sijbrandahuis	Sibrandahûs
St. Annaparochie	St. Anne
St. Jacobiparochie	St. Jabik
St. Johannesga	St. Jansgea
St. Nicolaasga	St. Nyk
Sloten	Sleat
Smallebrugge	Smelbrêge
Smalle Ee	Smelle Ie
Snakkerburen	Snakkerbuorren
Sneek	Snits
Snikzwaag	Sniksweach
Sonnega	Sonnegea
Spanga	Spangea
Stavoren	Starum
Stroobos	Strobos

Suameer	Sumar
Suawoude	Suwâld
Surhuisterveen	Surhústerfean
Surhuizum	Surhuzum
Teerns	Tearns
Terband	Terbant
Terhprne	Terherne
Ter Idzard	Teridzert
Terzool	Tersoal
Tietjerk	Tytsjerk
Tijnje	Tynje
Tirns	Turns
Tjalhuizum	Tsjalhuzum
Tjalleberd	Tsjalbert
Tjerkgaast	Tsjerkgaast
Tjerkwerd	Tsjerkwert
Twijzel	Twizel
Twijzelerheide	Twizelerheide
Tzum	Tsjom
Tzummarum	Tsjummearum
Uitwellingerga	Twellingea
Ureterp	Oerterp
Valom	Falom
Veenklooster	Feankleaster
Veenwouden	Feanwâlden
Vegelinsoord	Vegelinsoard
Vinkega	Finkegea
Vrouwenparochie	Froubuorren
Waaxens	Waaksens (both settlements with this name in Friesland)
Wanswerd	Wânswert
Warfstermolen	Warfstermûne
Warga	Wergea
Wartena	Warten
Waskemeer	Waskemar
Welsrijp	Wjelsryp
Westergeest	Westergeast
Westhem	Westhim
West-Terschelling	West-Skylge
Wieuwerd	Wiuwert
Wijckel	Wikel
Wijnaldum	Winaam
Wijnjewoude	Wynjewâld
Wijns	Wyns
Wirdum	Wurdum
Witmarsum	Wytmarsum
Wolvega	Wolvegea
Wons	Wûns
Workum	Warkum
Woudsend	Wâldsein
Wouterswoude	Wâlterswâld
Ypecolsga	Ypelkolsgea

Zurich	Surch
Zwaagwesteinde	Westerein
Zwagerbosch	Sweagerbosk
Zweins	Sweins

In all other cases, the settlement has a unilingular name.

Administrative districts

The Netherlands is split into 12 provinces:

Drenthe (Dr.)
Flevoland (Fl.)
Friesland (Fr.)
Gelderland (Gld.)
Groningen (Gr.)
Limburg (Lim.)
Noord Brabant (N.Br.)
Noord Holland (NH)
Overijssel (Ov.)
Utrecht (Utr.)
Zeeland (Zld.)
Zuid Holland (ZH)

These are not used in addresses unless no postcode is used and a town of the same name exists in more than one province.

These provinces are further split into *gemeentes*, municipalities which contain one or more settlements.

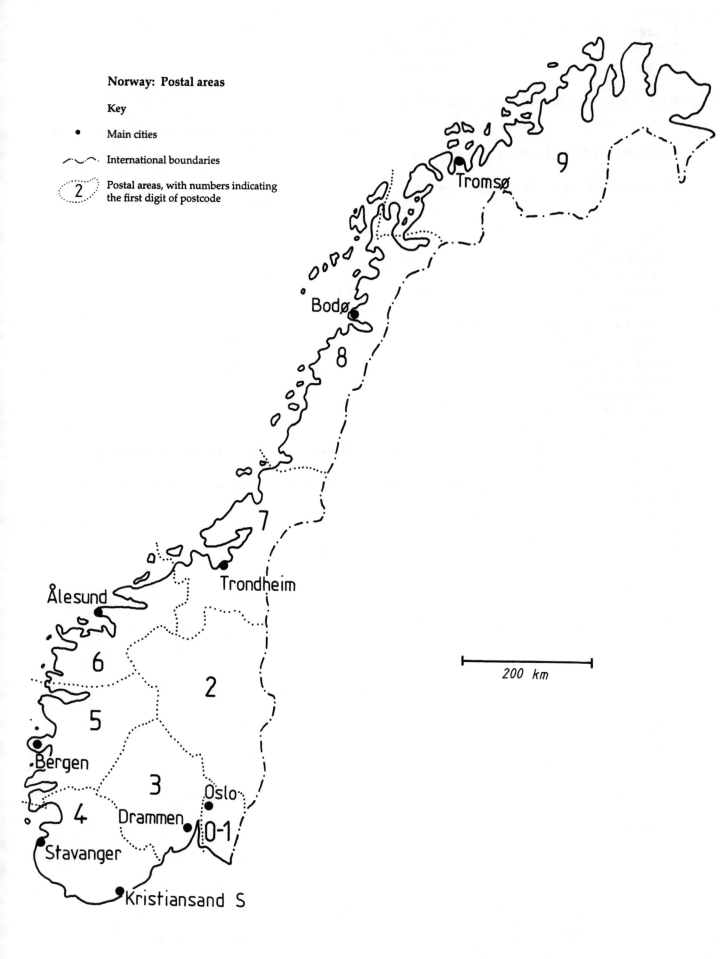

Norway: Postal areas

Key

●   Main cities

〜〜   International boundaries

2   Postal areas, with numbers indicating
the first digit of postcode

9

Tromsø

Bodø

8

7

Trondheim

Ålesund

6

200 km

2

5

Bergen

3

4   Drammen   Oslo

0-1

Stavanger

Kristiansand S

Norway
Norge

Area: 323,877 sq. km (125,050 sq. miles)

Population: 4,249,817 (1991 estimate)

Population density: 13.1 per sq. km

Capital: Oslo (population 458,364 (1989))

Currency: 1 Norwegian krone = 100 øre

Languages

Norwegian, the official language, has two forms: Bokmål or Riksmål and Nynorsk or Landsmål. All children in Norway learn both forms at school. The former is that spoken in Oslo and most other urban areas. The two forms together are spoken by 99 per cent of the population. Lapp is spoken by the 22,500 Lapps living in the far north of the country.

Company types

The following company types may be found in Norwegian address databases:

    AL
    ANS
    AS
    Gruppen

Addresses

Addresses are written in this format:

    Recipient name
    Street name[ ]number
    postcode[ ]TOWN NAME{[ ]sorting code}

For example:

Hans Hansen
Svingen 22
0107 OSLO 1

The thoroughfare type is suffixed to the street name without a space. As with other Scandinavian languages, the definite article does not appear as a separate word but as -en or -et at the end of a word (see language rules below). Thus 'way' is *vei*, 'the way' is *veien*.

Thoroughfare types

The most commonly occurring thoroughfare types, with their abbreviations, are listed below:

Allè	
Allèen	
Bakken	
Bukt	
Byen	
Dalen	
Flate	
Gata (dialect)	G, Gt
Gate(n)	G, Gt
Lia	
Park	
Plassen	Pl
Stortorget	
Stredet	
Svingen	
Torget	
Vegen (dialect)	V.
Vei(en)	V.

Other common nouns, adjectives and prepositions commonly found in address databases

NB : This list is for Bokmål. The ending of the adjectives changes according to the gender of the noun to which it refers and whether it is singular or plural. The plural in Norwegian is made by adding -(e)r to the end of a word, or -(e)ne when the word is preceded by the definite article.

den, det	= the (but only when followed by an adjective preceding a noun. Otherwise -en (gendered) or -et (neuter) is added to the end of the noun. So, for example, vei = road, den store vei= the big road, but … veien)
en, et	= a, an
og	= and
til, inntil	= till, until, up to
for, til	= for
fra	= of
av, fra	= from
til	= to, towards
ved, nær	= near, by
på	= on
i	= in
overfor	= opposite

ved siden av, nærmest, nest	= next to
bak, bakerst	= behind
foran	= in front of
mellom, imellom	= between
over	= over
under	= under
med	= with
ny	= new
gammel	= old
kort	= short
lang	= long
stor	= big
liten, lita, lite, lille, små (plural)	= small
nord	= north
øst	= east
syd	= south
vest	= west

(NB: When used with nouns, the words for north, south, east and west are prefixed without a space to the noun to which they refer. For example, Sydgate = South Street).

Industriebygget	= Industrial estate

Postbox

This is written as Postboks, abbreviated to PB.

Postcodes

Norwegian postcodes consist of 4 consecutive digits, beginning with a number from 0 to 9. The postcode is placed on the last line of the address and precedes the town name. In the larger cities, a number indicating the sorting office may be written after the town name, for example:

0501 OSLO 5

Administrative districts

Norway has 19 counties (*Fylker*), which do not appear in addresses. They are listed below:

Akerhus	Oslo
Aust-Agder	Østfold
Buskerud	Rogaland
Finnmark	Sogn og Fjordane
Hedmark	Sør-Trøndelag
Hordaland	Telemark
More og Romsdal	Troms
Nord-Trøndelag	Vest-Agder
Nordland	Vestfold
Oppland	

Poland
Polska

Area: 312,683 sq. km (120,727 sq. miles)

Population: 38,183,200 (1990 estimate)

Population density: 122.1 per sq. km.

Capital: Warsaw (Warszawa), (population 1,655,700 (1990 estimate))

Currency: 1 Złoty = 100 groszy

Languages

The official language, Polish, is spoken by 98 per cent of the population. Ukrainian is spoken by 1 per cent, and there is a German-speaking minority.

Addresses

Addresses are written in this format:

Recipient name
thoroughfare type[   ]Thoroughfare name[   ]number
postcode[   ]SETTLEMENT

for example:

Mr Jan Kalinkowski
ul Cicha 5
62–806 KALISZ

Postcodes

Polish postcodes have 5 digits and are written in this format:

99[-]999

Towns

Polish borders have changed greatly throughout history; many settlements have corresponding names in German and Russian in particular. The following list gives the foreign language equivalents of the main Polish town names:

Polish	English	German	Spanish	Italian
Gdańsk	Danzig	Danzig		Danzica
Kraków	Crakow	Krakau		Cracovia
Oświęcim	Auschwitz			
Szczecin	Stettin	Stettin		Stettino
Warszawa	Warsaw	Warschau	Varsovia	
Wroclaw	Breslau			

All accented town names are usually written without accents in English.

Administrative districts

Poland has 49 provinces (*Voivodships*). They are not used in addresses. They are listed below:

Biała Podlaska	Opole
Białystok	Ostrołęka
Bielsko-Biała	Piotrków Trrybunalski
Bydgoszcz	Piła
Chełm	Płock
Ciechanów	Poznań
Częstochowa	Przemyśl
Elbląg	Radom
Gdańsk	Rzeszów
Gorzów Wielkopolski	Siedlce
Jelenia Góra	Sieradz
Kalisz	Skierniewice
Katowice	Słupsk
Kielce	Suwałki
Konin	Szczecin
Koszalin	Tarnobrzeg
Kraków	Tarnów
Krosno	Toruń
Legnica	Wałbrzych
Leszno	Warszawa
Łódź	Włocławek
Łomża	Wrocław
Lublin	Zamość
Nowy Sącz	Zielona Góra
Olsztyn	

Portugal

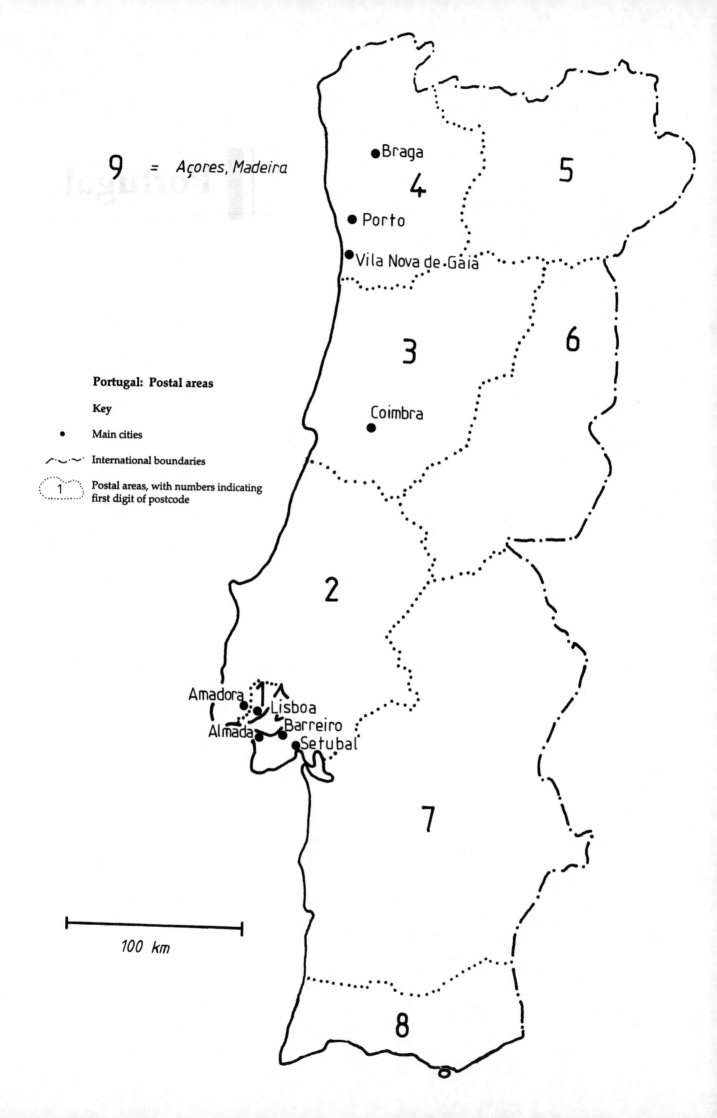

9 = Açores, Madeira

● Braga

4

● Porto

● Vila Nova de Gaia

5

3

6

● Coimbra

Portugal: Postal areas

Key

●   Main cities

⌐·⌐·⌐   International boundaries

⟨1⟩   Postal areas, with numbers indicating first digit of postcode

2

Amadora ●

1

Lisboa

Almada ●   Barreiro

Setubal

7

100 km

8

Portugal

Area: 92,389 sq. km (35, 672 sq. miles)

Population: 10,249,900 (1988 estimate)

Population density: 111.3 per sq. km

Capital: Lisbon (Lisboa) (population 807,937 (1981))

Currency: 1 Portuguese escudo = 100 centavos

Languages

Portuguese is spoken by the whole population. There are no indigenous language minorities.

Company types

C.ª in a company name means *Companhia* (Company).

Contact names

The Portuguese each have four names: two first names and two surnames, which will differ within the same family. The first surname comes from the mother, the second from the father. When addressing women, the first name should be used after the salutation. When addressing men, a first name *or* a surname may be used after the salutation. First names are more important in Portugal than in many other European countries, for example. The whole name should be written in addresses.

Addresses

Addresses consist of three or four lines, comprising the following:

1.   The recipient's name

2.   The street name and number
3,   The region (not obligatory)
4,   The postcode and town.

Addresses are written in this format:

> Recipient name
> Thoroughfare type[ ]Thoroughfare name[ ]number
> {Region}
> postcode[ ]TOWN NAME{[CODEX]}

For example:

> Senhor Carlos Manuel Pereira
> Rua Conde Redondo 80
> 1192 LISBOA CODEX

As in Spain, the house number is often followed by a series of letters and punctuation to indicate floor numbers, stairway numbers and so on.

The name and address of the sender should not be written on the back but on the top left-hand corner of the front of the envelope.

Thoroughfare types

Thoroughfare types are written before and separately from the thoroughfare name. Here is a list of the most commonly occurring thoroughfare types with their common abbreviations:

Alaineda	
Avenida	Av., Avda.
Beco	
Calçada	Cc.
Calçadinha	
Caminho	
Escadas	
Escadinhas	
Estrada	Est.
Largo	L., Lgo.
Praça	Pr.
Quarto, Quarta	Qt., Qto., Qta.
Rua	R.
São, Santa, Santo	S.
Travessa	
Volta	

The exact form of the thoroughfare type and any prepositions within the address will be determined by grammar. For example, you will find the following:

Rua de	masculine singular before a proper noun
Rua do	masculine singular before any other noun
Rua da	feminine singular
Rua dos	masculine plural
Rua das	feminine plural

Other address indications

Portuguese addresses often contain indications of floor or staircase number and so on, which are needed for the correct delivery of a package. The following words give these indications:

andar	floor
direito (dto.)	right
esquerdo (esq.)	left
rés-do-chão (r/c)	ground floor

The words 'first', 'second' and so on are written as a number followed by a superscript 'o', for example:

1°, 2° etc.

Other nouns, adjectives and prepositions commonly found in address databases:

NB:The form of each word can change according to whether the following word is masculine or feminine, singular or plural, or the definite article. Where more than one form is given, they are in the order masculine singular, feminine singular, masculine plural and feminine plural.

o, a, os, as	= the
um, uma	= a, an
e	= and
até	= till, until, up to
para	= for
de	= of, from
do, da, dos, das	= of the, from the
a	= to, towards
ao, á, aos, ás	= to the, towards the
perto	= near, by
em	= on, in
no, na, nos, nas	= on the, in the
defronte de	= opposite (proper noun)
defronte do, da, dos, das	= opposite (other noun)
junto a	= next to (proper noun)
junto ao, á, aos, ás	= next to (other noun)
atrás de	= behind (proper noun)
atrás do, da, dos, das	= behind (other noun)
em frente de	= in front of (proper noun)
em frente do, da, dos, das	= in front of (other noun)
entre	= between
sobre	= over
debaixo de	= under (proper noun)
debaixo do, da, dos, das	= under (other noun)
com	= with
novo, nova, novos, novas	= new
velho, velha, velhos, velhas	= old
curto, curta, curtos, curtas	= short
longo, longa, longos, longas	= long
grande, grandes	= large
pequeno, pequena, pequenos, pequenas	= small
norte, do norte, setentrional	= north, northern

leste, este, do leste, do este, oriental	= east, eastern
sul, do sul, meridional	= south, southern
oeste, do oeste, ocidental	= west, western
São (male saint), Santa (female saint)	= Saint

Postcodes

Postcodes consist of 4 consecutive digits, starting with a number between 1 and 9, and are always followed on the last line of the address by the town name in capitals. Large users are indicated by the word CODEX after the name of the town.

Towns

Lisboa is Lisbon in English, Lissabon in German and Dutch, Lisbonne in French, Lisboa in Spanish and Lisbona in Italian.

Porto is Oporto in English, French, Spanish and Dutch.

Administrative districts

Portugal has 11 provinces, 18 districts and the two autonomous island groups of Açores (Azores) and Madeira:

Provinces

Algarve	Douro-Litoral
Alto-Alentejo	Estremadura
Baixo-Alentejo	Minho
Beira-Alta	Ribatejo
Beira-Baixa	Trás-os-Montes e Alto-Douro
Beira-Litoral	

Districts

Aveiro	Leiria
Beja	Lisboa
Braga	Porto
Bragança	Portalegre
Castelo Branco	Santarém
Coimbra	Setúbal
Évora	Viana do Castelo
Faro	Vila Real
Guarda	Viseu

Romania
România

Area: 237,500 sq. km (91,699 sq. miles)

Population: 23,190,000 (1990 estimate)

Population density: 97.6 per sq. km

Capital: Bucharest (Bucureşti) (population 2,200,000 (1989))

Currency: 1 leu (plural lei) = 100 bani

Languages

The official language, Romanian, is spoken by 87 per cent of the population. Other languages spoken are Hungarian (9 per cent), German (2 per cent) and Romany (1 per cent).

Addresses

Addresses are written in the following format:

Recipient name
Street name[ ]number
postcode[   ]CITY NAME

For example

Gheorghe Petraru
Bd olescu 38
77113 BUCHAREST

Towns

Bucureşti, is known as *Bucharest* in English, *Bukarest* in German, and *Bucarest* in Italian and Spanish.

237

Administrative districts

Romania has 41 counties (*Judet*). They are not used in addresses. They are listed below:

Alba	Harghita
Arad	Hunedoara
Argeş	Ialomiţa
Bacău	Iaşi
Bihor	Maramureş
Bistriţa-Năsăud	Mehedinţi
Botoşani	Mureş
Brăila	Neamţ
Braşov	Olt
Bucureşti	Prahova
Buzău	Sălaj
Călăraşi	Satu Mare
Caraş-Severin	Sibiu
Cluj	Suceava
Constanţa	Teleorman
Covasna	Timiş
Dîmboviţa	Tulcea
Dolj	Vaslui
Galaţi	Vîlcea
Giurgui	Vrancea
Gorj	

Telephone numbers

Area codes begin with a 9 in Romania. As the area code for Bucharest is 90, callers from outside Romania will use '0' as the area code in this case.

 # San Marino

San Marino is a tiny but completely independent state encircled by Italy. For most rules and formats relating to this republic, please refer to the chapter on Italy.

Area: 60.5 sq. km. (23.4 sq. miles)

Population: 23,243 (1990)

Population density: 384.18 per sq. km

Capital: San Marino (population 4,185 (1990))

Currency: Italian lira. (San Marino forms part of the Italian economic area.)

Languages

Italian is spoken by the whole population.

Company names, contact names, addresses, postbox

The same rules and formats are used as in Italy. Please refer to the chapter on Italy.

Postcodes

San Marino forms part of the Italian postal system. Its addresses will usually be found in Italian address databases. They can be identified by their postcode, 47031, and, where written, their region, which is (SM) for San Marino.

Administrative districts

San Marino is sub-divided into 9 Castles, each corresponding to a village.

Telephone numbers

San Marino forms part of the Italian telephone system. The international dialling code is 39 and the area code for San Marino is 0549.

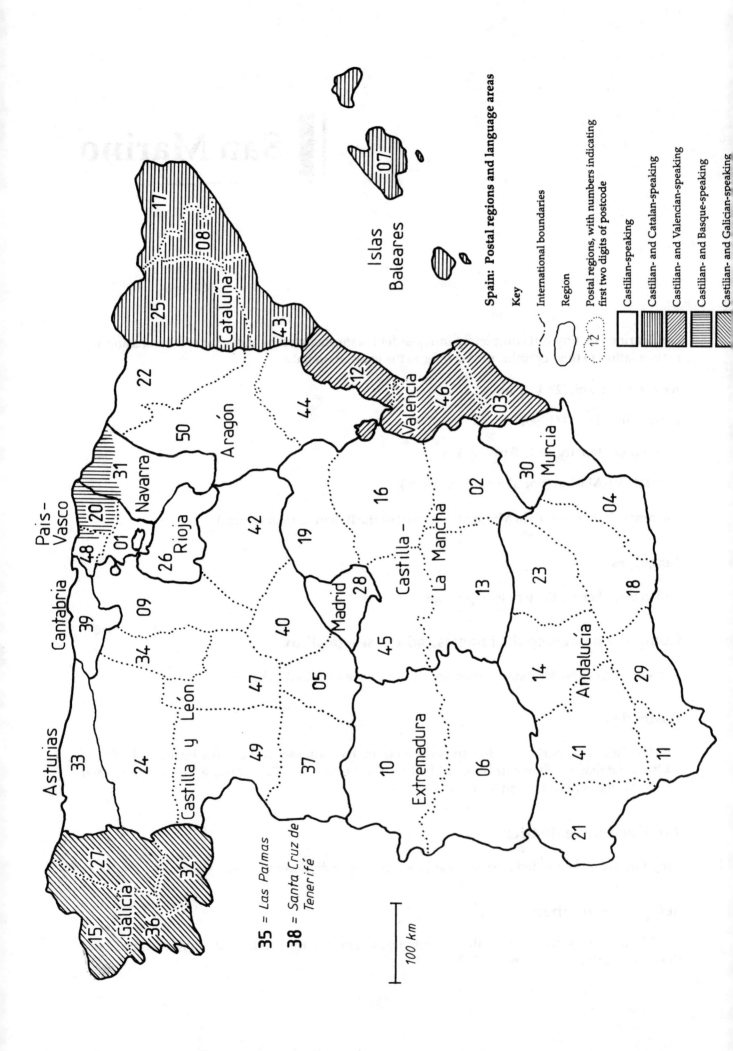

Spain: Postal regions and language areas

Key

International boundaries

Region

Postal regions, with numbers indicating first two digits of postcode · 12

Castilian-speaking

Castilian- and Catalan-speaking

Castilian- and Valencian-speaking

Castilian- and Basque-speaking

Castilian- and Galician-speaking

Islas Baleares

07

Cataluña
17
08
25
43

Aragón
22
50
44

Navarra
31

Pais-Vasco
20
48
01

Rioja
26

Valencia
12
46
03

Murcia
30

Cantabria
39

09

42
19

Madrid
28

Castilla - La Mancha
16
02
45
13
23

Andalucía
14
29
18
04

Asturias
33

Castilla y León
24
34
47
40
05
49
37

Extremadura
10
06

41
21
11

Galicia
15
27
32
36

35 = Las Palmas

38 = Santa Cruz de Tenerifé

100 km

Spain
España

Area: 504 ,782 sq. km (194,897 sq. miles)

Population: 39,321,604 (1990 estimate)

Population density: 77.9 per sq. km

Capital: Madrid (population 3,120,732 (1990 estimate))

Currency: 1 Spanish peseta = 100 centimos

Languages

Castellano (Castilian Spanish) is the official language for the whole of Spain, but several of Spain's autonomous regions have their own languages which are legally treated on a par with Castellano. Castellano is spoken by 70 per cent of the Spanish population. Català (Catalan) is spoken by 21 per cent of the population, and has official status in the regions of Catalonia, Valencia (where it differs very slightly from Catalan and is called Valencian) and the Balearic Islands. Galego (Galician) is spoken by 7 per cent of the population, and is recognized in Galicia. Euskera (Basque) is spoken by 1 per cent of the population, and is recognized in the Basque region and Navarre.

In Navarre, the official language is Castilian, but Basque is spoken and has legal protection. The province defines Basque as being the main language in the following municipalities:

Abaurrea	Arruazu
Alta	Bakáiku
Abaurrea Baja	Basaburua Mayor
Alsasua	Baztan
Anue	Bertizarana
Araitz	Betelu
Arantza	Burguete
Arano	Donamaría
Arakil	Etxalar
Arbizu	Etxarri-Aranatz
Areso	Elgorriaga
Aria	Erasun
Aribe,	Ergoien

Erro
Esteribar
Ezkurra
Garaioa
Garralda
Goizueta
Huarte-Arakil
Igantzi
Imotz
Inañeta
Ituren
Iturmendi
Labaien
Lakuntza
Lantz
Larraun
Leitza
Lesaka

Oitz
Olazagutia
Orbaitzeta
Orbara
Roncesvalles
Saldias
Santesteban
Sunbilla
Ultzama
Urdax
Urdiain
Urrotz
Valcarlos
Vera de Bidasoa
Villanueva
Ziordia
Zubieta y Zugarramurdi

Both Castilian and Basque are spoken in the following municipalities:

Abárzuza
Ansoain
Aoiz
Arce
Atez
Barañain
Burgui
Burlada
Ciriza
Cizur
Echarri
Echauri
Egüés
Ezcároz
Esparza
Estella
Ezcabarte
Garde
Goñi
Güesa
Guesálaz
Huarte
Isaba
Iza

Izalzu
Jaurrieta
Juslapeña
Lezaun
Lizoain
Ochagavía
Odieta
Oláibar
Olza
Ollo
Oronz
Oroz Betelu
Pamplona
Puente la Reina
Roncal
Salinas de Oro
Sarriés
Urzainqui
Uztárroz
Vidángoz
Vidaurreta
Villava
Yerri y Zabalza

All other municipalities have Castilian as their main language.

Note that the above lists give the municipality names in Castilian. For the equivalent Basque names, please refer to the Towns section.

There are no clear-cut geographical boundaries between the speakers of the different dialects and languages spoken in Spain.

Company types

The following company types will be found in company names:

Cooperativa	(Co-operative)
SA	Sociedad Anónima
Sociedad Civil	(non-profit entity)
Sociedad Colectiva	(General Partnership)
Sociedad Comanditaria	(General and Limited partnership)
Sociedad de Cartera	(Portfolio company)
Sociedad Limitada	(Limited company)

Contact names

Spanish people have two surnames, and members of the same family do not necessarily have the same surnames. A person's first surname is their father's first surname, their second surname is their mother's first surname. For example:

José Jimenez Perez marries Margarita Diaz Jimenez

their children, Manuel and Isabel, will be known as:

Manuel Jimenez Diaz and Isabel Jimenez Diaz

A woman keeps her maiden name after marriage. The first surname is considered the most important, but the full set of names will appear on official documents.

Addresses

Addresses are written in the following format:

Recipient name
{thoroughfare type[ ]}Thoroughfare name[,]house number{[–]floor/flat/staircase number etc.}
postcode[ ]TOWN[(]Province[)]

For example:

Sra Ana Jimenez
calle Alcalá, 142 – 2°D
03201 ELCHE (Alicante)

Calle, the Spanish word for street, is by far the most commonly occurring thoroughfare type and for this reason is rarely written. You would be more likely to find the example address given above written as:

Alcalá, 142 – 2°D

The floor/flat/staircase number can be followed by a superscripted 'o' (a masculine word) or 'a' (a feminine word).

The 'D' in this example means *derecha*, right. An 'I', *izquierda*, would indicate left.

The words for right and left in Catalan are *dreta* and *esquerra* respectively, *dereita* and *esquerda* in Galician and *zuzen* and *ezkerkada* in Basque.

The thoroughfare type, when included, is written before, and separately from, the thoroughfare name. It should be written with the first letter in lower case.

Spanish addresses may contain the kilometre number of a house or company on long or intercity routes.

The return address of the sender can be written either on the back of the envelope or in the top left-hand corner of the front of the envelope.

Thoroughfare types

Below is a list of the most commonly occurring thoroughfare types, with the abbreviated form(s) which you are most likely to find in address databases:

Castilian	Abbreviation	Catalan	Galician	Basque
avenida	av.	avinguda	avenida ampla alameda chea	bidezabal, bidehandi, bidenausi
bajada		baixada	baixada	
calle	c/	carrer	rúa	bide, autobide, zidor, bida
callejón	cj.		ruela, viela	kaletarte, karrika, zeharkale
callejuela			ruela, viela	
camino	cm.	camí	camiño	
carretera	ctra., cr., cte	carettera	estrada	autobidezebal, autopista
cuesta		pujada	costa, encosta	
glorieta	g.		glorieta	
paseo		passeig	paseo	
plaza	p.	plaça	praza	plaza, enparantza
plazuela		plaçeta	praciña	
rambla	rbla.	rambla	rambla	
ronda	rd.	ronda	ronda	
rotonda			rotunda	
rúa			rúa	kale, karrika
sendero		dreçera	sendeiro	basabide, bidexka bidetxo, bidezidor, Zaldibide, bideska
subida		pujáda	subida, costa, suba	
travesía		travessera	travesía	bidegurutze, bidebieta, karrikagurutze, gurutzagune
vía		via	vía	pasabide, pasagune, iraganleku, pasaleku, pasatoki, pasarte

Other nouns, adjectives and prepositions commonly found in address databases

Castilan

NB: Prepositions retain a lower case first letter when used in a mixed-case field The following abbreviations are used: (m) = masculine; (f) = feminine; (s) = singular; (pl) = plural

el (m s) / la (f s) / los (m pl) / las (f pl)	= the
un (m) / una (f)	= a, an
y (before a word beginning with i- or hi-, this becomes 'e')	= and
hasta	= till, up to, until
para	= for
de	= of
a	= to, towards
en	= in
cerca de	= near
junto a	= near, next to
enfrente de	= opposite
detrás de	= behind
entre	= between
debajo de	= under
al lado de	= next to
encima de	= on (top of)
con	= with
nuevo (m)/nueva (f)	= new
viejo (m)/vieja (f)	= old
corto (m)/corta (f)	= short
largo (m)/larga (f)	= long
gran (before the noun to which it refers), grande (after the noun to which it refers)	= large
pequcño (m)/perqueña (f)	= small
norte	= north
este	= east
oeste	= west
sur	= south
San (m) / Santa (f)	= Saint

Adjectives referring to plural nouns add an 's' on the end.

Catalan

al(m s)/la (fs)/els (m pl)/les (f pl)	= the
un (m)/una (f)	= a, an
i (before a word beginning with i- or hi-, this becomes 'e')	= and
fins	= till, up to, until
per	= for
de	= of
a	= to, towards
en/a/amb/en	= in
prop de	= near
al constat de	= near, next to
davant de	= opposite
darrera de	= behind
entre	= between
sota	= under
al costat de	= next to

sobre/damunt	= on (top of)
amb	= with
nou (m)/nova (f)	= new
vell (m)/vella (f)	= old
curt (m)/curta (f)	= short
llarg (m)/llarga (f)	= long
gran	= large
petit (m)/petita (f)	= small
nort	= north
est	= east
oest	= west
sud	= south
Sant (m)/Santa (f)	= Saint

Galician

o, lo, a, la, os, los, as, las	= the
un, unha	= a, an
y, e	= and
ata	= till, up to, until
para	= for
de, del, dela, deles, delas	= of
en, nel, nela, neles, nelas	= in
a	= to, towards
cerca de	= near
xunto a	= near, next to
defronte de, enfronte de	= opposite
detrás de	= behind
entre	= between
debaixo de, so	= under
al lado de	= next to
encima de, enriba de	= on (top of)
con	= with
nove, novo	= new
vello, vella	= old
curto, curta	= short
largo, larga, longo, longa	= long
gran	= large
pequeno	= small
norte	= north
este, leste	= east
oeste	= west
sur	= south
San, Santa	= Saint

Basque

Basque is a tremendously complex language with a large number of delensions which make recognition of certain words for a non-speaker very difficult. The definite article, for example, is suffixed to another word and can take one of four forms (-a, -ak, -ek and -ok) depending on whether the word is singular, plural, transitive or denoting a group. Many prepositions and adjectives form prefixes or suffixes to other words, and change their form according to their context. As their form and case are dependent on their context, no list of prepositions or adjectives is given here.

Postbox

This is written as Apartado in Castilian and Galician, Apartat or Apartat de Correus in Catalan.

Postcodes

Postcodes in Spain consist of 5 consecutive digits which should be placed before the town name on the last line of the address.

The first two digits of the postcode, ranging from 01 to 50, indicate the province. The third digit indicates a place within the province. If this digit is 0, the address is in the capital of the province, if it is 1 it is in the vicinity of the capital, and so on. The higher this number, the further the address is from the region's capital. The last two digits are split into three ranges of numbers to indicate:

* Postboxes
* Delivery addresses
* Large users

More than one municipality can share the same postcode, whilst in larger cities the postcodes refer to groups of streets.

Certain codes are fixed:

nn 080: for private postboxes
nn 071: for official (governmental) postal address/postboxes
nn 070: for Post Office boxes

Towns

The following two lists give alternative town names, the first for indigenous languages, the second for other European languages. The first list gives only the alternatives for the larger settlements – many smaller settlements will also have two names. It is important to try to use the version corresponding to the language of the respondent rather than just the Castilian version.

Castilian	*Catalan/Valencian*	*Basque*	*Galician*
Abárzuza		Abartzuza	
Abaurrea Alta		Abaurregaina	
Abaurrea Bzaja		Abaurrepea	
Alsasua		Altsasu	
Ansoain		Antsoain	
Aoiz		Agoitz	
Arce		Artzibar	
Bakáiku		Bakaiku	
Baracaldo		Barakaldo	
Basaburua Mayor		Basaburua	
Bilbao		Bilbo	

Castilian	*Catalan/Valencian*	*Basque*	*Galician*
Burguete		Auritz	
Burgui		Burgi	
Burlada		Burlata	
Castellón	Castelló de la Plana		
Ciriza		Ziriza	
Cizur		Zizur	
Donamaría		Donamaria	
Echarri		Etxarri	
Echauri		Etxauri	
Egüés		Eguesibar	
Elche	Elx		
Erasun		Eratsun	
Erro		Erroibar	
Escabarte		Ezkabarte	
Esparza		Espartza	
Estella		Lizarra	
Ezcároz		Ezkaroze	
Figueras	Figueres		
Gerona	Girona		
Goñi		Goñerri	
Guernica		Gernika	
Güesa		Gorza	
Guesálaz		Gesalatz	
Huarte		Uharte	
Huarte-Arakil		Uharte-Arakil	
Ibiza	Eivissa		
Isaba		Izaba	
Iza		Itza	
Izalzu		Itzaltzu	
Jaurrieta		Eaurta	
Juslapeña		Xulapain	
La Coruña			A Coruña
Lérida	Lleida		
Mahón	Maó		
Ochagavía		Otsagi	
Oláibar		Olaibar	
Olazagutia		Olazti	
Ollo		Ollaran	
Olza		Oltza	
Orense			Ourense
Oronz		Orontze	
Oroz Betelu		Orotz-Betelu	
Pamplona		Iruñea	
Puente la Reina		Gares	
Roncal		Erronkari	
Roncesvalles		Orreaga	
Salinas de Oro		Jaitz	
San Sebastián		Donostia	
Santesteban		Doneztebe	
Sarriés		Sarze	
Tarrasa	Terrassa		
Urdax		Urdazubi	

Urzainqui	Urzainki
Uztárroz	Uztarroze
Valcarlos	Luzaide
Vera de Bidasoa	Bera
Vich Vic	
Vidángoz	Bidankoze
Vidaurreta	Bidaurreta
Villanueva	Hiriberri
Villava	Atarrabia
Vitoria	Gastéiz
Yerri y Zabalza	Deierri eta Zabaltza
Zubieta y Zugarramurdi	Zugarramurdi

Castilian	English	French	Italian	Dutch
Barcelona		Barcelone	Barcellona	
Cádiz	Cadiz	Cadix	Cadice	
Cartagena		Carthagène		
Córdoba	Cordoba	Cordoue		
Grenada		Grenade		
Málaga	Malaga			
Murcia		Murcie		
Pamplona		Pampelone		
Salamanca		Salamanque		
San Sebastián		Saint Sébastien		
Segovia		Ségovie		
Sevilla	Seville	Séville	Siviglia	
Toledo		Tolède		
Zaragoza	Saragossa	Saragosse		Sarragossa

Administrative districts

The name of the province in which an address is situated should be written in full brackets after the name of the town.

Spain has 17 regions split into 50 provinces. The names of the provinces are usually the same as those of their capital cities. Exceptions have been specified in the table below.

Region	Province	First 2 digits of postcode
Andalucía	Almería	04
	Cádiz	11 (includes Ceuta)
	Córdoba	14
	Granada	18
	Huelva	21
	Jaén	23
	Málaga	29 (includes Melilla)
	Sevilla	41
Aragón	Huesca	22
	Teruel	44
	Zaragoza	50
Asturias	Oviedo	33

Region	*Province*	*First 2 digits of postcode*	
Canarias	Las Palmas	35	
	Santa Cruz de Tenerifé	38	
Cantabria	Santander	39	
Castilla – La Mancha	Albacete	02	
	Ciudad Real	13	
	Cuenca	16	
	Guadalajara	19	
	Toledo	45	
Castilla y León	Ávila	05	
	Burgos	09	
	León	24	
	Palencia	34	
	Salamanca	37	
	Segovia	40	
	Soria	42	
	Valladolid	47	
	Zamora	49	
Cataluña (Catalonia)	Barcelona	08	
	Gerona	17	
	Lérida	25	
	Tarragona	43	
Comunidad Valenciana	Alicante	03	
	Castellón	12	
	Valencia	46	
Extremadura	Badajoz	06	
	Cáceres	10	
Galicia	La Coruña	15	
	Lugo	27	
	Orense	32	
	Pontevedra	36	
Islas Baleares	Palma de Mallorca	07	
La Rioja	La Rioja	26	(Capital: Logroño)
Madrid	Madrid	28	
Murcia	Murcia	30	
Navarra	Navarra	31	(Capital: Pamplona)
País-Vasco	Álava	01	(Capital: Vitoria/Gastéiz)
	Guipúzcoa	20	(Capital: San Sebastián/Donostia)
	Vizcaya	48	(Capital: Bilbao/Bilbo)

Sweden
Sverige

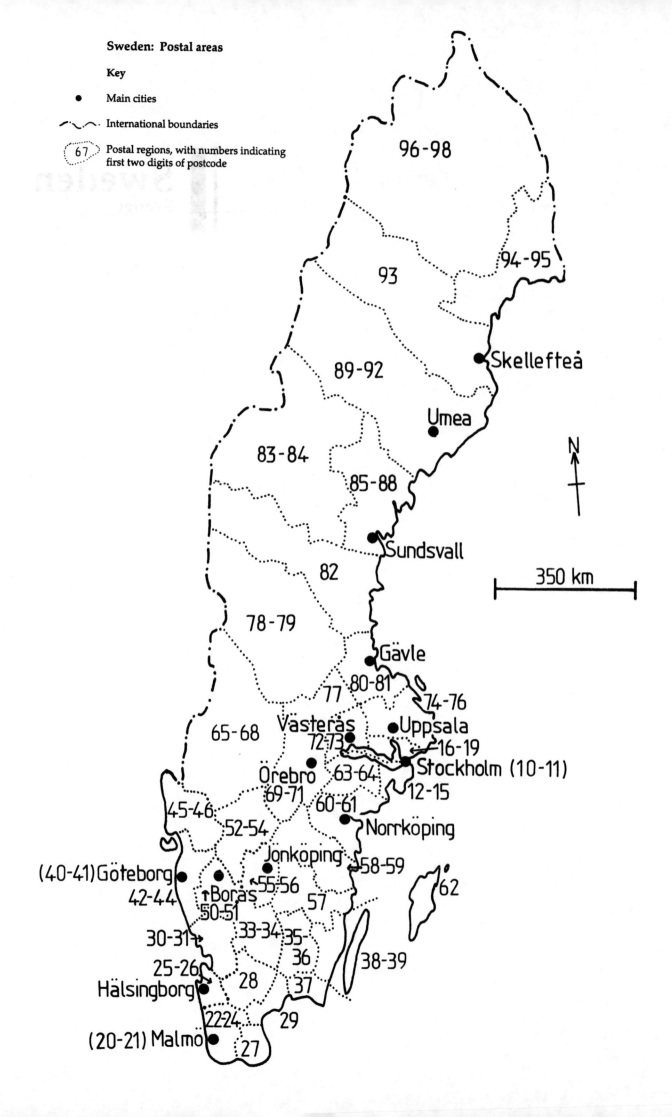

Sweden: Postal areas

Key

●   Main cities

⌁   International boundaries

(67)   Postal regions, with numbers indicating first two digits of postcode

96-98

94-95

93

● Skellefteå

89-92

Umea ●

83-84

85-88

● Sundsvall

82

N

350 km

78-79

● Gävle

80-81

77   74-76

65-68

Västerås   ● Uppsala

72-73   16-19

●   Stockholm (10-11)

Örebro   63-64

69-71   12-15

45-46   60-61

52-54   ● Norrköping

Jonköping

(40-41)Göteborg ●   58-59

42-44   ↑Borås 55-56   62

50-51   57

30-31↑ 33-34 35

36

25-26   38-39

Hälsingborg ● 28   37

22-24   29

(20-21) Malmö ● 27

Sweden
Sverige

Area: 440,945 sq. km (170,250 sq. miles)

Population: 8,590, 630 (1990 estimate)

Population density: 19.5 per sq. km

Capital: Stockholm (population 674,452 (1990))

Currency: 1 Swedish krona = 100 öre

Languages

The official language, Swedish, is spoken by 93 per cent of the population. Finnish is spoken by 3 per cent. Other languages are Toroyo and Lapp, spoken by some 8,000 people in the far north.

Company names

The company type *AB* will often be found in company databases.

Contact names

Generally in Sweden, you can indicate on your correspondence whether the contents are private or may be opened by others. Two formats are used. The following format indicates that your mail may be opened by others:

    Company name
    Department name
    Contact name
    Rest of address

The following format indicates that the mail is private and personal:

    Contact name
    Company name

Department name
Rest of address

Addresses

Addresses are written in the following format:

Recipient name
Street name[ ]number
postcode[ ]TOWN NAME

For example:

Fru Inger Lilja
Vasavagen 3
582 20 LINKOPING

Thoroughfare types are written after the thoroughfare name, without a space between them.

As with other Scandinavian languages, the definite article does not appear as a separate word in Swedish but as a suffix (-en) at the end of a word. By far the most common thoroughfare types that will be encountered are -gaten and -vägen. A fuller list of thoroughfare types follows:

alle
dallen
gata
gaten
grand
granden
lerig
liden
plan
promenaden
rade
stigen
strand
torg
vag
vägen

The settlement name to be given in the address is that of the post-office distribution centre. Villages within an area served by a distribution centre in a larger settlement do not have to be separately mentioned on the address – the name of the larger centre with the postcode is sufficient.

Isolated farmsteads, of which Sweden has many, are often addressed without a street address. The following form would be used:

Recipient name
Village[,]Farmstead name
postcode[ ]TOWN NAME

For example:

Jorgen Walgren
Hemsjöl, Långsmon
441 96 ALINGSÅS

Nouns, adjectives and prepositions commonly found in address databases:

NB: In Swedish the form of an adjective depends on the gender of the noun to which it refers and whether it is singular or plural. The following abbreviations are used: (s) = singular, (p) = plural.

den (s), de (pl.)	= the (but only when followed by an adjective preceding a noun. Otherwise the gender is indicated by adding a suffix to the noun)
en	= a, an
och	= and
till, intill	= till, until, up to
för, framför, före, inför	= for
av	= of
från	= from
till, åt	= to, towards
vid, i närheten	= near, by
på	= on
i, in	= in
motliggande, på andra sidan	= opposite
närmast	= next to
bak, bakom	= behind
framme, framför	= in front of
mellan, emellan	= between
över	= over
under	= under
med	= with
ny, nya	= new
gammal, gamla, gammalt	= old
kort	= short
lång	= long
stor	= big
liten (s), små (pl)	= small
nord	= north
ost	= east
syd	= south
väst	= west

Postbox

This is written as Box.

Postcodes

Postcodes consist of 5 digits, beginning with a number between 1 and 9, and written in the following structure:

999[ ]99

The first digits usually indicate the borough, the last indicate areas or streets within the borough. With larger cities, a whole range of postcodes exists and only the first digit is the same for the whole city. In medium-sized towns the first two digits are likely to be the same, whilst all three digits will be the same in more rural areas. Large companies and post-office boxes may have individual postcodes. Although the first three digits indicate an area, the name of the town given may differ. For example:

311 42 Falkenberg
311 96 Heberg

There are no postcodes in Sweden beginning with these numbers:

0, 32, 47, 48, 49, 99

Towns

Stockholm is known as Stoccolma in Italian and Estocolmo in Spanish.

Administrative districts

Sweden has 24 counties (*Län*). They are not used in addresses. They are listed below:

Alvsborgs Län	Malmöhus Län
Blekinge Län	Norbottens Län
Gävleborgs Län	Örebro Län
Göteborgs och Bohus Län	Östergötlands Län
Gotlands Län	Skaraborgs Län
Hallands Län	Södermanlands Län
Jämtlands Län	Stockholms Län
Jönköpings Län	Uppsala Län
Kalmar Län	Värmlands Län
Kopparbergs Län	Västerbottens Län
Kristianstads Län	Västernorrlands Län
Kronobergs Län	Västmanlands Län

Switzerland
Schweiz/Suisse/Svizzera

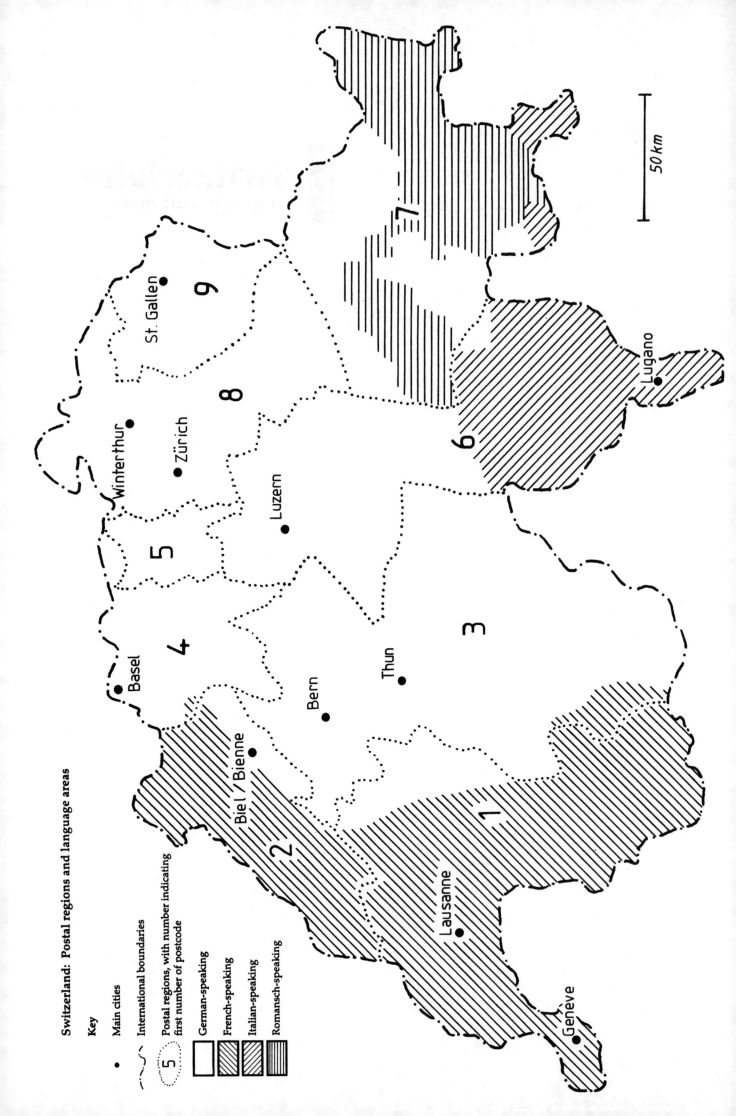

Switzerland: Postal regions and language areas

Key

●   Main cities

◞‒◞   International boundaries

⑤   Postal regions, with number indicating
      first number of postcode

☐   German-speaking

▨   French-speaking

▧   Italian-speaking

▥   Romansch-speaking

50 km

St. Gallen

Lugano

Winterthur

Zürich

Luzern

Basel

Bern

Thun

Biel / Bienne

Lausanne

Genève

9

8

5

4

7

6

3

2

1

Switzerland
Schweiz/Suisse/Svizzera

Area: 41,293 sq. km (15,953 sq. miles)

Population: 6,883,750 (1991 estimate)

Population density: 166.7 per sq. km

Capital: Bern/Berne/Berna (population 134,393 (1989 estimate))

Currency: 1 Swiss franc/Franken = 100 centimes/Rappen

Languages

Switzerland has four official languages: German, French, Italian and Romansch. The percentage of people speaking each language as a mother tongue is as follows:

German	63.6%
French	19.2%
Italian	7.6%
Romansch	0.6%

The remaining 9 per cent speak other, non-indigenous, languages.

Switzerland does not suffer the same kind of tension between members of different language groups as do many other multilingular European countries, and most Swiss speak more than one of the national languages. Although some kind of border can be drawn between the areas where the different languages are spoken, in many areas there is a great deal of mixing of peoples from the different language groups.

The smallest language group, Romansch, is only spoken in a few isolated Alpine valleys. Despite this, it exists in a number of different dialectical forms, and until recently there was no agreement of which form should be taken as a written standard. For this reason it is rare to come across Romansch in addresses or names.

Company names

In the German, French and Italian language areas, it is more correct, where the *nature* of a company is mentioned in its name, that this *precedes* the name of the company, thus:

Bäcker Schmidt
Boulangerie Dupont
Fornaio Andretti

You will often, however, find these activity indications *after* the company name, thus:

Schmidt, Bäcker
Schmidt (Bäcker)
Dupont, Boulangerie
Dupont (Boulangerie)
Andretti, Fornaio
Andretti (Fornaio)

Company types

The following company types will be found in company address databases:

German: AG
French: SA
Italian: SA

These abbreviations will also often be encountered in company names:

Gebr. = Gebrüder (brother, German)
Ste. = Société (company, French)
Cie. = Compagnie (company, French)

Contact names

In the German-speaking areas, the words *zu Händen*, abbreviated to z.H. or z.Hd. mean 'For the attention of'.

Addresses

Structure

Addresses will be written in German, French, Italian or Romansch according to the language of the region. In bilingual regions, addresses may be written in either or both languages. In German-speaking areas, addresses are written in this format:

Salutation
Recipient name
Thoroughfare name thoroughfare type[ ]number
postcode[ ]TOWN NAME

For example:

Herrn Heinz Schmidt
Bahnhofstrasse 15
8000 ZÜRICH

In Italian-speaking areas, the address should be written in the following format:

Recipient name
thoroughfare type[ ]Thoroughfare name[ ]number
postcode[ ]TOWN NAME

For example:

Gaspare Andretti
Via Basilea 12
6500 BELLINZONA

In French-speaking areas, the address should be written in either of the following formats:

Recipient name
number[ ]thoroughfare type[ ]Thoroughfare name
postcode[ ]TOWN NAME

or

Recipient name
number[,]thoroughfare type[ ]Thoroughfare name
postcode[ ]TOWN NAME

For example:

Fernand Genoud
8 rue du Marché
1000 LAUSANNE

or

Fernand Genoud
8, rue du Marché
1000 LAUSANNE

In German-speaking areas, the general rule is that the thoroughfare type part of the street address is suffixed to the rest of the address, thus:

Zentralstrasse
Zwingliplatz

However, there are two important exceptions. If the thoroughfare name refers to the real name of a place (e.g. a town name, a castle name, a forest name, etc.) then there is a space between the thoroughfare name and the thoroughfare type. The second exception is where complete personal names are used. In these cases, each component of the name and each thoroughfare type are separated with hyphens. Surnames *only* are *not* covered by this exception. Thus:

Züricher Strasse 2
William-Tell-Strasse 9
Calvinstrasse

In streets beginning with prepositions or some adjectives ('Am', 'An', 'Alter' etc.), the preposition is followed by a space, thus:

Alter Marktstrasse 3

In the French and Italian language regions, thoroughfare types should correctly begin with a lower case letter. Prepositions, articles etc. (e.g. 'de', 'la' etc.) should also be written without a capital letter. In both the French- and the Italian-speaking regions, the thoroughfare type is written before and separately from the thoroughfare name, thus:

rue des Noirettes
route de Genève
via Ospedale
viale Cattaneo

Thoroughfare types

Below is a list of the most commonly occurring thoroughfare types, with the abbreviated form(s) which you are most likely to find in address databases:

German	*Abbreviations*	*German*	*Abbreviations*
Allee		Hof	
Berg		Kamp	
Boulevard	Bd.	Markt	
Bruch		Platz	Pl.
Bühl		Ring	
Chaussee	Ch.	Strasse	Str.
Damm		Ufer	
Gasse		Wall	
Graben		Weg	
Hafen		Weide	

French	*Abbreviations*	*French*	*Abbreviations*
allée		mont/	mt.
avenue	ave.	montagne	
boulevard	bd., bld.	parc	
canal		place	pl.
centre		quai	
champ		quartier	qu.
chaussée	ch., chee., chée	route	rte.
chemin		Route	
clos		National	RN
cour		rue	r.
digue		square	sq.
impasse	imp.	val/vallée	
marché			

Italian	*Abbreviations*	*Italian*	*Abbreviations*
borgo			
contrada	c.da	corso	c., cso., c.so

frazione	fraz., fr.
largo	lgo.
lungofiume	(fiume can be replaced with the name of a river)
lungolago	(lago can be replaced with the name of a lake)
lungomare	(mare can be replaced with the name of a sea)
piazza	p., pza.
piazzale	p.^{le}
strada	
traversa	
via	v.
viale	vle., vl.
vicolo	

Other nouns, adjectives and prepositions commonly found in address databases:

German

NB: German grammar rules governing articles, prepositions and adjectives are complex, and there is no need to explain them here. It is only necessary to be able to recognize them when and where they occur in addresses. For this reason a list without further explanation is provided. As a very general rule of thumb, the prepositions and adjectives listed may have one of the following endings added: nothing; e; er; em; en or es.

der/die/das/den/dem/des	= the
ein/eine/eines/einen/einem/einer	= a, an
und	= and
bis	= till, until, up to
für	= for
von	= of, from
zu, nach	= to, towards
bei, bei der/den/dem (beim)	= near, at
an, an der/den/dem (am)	= at, by, towards
auf, auf der/den/dem	= on
in, in der/den/dem (im)	= in
gegenüber	= opposite, facing
nächst, neben, neben der/dem/den	= next to
hinter, hinter der/den/dem	= behind
vor, vor der/den/dem	= before, in front of
zwischen, zwischen der/den/dem	= between, amongst
über, über der/den/dem	= over, above, beyond
unter, unter der/dem/den	= under, beneath, below
mit	= with
neu/neue	= new
alt/alte	= old
kurz/kurze/kurzen/kurzer/kurzem/kurzes (K.)	= short
lang/lange/langen/langer/langem/langes (L./Lge.)	= long
gross/grosse/grossen/grosser/grossem/grosses (G.)	= large
klein/kleine/kleinen/kleiner/kleinem/kleines (K./Kl./Kle.)	= small
nord	= north
ost	= east
süd	= south
west	= west

sankt (St.)	= saint
Industrieterrein, Industriegebiet	= industrial estate

French

NB: Except where specified, the plural form of adjectives is the correctly gendered singular form followed by an 's'. The following abbreviations are used: (m) = masculine form; (f) = feminine form; (pl) = plural form.

le (m)/la (f)/les (pl)	= the
(NB: le and la are written l' before a vowel or an unaspirated h)	
un (m)/une (f)	= a, an
et	= and
à/au (m)/à la (f)/aux (pl)	= till, until, up to, to
pour	= for
de (before a proper noun)/du (m)/de la, de l' (f)/des (pl)	= of, from
à	= at
près de	= by, near to
sur	= on (a river, the sea)
dans	= in
en face de	= opposite
à côté de	= next to
derrière	= behind
devant	= in front
entre	= between
avec	= with
sous	= under
lès (occurs *only* in place names)	= near
nouveau (m)/nouvelle (f)/nouveaux (m.pl.)/nouvelles (f.pl.) / nouvel (m, before a vowel or unaspirated h)	= new
vieux (m, pl)/vieille (f)/vielles (f.pl.)/vieil (m, before a vowel or an unaspirated h)	= old
court (m) (Ct.)/courte (f) (Cte.)	= short
long (m) (Lg.)/longue (f) (Lgue.)	= long
grand (m) (Gr./Grd.)/grande (f) (Gr./Grde.)	= large
petit (m) (P./Pt.)/petite (f) (P./Pte.)	= small
nord	= north
est	= east
sud	= south
ouest	= west
saint (m) (St.)/sainte (f) (Ste.)	= saint
Parc Industriel	= industrial estate
Zone d'Activités (Z.A.C.)	
Zone Industrielle (Z.I.)	
Zone Artisanale (Z.A.)	

Italian

NB: The form which certain common words take in Italian depends on a number of factors such as the gender of the following word, whether the next word is the definite article, whether the first letter of the next word is a vowel or a consonant, and whether that consonant is a z, ps or an s

+ consonant. As this is rather complex, no explanation is given for each form but, where more than one form exists, each form is given.

il/i/l'/gli/lo/la/le	= the
un/uno/una/un'	= a, an
e	= and
fino a, sino a	= till, until
per	= for
di	= of
del/dei/dell'/ degli/dello/della/delle	= of the
verso, a, in	= to, towards
al, allo, alla, ai, agli, alle	= towards the
presso, vicino a, accanto a	= near, by, next to
su	= on (sea, a river), over
sul, sulla, sullo, sulle, sella	= on the
in	= in
nel, nello, nella, a	= in the
in faccia a, di fronte (a), dirimpetto (a)	= opposite
dietro, dopo, addietro, didietro	= behind
davanti a, dinanzi a	= in front of
fra, tra	= between
sotto	= under
sopra	= over
con	= with
nuovo, nuova, nuovi, nuove	= new
vecchio, vecchie, vecchia, vecchi	= old
corto, corta, corte, corti	= short
lungo, lunga, lunghi, lunghe	= long
grande, grandi	= large
piccolo, piccola, piccoli, piccole	= small
nord, del nord, settentrionale	= north
est, dell'est, orientale	= east
ovest, dell'ovest, occidentale,	= west
sud, del sud, meridionale	= south

Sann (masculine), Santa (feminine), Sant' (before a vowel),
Santo (before a name beginning with a z, ps or s + consonant;
e.g. Santo Stefano) (abbreviated to S., St., Sta.)   = Saint

Zona Industriale   = industrial estate

Postbox

This is written as Postfach, abbreviated to PF, in German; Case Postale, abbreviated to CP, in French; and Casella Postale, abbreviated to CP in Italian.

Postcodes

Postcodes consist of 4 consecutive digits. The initial digit indicates the largest postal regions, and can be any number between 1 and 9 (not 0). The second digit indicates the region within this area. The postcode areas do not correspond well to administrative boundaries. Most municipalities have their own number, although some numbers are shared and some numbers cover more than one municipality. In the latter cases, the municipality containing the distribution centre is used in the address, with the actual habitation address on the preceding line. The postcode is placed before and on the same line as the town name. Larger population centres have an additional digit after the town name to indicate the sorting district. The streets belonging to each postal district are listed in the telephone book of the area concerned.

The towns of Büsingen in Germany and Campione d'Italia in Italy are also ascribed the following postal codes by the Swiss Post Office:

8238 Büsingen (D-7701)
6911 Campione d'Italia (I-22060)

Liechtenstein has been assigned the Swiss postcodes between 9485 and 9497.

As mentioned above, although most parts of Switzerland belong firmly to one or other language region, there are a number of areas where a language mix occurs. Romansch was, until recently, only a spoken language, so addresses in Romansch-speaking regions are usually written in German. This is a fluid situation and may change. Using the postcode, it is usually possible with a fair degree of accuracy to identify the language in which the address will be given, although, of course, the contents of the mailing should be done in the language of the recipient rather than the language of the area. The lists below show the postcodes belonging to each language area. Note that not all numbers in the sequence from 1000 to 9999 have been utilized; you can find out which postcodes do *not* exist by referring to the post-code lists published by the Swiss PTT.

French

1000–1589, 1602–1654, 1661–1699, 1701, 1720–1721, 1723–1728, 1730–1733, 1740–1782, 1785–1789, 1800–2074, 2087–2416, 2515–2525, 2534–2539, 2603–2746, 2748–2812, 2822–2826, 2828–2954, 3960–3968, 3971–3979.

German

1655–1657, 1711–1719, 1734–1738, 1792–1795, 1797, 2076, 2512–2514, 2540–2578, 2813–2814, 3000–3274, 3282–3284, 3286–3954, 3969–3970, 3981–6493, 7000–7563, 7710, 8000–8236, 8239–9479, 9500–9658

(Note that postcodes 9485–9497 belong to Liechtenstein and not Switzerland.).
(Note that 8238 Büsingen is in Germany, German postcode = D-7701.)

Italian

6500–6910, 6912–6999, 7602-7610, 7741–7748

(Note that 6911 Campione d'Italia is in Italy, Italian postcode = I-22060.)

Predominantly French with German

1595 (Faourg), 1700 (Fribourg, German minority very small), 1722 (Bourgillon), 1729 (Bonnefontaine), 1783 (Pensier), 1784 (Courtepin), 1791 (Courtaman), 1796 (Courgevaux), 2075 (Thielle-Wavre), 2747 (Corcelles BE only – Seehof, with the same postcode, is German speaking), 2827 (Mervelier)

Predominantly German with French

2532 (Magglingen/Macolin), 2533 (Evilard), 3280 (Murten), 3285 (Galmiz)

Bilingual German/French

2500-2505 (Biel/Bienne)

Towns

In the French-speaking areas, town names consisting of more than one word are hyphenated with the exception of towns beginning with the words 'LE' or 'LA', where there is a space between this word and the next (other words in the same town name will be hyphenated).

As Switzerland has four official languages, most large towns have equivalent names in the other languages. The following lists give the correct town name in the local language and the equivalent names in the other official languages. As well as a list for each indigenous language, a list is provided of equivalent names in other European languages. Whatever the name of the town in the local language, the Swiss Post Office will process equally efficiently mail with towns names spelt in one of the other official languages.

The lists of alternative town names include the postcodes and the canton abbreviation for each of the settlements concerned.

German-speaking areas

	German	*French*	*Italian*	*Romansch*
BS 4000–4091	Basel	Bâle	Basilea	
BE 3000-3030	Bern	Berne	Berna	
VS 3900	Brig	Brigue		
GR 7000–7007	Chur	Coire	Coira	Cuera
GR 7142	Cumbel			Cumbels
FR 3284	Fräschels	Frasses (Lac)		
BE 2076	Gals	Chules		
BE 3236	Gampelen	Champion		
FR 3215	Gempenach	Champagny		
FR 1735	Giffers	Chevrilles		
GL 8750	Glarus		Glarona	
SO 2540	Grenchen	Granges		
FR 3212	Gurmels	Cormondes		
FR 1655	Im Fang	La Villette		
FR 3210	Kerzers	Chiètres		
SO 4245	Kleinlützel	Petit-Lucelle		
LU 6000–6009	Luzern	Lucerne	Lucerna	
SA 3953	Leuk Stadt	Loèche-la-Ville		
SA 3954	Leukerbad	Loèche-les-Bains		
BE 2514	Ligerz	Gléresse		
BE 1797	Münchenwiler	Villars-les-Moines		
FR 3286	Muntelier	Montilier		
BE 3225	Müntschemier	Monsmier		
FR 3280	Murten	Morat		
VD 1595	Pfauen	Faoug		
BE 2542	Pieterlen	Perles		
FR 1716	Plaffeien	Planfayon		
VS 3942	Raron	Rarogne		
BE 3792	Saanen	Gessenay		
GR 7151	Schluein			Schleuis
FR 1711	Schwarzsee	Lac-Noir		

	German	French	Italian	Romansch
FR 1718	Rechthalten	Dirlaret		
VS 3970	Salgesch	Salquenen		
FR 1794	Salvenach	Salvagny		
SG 9000	Sankt Gallen	Saint-Gall	San Gallo	
FR 1717	Sankt Ursen	Saint-Ours		
SH 8200	Schaffhausen	Schaffhouse	Sciaffusa	
BE 2747	Seehof	Elay		
SO 4500	Solothurn	Soleure	Soletta	
VS 3952	Susten	La Souste		
FR 1712	Tafers	Tavel		
FR 3912	Termen	Thermen		
BE 3600	Thun	Thoune		
VS 3946	Turtmann	Tourtemagne		
BE 2513	Twann	Douanne		
FR 3214	Ulmiz	Ormay		
VS 3969	Varen	Varonne		
VS 3930	Visp	Viège		
SP 4716	Welschenrohr	Rosières		
ZG 6300-6310	Zug	Zoug	Zugo	
ZH 8000-8099	Zürich	Zurich	Zurigo	

French-speaking areas

	French	German	Italian
FR 1722	Bourguillon	Bürglen	
FR 1792	Cordast	Grossguschelmuth	
FR 1796	Courgevaux	Gurwolf	
JU 2800	Delémont	Delsberg	
FR 1700–1701	Fribourg	Freiburg	Friburgo
BE 2535	Frinvillier	Friedliswart	
GE 1200–1211 +1289	Genève	Genf	Ginevra
BE 2520	La Neuveville	Neuenstadt	
VD 1000-1007 +1010-1018	Lausanne		Losanna
JU 2807	Lucelle	Lützel	
BE 2740	Moutier	Münster	
BR 2534	Orvin	Ifflingen	
JU 2900	Porrentruy	Pruntrut	
BE 2515	Prêles	Prägelz	
BE 2732	Reconvilier	Rokwiler	
BE 2610	Saint-Imier	Sankt Immer	
VS 1950	Sion	Sitten	
BE 2710	Tavannes	Dachsfelden	
BE 2720	Tramelan	Tramlingen	
BE 2512	Tüscherz-Alfermée	Daucher	
BE 2537	Vauffelin	Füglisthal	

Italian-speaking areas

	Italian	German	French
TI 6500–6506	Bellinzona	Bellinzonae	Bellenz
TI 6951	Odogno	Lelgio	

Romansch-speaking areas

	Romansch	*German*	*Italian*
GR 7153	Falera	Fellers	
GR 7130	Ilanz	Glion	
GR 7145	Degen	Igels	
GR 7265	Davos Wolfgang	Laret	
GR 6563	Mesocco	Misox	
GR 7537	Müstair	Münster	
GR 7522	La-Punt-Chamues-ch		Pont-Campovasto
GR 7550	Scuol	Schuls	
GR 7127	Sevgein	Seewis im Oberland	
GR 7174	S. Benedetg	St. Benedikt	San Benedetto
GR 7175	Sumvitg	Somvix	
GR 7166	Trun	Truns	
GR 7147	Vignogn	Vigens	

NB: 2500–2505 Biel/Bienne is a virtually bilingual (French/German) town, and therefore is usually known by its French and German names together – hence Biel/Bienne. Its Italian equivalent is Bienna. There is another town called Biel, with the postcode 4105, known as Biel-Benken.

Other European Languages

	Indigenous	*English*	*Spanish*	*Dutch*
BS 4000-4091	Basel			Bazel
BE 3000-3030	Bern	Berne	Berna	
GE 1200-1211+ 1289	Genève	Geneva		
ZH 8000-8099	Zürich	Zurich		

Administrative districts

Switzerland is a federation of 23 cantons (of which 6 are demi-cantons). These, with their abbreviations and languages spoken are listed below:

NB: * = demi-canton
     (G) = German; (F) = French; (I)= Italian; (R) = Romansch

Aargau	AG (G)	* Nidwalden	NW (G)
* Appenzell IR	AI (G)	* Obwalden	OW (G)
* Appenzell AR	AR (G)	Sankt Gallen	SG (G)
* Basel Landschaft	BL (G)	Schaffhausen	SH (G)
* Basel Stadt	BS (G)	Solothurn	SO (G)
Bern/Berne	BE (G & F)	Schwyz	SZ (G)
Fribourg	FR (F & G)	Thurgau	TG (G)
Genève	GE (F)	Ticino	TI (I)
Glarus	GL (G)	Uri	UR (G)
Graubünden	GR (G & R & I)	Vallais/Wallis	VS (F & G)
Jura	JU (F)	Vaud	VD (F)
Luzern	LU (G)	Zug	ZG (G)
Neuchâtel	NE (F)	Zürich	ZH (G)

The canton abbreviations are often added to addresses after, and on the same line as, the town name, but they are not necessary provided that the postcode is used, and the Swiss PTT prefers that they are excluded from addresses.

Towns with the abbreviation FL (Fürstentum Liechtenstein) following their name are not in Switzerland but in the neighbouring country of Liechtenstein.

United Kingdom of Great Britain and Northern Ireland

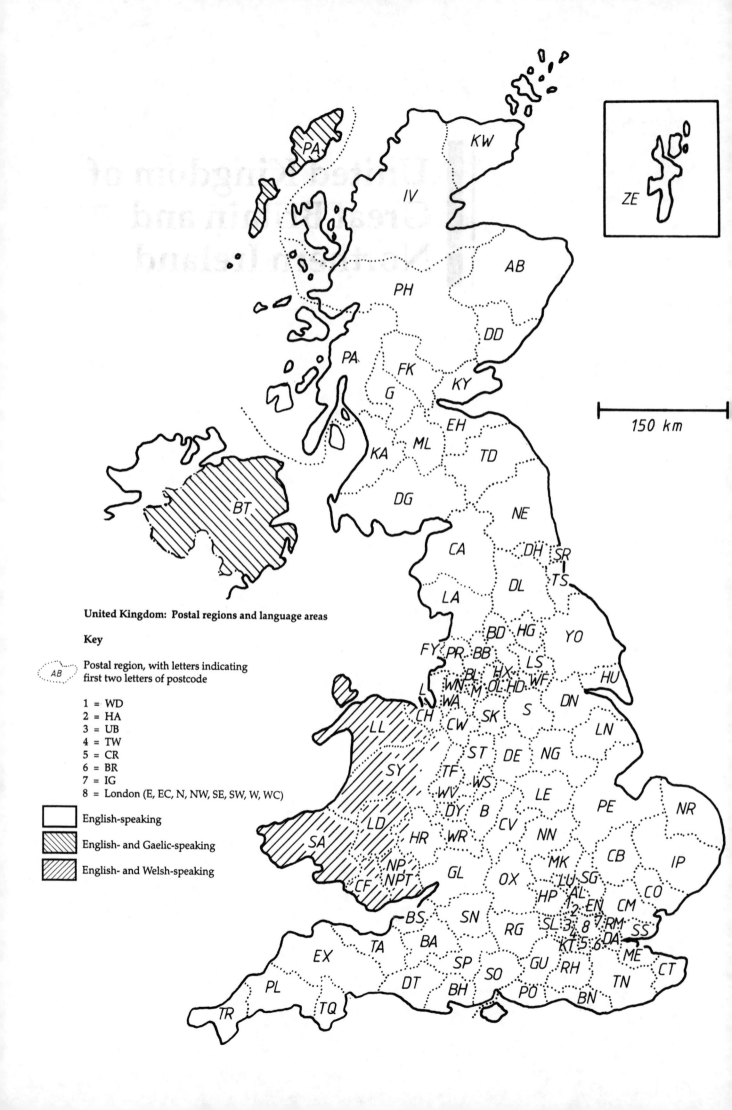

United Kingdom: Postal regions and language areas

Key

Postal region, with letters indicating first two letters of postcode

1 = WD
2 = HA
3 = UB
4 = TW
5 = CR
6 = BR
7 = IG
8 = London (E, EC, N, NW, SE, SW, W, WC)

English-speaking

English- and Gaelic-speaking

English- and Welsh-speaking

150 km

United Kingdom of Great Britain and Northern Ireland

The United Kingdom comprises the nations of England and Scotland, the principality of Wales and the Constituent Region of Northern Ireland. It excludes the Crown Dependencies of the Isle of Man, Jersey and Guernsey. Great Britain is the island which comprises England, Scotland and Wales. Letters from outside the United Kingdom should be addressed correctly. Avoid especially using 'England' for destinations in other parts of the United Kingdom.

Area: 256,668 sq. km. (160,418 sq. miles)

Population: 58,819,200 (1989 estimate)

Population density: 229 per sq. km.

Capital: London (population 6,756, 400 (Greater London, 1989 estimate))

Currency: 1 Pound Sterling = 100 pence

Languages

English, the official language, is spoken by 98 per cent of the population. Welsh is spoken by 1 per cent of the population, mainly in northern and central Wales. Scottish Gaelic is spoken by 19,738 people in the Western Isles of Scotland and Irish Gaelic is spoken in areas of Northern Ireland.

Company names

Words indicating the *nature* of a company, when forming part of the company name, will always follow the *name* of the company, either after a comma or in brackets, thus:

John Smith, Bakers
John Smith (Bakers)

Company types

The company types Limited (abbreviated to Ltd, and PLC (Public Limited Company) are those most commonly found in address databases.

Addresses

Addresses in the United Kingdom are the least formatted of any country in Europe. Whilst many countries limit addresses to, at most, three lines, the structure of addresses in the United Kingdom seems very much to have been left to the discretion of the sender, with the result that addresses are often long, contain not strictly necessary information and some almost provide the postman with a route description from the nearest large town to the address concerned. Naming houses or company locations is as common in the United Kingdom as it is rare in other parts of Europe. The postcode is also not as instinctively used as it is in other European countries.

The address is written in the following format:

Contact name
{Job Title}
Company Name
number[ ]Thoroughfare name[ ]Thoroughfare type
District/suburb of town etc. or village name
Town
{County}
Postcode

The street address may also be written as follows:

Number[,]Thoroughfare name[ ]Thoroughfare type

The address may also contain one or more of the following parameters:

Floor number
Unit number
Industrial Estate name
Building name

The order of these parameters varies. Punctuation (commas at the end of lines) is optional. There must be no punctuation on the same line as the postcode.

For example:

Smiths the Bakers
Flour House
Unit 3, Mary Street Industrial Estate
Benson
Oxford
OX9 1AA

Smiths the Bakers
3 Mary Street
Benson
OX9 1AA

Smiths the Bakers
Flour House, 1st floor
Unit 3
Mary Street Industrial Estate
Benson
Nr. Oxford
OX9 1AA

The thoroughfare type is written after and separately from the thoroughfare name, thus:

Saint Helen's Avenue

An exception is the thoroughfare type '-gate', which is of Scandinavian origin and is usually attached to the thoroughfare name, thus:

Friargate

UK addresses will also often use a whole series of other directional indications, such as 'c/o' (care of), 'r/o' (rear of), 'near', 'off' and so on.

Thoroughfare types

Below is a list of commonly occurring thoroughfare types, with the abbreviated form(s) which you are most likely to find in address databases:

Alley		Hill	
Avenue	Ave.	Lane	
Boulevard	Bd.	Market	Mkt.
Centre	Ctr.	Mews	
Chambers		Parade	
Circus		Park	
Close		Place	Pl.
Court	Ct.	Quay	
Crescent	Cr.	Road	Rd.
Drive		Route	Rte.
Drove		Row	
Estate		Square	Sq.
Field		Street	St.
Gardens		Terrace	
Gate		Way	
Grove		Yard	

NB : The abbreviation for Saint is the same as that commonly used for Street, 'St.'.

Postbox

This is written as P.O. Box, Post Office Box, PO Box, Postbox.

Note that in the United Kingdom, a postbox is not necessarily a number. It can also be a part (usually the last part) of a postcode. Thus, for example:

Mr Bun the Bakers
P.O. Box 1PT
NE17 1PT

Postcodes

Postcodes must be placed on a separate line at the bottom of the address, after the town name. There must be nothing else written on this line.

Postcode areas do not correspond to administrative districts. Each code represents a single large user or a small number of addresses in a street or neighbourhood.

Each postcode has two parts, separated by a space. No postcode is longer than 8 characters. The first part of the postcode can take the following forms:

A9   e.g. E1
A99   e.g. E11
A9A   e.g. E1A
AA9   e.g. EX1
AA99   e.g. EX11
AA9A   e.g. EC1A
AAA   (This pattern occurs only for the Newport postal area, with the letters being NPT)

The second part of the postcode is always a digit followed by 2 letters, e.g. 1AP.

The format AA9A is found only in London.

The first part of the postcode relates to the postal distribution centre, the letters deriving from the town name, and the part of that district. The second part relates to a street and to which side of the street the house is found or whether the house is odd- or even-numbered; or it may be unique to a single large user. The user cannot derive these details from the code itself.

The following list gives all possible initial characters of U.K. postcodes, with their corresponding postal town:

AB	Aberdeen	EX	Exeter
AL	St. Albans	FK	Falkirk
B	Birmingham	FY	Blackpool
BA	Bath	G	Glasgow
BB	Blackburn	GL	Gloucester
BD	Bradford	GU	Guildford
BH	Bournemouth	HA	Harrow
BL	Bolton	HD	Huddersfield
BN	Brighton	HG	Harrogate
BR	Bromley	HP	Hemel Hempstead
BS	Bristol	HR	Hereford
BT	Belfast	HU	Kingston upon Hull
CA	Carlisle	HX	Halifax
CB	Cambridge	IG	Ilford
CF	Cardiff	IP	Ipswich
CH	Chester	IV	Inverness
CM	Chelmsford	KA	Kilmarnock
CO	Colchester	KT	Kingston upon Thames
CR	Croydon	KW	Kirkwall
CT	Canterbury	KY	Kirkcaldy
CV	Coventry	L	Liverpool
CW	Crewe	LA	Lancaster
DA	Dartford	LD	Llandrindod Wells
DD	Dundee	LE	Leicester
DE	Derby	LL	Llandudno
DG	Dumfries	LN	Lincoln
DH	Durham	LS	Leeds
DL	Darlington	LU	Luton
DN	Doncaster	M	Manchester
DT	Dorchester	ME	Medway
DY	Dudley	MK	Milton Keynes
E	London	ML	Motherwell
EC	London	N	London
EH	Edinburgh	NE	Newcastle upon Tyne
EN	Enfield	NG	Nottingham

NN	Northampton	SR	Sunderland
NP,NPT	Newport	SS	Southend-on-Sea
NR	Norwich	ST	Stoke-on-Trent
NW	London	SW	London
OL	Oldham	SY	Shrewsbury
OX	Oxford	TA	Taunton
PA	Paisley	TD	Galashiels
PE	Peterborough	TF	Telford
PH	Perth	TN	Tunbridge Wells
PL	Plymouth	TQ	Torquay
PO	Portsmouth	TR	Truro
PR	Preston	TS	Cleveland
RG	Reading	TW	Twickenham
RH	Redhill	UB	Southall
RM	Romford	W	London
S	Sheffield	WA	Warrington
SA	Swansea	WC	London
SE	London	WD	Watford
SG	Stevenage	WF	Wakefield
SK	Stockport	WN	Wigan
SL	Slough	WR	Worcester
SM	Sutton	WS	Walsall
SN	Swindon	WV	Wolverhampton
SO	Southampton	YO	York
SP	Salisbury	ZE	Lerwick

As both the International sorting code and UK postcodes begin with letters, confusion can occur (e.g. CH indicating Switzerland can be confused with CH indicating Chester), and for this reason the British Post Office prefers that the International sorting code is not used for international mail posted within the United Kingdom.

Postcodes beginning GY are in the crown dependency of Guernsey, those beginning JE are in Jersey and those beginning IM in the Isle of Man.

Towns

London is known as Londres in French and Spanish, Londra in Italian and Londen in Dutch.

Edinburgh is known as Edimbourg in French, Edimburgo in Spanish and Italian, and Edinburg in Dutch.

Welsh is still widely spoken in Wales, and many settlements in Wales have both Welsh and English names. These alternative names are listed below. Where more than one settlement of the same name exists in Wales, the county in which it is situated is given in brackets after the English version of the name. Much of this information is derived from Oliver Mason's *Bartholomew Gazetteer of Places in Britain* (latest edition 1989).

Welsh	*English*
Abaty Cwmhir	Abbeycwmhir
Aberafan	Aberavon
Aberbargod	Aberbargoed
Aberbig	Aberbeeg
Abercastell	Abercastle
Abercynffig	Aberkenfig
Aberdaugleddau	Milford Haven
Aberddawan	Aberthaw

Aberdyfi	Aberdovey
Abergwaun	Fishguard
Aberhonddu	Brecon
Aberllynfi	Three Cocks
Abermiwi	Abermule
Abermo	Barmouth
Aberogwr	Ogmore-by-Sea
Aberpennar	Mountain Ash
Aberriw	Berriew
Abertawe	Swansea
Aberteifi	Cardigan
Abertyleri	Abertillery
Allt Melyd	Meliden
Arberth	Narberth
Arddleen	Ardd-lin
Bangor-is-y-Coed	Bangor-on-Dee
Bargod	Bargoed
Basaleg	Bassaleg
Bedwellte	Bedwellty
Begeli	Begelly
Bers	Bersham
Betws	Bettws
Betws Bledrws	Bettws Bledrws
Biwmares	Beaumaris
Blaenafon	Blaenavon
Blaenau	Blaina
Blaendulais	Seven Sisters
Bochrwyd	Boughrood
Breudeth	Brawdy
Bugeildy	Beguildy
Bwcle	Buckley
Caerdydd	Cardiff
Caerffili	Caerphilly
Caerfyrddin	Carmarthen
Caergybi	Holyhead
Caeriw	Carew
Caernarfon	Caernarvon
Camros	Camrose
Capel Newydd	Newchapel
Capel Uchaf	Upper Chapel
Carwe	Carway
Cas-bach	Castleton
Cas-blaidd	Wolf's Castle
Cas-fuwch	Castlebythe
Cas-gwent	Chepstow
Casilwchwr	Loughor
Cas-mael	Puncheston
Casmorys	Castle Morris
Casnewydd-ar-Wysg	Newport (Gwent)
Casnewydd-bach	Little Newcastle
Castellhaidd	Hayscastle
Castellhenri	Henry's Moat
Castellmartin	Castlemartin
Castell-nedd	Neath

Castell-paen	Painscastle
Cas-wis	Wiston
Cathedin	Cathedine
Ceigidfa	Guilsfield
Ceinewydd	New Quay
Cemais	Kemeys Inferior
Cemais Comawndwr	Kemeys Commander
Cendl	Beaufort
Chwitffordd	Whitford
Cilgeti	Kilgetty
Cilmeri	Cilmery
Cleirwy	Clyro
Clunderwen	Clynderwen
Clydau	Clydey
Coed-duon	Blackwood
Coed-llai	Leeswood
Coed-y-paun	Coed-y-paen
Coedcernyw	Coedkernew
Coety	Coity
Conwil Elvet	Cynwyl Elfed
Corntwn	Corntown
Crai	Cray
Crindai	Crindau
Cronwern	Crunwear
Crucywel	Crickhowell
Crugion	Criggion
Crymlyn	Crumlin
Crynwedd	Crinow
Cwmafan	Cwmavon (West Glamorgan)
Cwmafon	Cwmavon (Gwent)
Cwmbrân	Cwmbran
Cwmcarfan	Cwmcarvan
Cwmcou	Cwmcoy
Cwmlline	Cwm Llinau
Cwmtyleri	Cwmtillery
Cydweli	Kidwelly
Cynffig	Kenfig
Cyncoed	Kingcoed
Derwen-fawr	Broad Oak
Derwen-gam	Oakford
Dinbych	Denbigh
Dinorwic	Dinorwig
Diserth	Dyserth
Drenewydd	Newton (Mid Glamorgan)
Drenewydd Gelli-farch	Shirenewton
Dynbych-y-pysgod	Tenby
Dynfant	Dunvant
Eglwys Fair y Mynydd	St. Mary Hill
Eglwys Wen	Whitechurch
Eglwys Wythwr	Monington
Erbistog	Erbistock
Ewenni	Ewenny
Faerdre	Vardre
Felindre	Velindre (2 in Dyfed, Powys)

Felin-wen — White Mill
Ffontygari — Font-y-gary
Ffwl-y-mwn — Fonmon
Ffynnongroew — Ffynnongroyw
Ffynnon Taf — Taff's Well

Gelli — Gelly
Glan-bad — Upper Boat
Glasgoed — Glascoed
Glyn-nedd — Glyn-neath
Gresffordd — Gresford
Gwenfo — Wenvoe
Gwerneshi — Gwernesney
Gwndy — Undy

Helygain — Halkyn
Hendy-gwyn — Whitland
Hwiffordd — Haverfordwest

Lacharn — Laugharne
Landimor — Landimore
Larnog — Lavernock
Lecwydd — Leckwith
Llanandras — Presteigne
Llanarthne — Llanarthney
Llanbadog — Llanbadog
Llanbedr — Llanbeder
Llanbedr Felffre — Lampeter Velfrey
Llanbedr Pont Steffan — Lampeter
Llanbydderi — Llanbethery
Llancaeach — Llancaiach
Llancaeo — Llancillo
Llancatal — Llancadle
Llandaf — Llandaff
Llan-dawg — Llandawke
Llanddewi Felffre — Llanddewi Velfrey
Llanddewi Nant Hodni — Llanthony
Llanddingad — Dingestow
Llanddinol — Itton
Llandeilo Bertholau — Llantilio Pertholey
Llandeilo Gresynni — Llantilio Crossenny
Llanddunwyd — Welsh St. Donats
Llandegfedd — Llandegveth
Llandeilo Ferwallt — Bishopston
Llandenni — Llandenny
Llandudoch — St. Dogmaels
Llandw — Llandow
Llandyfai — Lamphey
Llandyfalle — Llandefalle
Llanedern — Llanedeyrn
Llanedi — Llanedy
Llaneirwg — St. Mellons
Llanelen — Llanellen
Llaneleu — Llanelieu
Llanelltud — Llanelltyd

Llanelwy	St. Asaph
Llanfable	Llanvapley
Llanfaches	Llanvaches
Llanfaes	Llanmaes
Llan-fair	St. Mary Church
Llanfair Isgoed	Llanvair Discoed
Llanfair Llythynwg	Gladestry
Llanfair-ym-Muallt	Builth Wells
Llanfarthin	Llanmartin
Llanfeuthin	Llanvithyn
Llanfihangel-ar-Elai	Michaelston-super-Ely
Llanfihangel Crucornau	Llanvihangel Crucorney
Llanfihangel Troddi	Mitchel Troy
Llanfihangel y Bont-faen	Llanmihangel
Llanfihangel-y-fedw	Michaelston-y-Vedw
Llanfihangel-y-gofion	Llanvihangel Gobion
Llanfihangel-y-pwll	Michaelston-le-Pit
Llanfihangel Ystum Llywern	Llanvihangel Ystern Llewern
Llanfleiddan	Llanblethian
Llanfocha	St. Maughan's
Llangatwg	Llangattock
Llangatwg Dyffryn Wysg	Llangattock nigh Usk
Llangatwg Feibion Afel	Llangattock Vibon Avel
Llangatwg Lingoed	Llangattock Lingoed
Llangeinwyr	Llangeinor
Llangiwa	Llangua
Llangofen	Llangofen
Llangors	Llangorse
Llangrallo	Coychurch
Llangybi	Llangibby
Llangyfiw	Llangeview
Llamgynnwr	Llangunnor
Llangynydd	Llangennith
Llanhari	Llanharry
Llanhiledd	Llanhilleth
Llanilltern	Capel Llanilltern
Llanilltud Faerdref	Llantwit Fardre
Llanilltud Fawr	Llantwit Major
Llanisien	Llanishen
Llanismel	St. Ishmael
Llan-lwy	Llandeloy
Llannarth	Llanarth
Llannewydd	Newchurch (Dyfed)
Llanofer Fawr	Llanover
Llanrheithan	Llanreithan
Llanrhian	Llanrian
Llan Sain Siôr	St. George (Clwyd)
Llan Sain Siôr	St. George's (South Glamorgan)
Llansanffraid-ar-Elai	St. Bride's-super-Ely
Llansanffraid Gwynllwg	St. Bride's Wentlloog
Llansanwyr	Llansannor
Llansawel	Briton Ferry
Llan-soe	Llansoy
Llansteffan	Llanstephan
Llantrisaint (or Llantrissent)	Llantrisant

Llantydewi	St. Dogwells
Llanwarw	Wonastow
Llanwytherin	Llanvetherine
Llanychar	Llanychaer Bridge
Llanymddyfri	Llandovery
Llwyneliddon	St. Lythans
Llysfaen	Lisvane
Llyswyrny	Llysworney
Maenorbyr	Manorbier
Maerdy	Mardy
Maerun	Marshfield
Maesyfed	New Radnor
Magwyr	Magor
Mamheilad	Mamhilad
Marcroes	Marcross
Matharn	Mathern
Mathri	Mathry
Meisgyn	Miskin
Melin Ifan Ddu	Blackmill
Morfil	Morvil
Mynwar	Minwear
Mynwent y Crynwyr	Quaker's Yard
Nant-y-deri	Nant-y-derry
Niwdwl	Newgale
Nyfer	Nevern
Ogwr	Ogmore
Pant-teg	Panteg
Pedair-hewl	Four Roads
Penarlag	Hawarden
Pen-bre	Pembrey
Pencam	Pelcomb
Pencraig	Old Radnor
Pendeulwyn	Pendoylan
Penffordd-Las	Staylittle
Penfro	Pembroke
Pengelli-ddrain	Grovesend
Penhelyg	Penhelig
Penmarc	Penmark
Pentremeurig	Pentre Meyrick
Pomtarfynach	Devil's Bridge
Pontaman	Pontamman
Pont-henri	Pont Henry
Pontneddfechan	Pontneathvaughan
Pontrhydyrynn	Pontrhydyrun
Pontsenni	Sennybridge
Pont-y-pwl	Pontypool
Port Einon	Port Eynon
Porth Sgiwed	Portskewett
Radur	Radyr (South Glamorgan)
Radur	Rhadyr (Gwent)
Rhaeadr Gwy	Rhayader

Rhaglan	Raglan
Rhisga	Risca
Rhiwabon	Ruabon
Rhiwbeina	Rhiwbina
Rhiwderyn	Rhiwderin
Rhoscrowdder	Rhoscrowther
Rhos-goch	Red Roses
Rhos-hyl	Rhos-hill
Rhuthun	Ruthin (Clwyd)
Rhuthun	Ruthin (South Glamorgan)
Rhydri	Rudry
Rhymni	Rhymney
Sain Dunwyd	St. Donats
Sain Ffagan	St. Fagans
Sain Ffred	St. Brides
Sain Nicolas	St. Nicholas (Dyfed and South Glamorgan)
Sain Pedrog	St. Petrox
Sain Silian	St. Julians
Saint Andras	St. Andrews Major
Sain Tathan	St. Athan
Saint-y-brid	St. Bride's Major
Sancler	St. Clears
Sgethrog	Scethrog
Sgiwen	Skewen
Sili	Sully
Silstwn	Gileston
Slebets	Slebech
Solfach	Solva
Sychdyn	Soughton
Talbenni	Talbenny
Talyllychau	Talley
Trap	Trapp
Trawsgoed	Crosswood
Trebefered	Boverton
Tredynog	Tredunnock
Trefaldwyn	Montgomery
Trefalun	Trevalyn
Trefaser	Trefasser
Trefdraeth	Newport (Dyfed)
Trefelen	Bletherston
Trefesgob	Bishton
Trefflemin	Flemingston
Trefforest	Treforest
Treffynnon	Holywell
Trefin	Trevine
Trefonnen	Nash
Trefor	Trevor (Clwyd and Gwynedd)
Treforgan	Morganstown
Trefwrdan	Jordanston
Trefyclo	Knighton
Trefynwy	Monmouth
Tregolwyn	Colwinston
Tre-groes	Whitchurch (Dyfed)

Tre-gŵyr	Gowerton
Trelales	Laleston
Treletert	Letterston
Treopert	Granston
Treorci	Treorchy
Tre'r-gaer	Tregare
Tresimwn	Bonvilston
Treteio	Tretio
Tretomas	Thomastown
Tretwr	Tretower
Trewallter	Walterston
Trewiliam	Williamstown
Trewyddel	Moylgrove
Trostre	Trostrey
Tryleg	Trelleck
Tyddewi	St. David's
Tŷ-dû	Rogerstone
Waltwn Dwyrain	Walton East
Waltwn Gorllewin	Walton West
Wrecsam	Wrexham
Y Barri	Barry
Y Batel	Battle
Y Bont-faen	Cowbridge (South Glamorgan)
Y Bont-faen	Pontfaen (Dyfed)
Y Clas-ar-Wy	Glasbury
Y Crwys	Three Crosses
Y Ddraenen Wen	Hawthorn
Y Ddwyryd	Druid
Y Drenewydd	Newton (South Glamorgan)
Y Drenewudd	Newtown (Powys)
Y Faenor	Vaynor
Y Fan	Van (Powys)
Y Farteg	Varteg
Y Ferwig	Verwick
Y Fflint	Flint
Y Forlan	Vorlan
Y Garn	Roch
Y Gelli	Hay-on-Wye
Y Goetre-hen	Coytrahen
Ynysgynwraidd	Skenfrith
Ynysowen	Merthyr Vale
Y Pil	Pyle
Yr As Fawr	Monknash
Yr Eglwys Lwyd	Ludchurch
Yr Eglwys Newydd	Newchurch (Powys)
Yr Eglwys Newydd ar y Cefn	Newchurch (Gwent)
Yr Hengastell	Oldcastle
Y Rhws	Rhoose
Yr Orsedd	Rossett
Yr Wyddgrug	Mold
Y Sblot	Splottlands
Ystras-fflur	Strata Florida
Y Trallwng	Welshpool

Y Transh	Tranch
Y Tymbl	Tumble
Y Waun	Chirk
Y Wig	Wick

There are few rules to govern the correct punctuation of town names. A good place to look for correct spellings is Oliver Mason's *Bartholomew Gazetteer of Places in Britain* (latest edition 1989). The UK has many charmingly and idiosyncratically named settlements, and space limitations do not allow me to list all of them. However, the list below, limited to settlements with more than 5,000 inhabitants (2,000 for settlements in Scotland or Wales) shows the correct way of writing the names of settlements which can be wrongly or alternatively spelt:

Ackworth Moor Top
Adwick le Street
Alderley Edge
Annfield Plain
Ashby-de-la-Zouch
Ashton-in-Makerfield
Ashton-under-Lyne

Barnard Castle
Barrow-in-Furness
Barton on Sea
Barton-upon-Humber
Bayston Hill
Berwick-upon-Tweed
Bettws-y-Coed
Bexhill-on-Sea
Bishop Auckland
Bishop's Cleeve
Bishop's Stortford
Blackhall Colliery
Blaenau Ffestiniog
Blandford Forum
Blaydon-on-Tyne
Boar's Hill
Bognor Regis
Bolton-le-Sands
Bo'ness
Boston Spa
Bourne End
Bradford-on-Avon
Bridge of Allan
Bridge of Weir
Bromley Cross
Builth Wells
Burgess Hill
Burley in Wharfedale
Burnham-on-Crouch
Burnham-on-Sea
Burry Port
Burscough Bridge
Burton Latimer
Burton upon Trent
Bury St. Edmunds

Caister-on-Sea
Canvey Island
Carlton in Lindrick
Castle Donington
Catterick Garrison
Cefn-Mawr
Chalfont St. Giles
Chalfont St. Peter
Chapel-en-le-Frith
Charlton Kings
Chester-le-Street
Chipping Norton
Chipping Ongar
Chipping Sodbury
Church Village
Clacton on Sea
Clay Cross
Clayton-le-Moors
Cleator Moor
Colwyn Bay
Connah's Quay
Conon Bridge
Coupar Angus
Cove Bay
Cross Hands

Dalgety Bay
Dalton-in-Furness
Dinas Powis

Easton-in-Gordano
Eaton Socon
Ebbw Vale
Ellesmere Port

Farnham Royal
Fort William

Gilfach Goch
Glyn-Neath
Guide Post
Gwaun-Cae-Gurwen

Hayling Island
Haywards Heath

Hazel Grove
Hedge End
Hemel Hempstead
Henley-in-Arden
Henley-on-Thames
Herne Bay
Hetton-le-Hole
Higham Ferrers
Higher Walton
Houghton-le-Spring
Hoyland Nether
Huyton-with-Roby

Ince-in-Makerfield
Isle of Walney
Iver Heath

Kings Langley
King's Lynn
Kingston upon Hull
Kingston upon Thames
Kirby Muxloe
Kirkby in Ashfield

Lee-on-the-Solent
Leighton Buzzard
Little Lever
Llandrindod Wells
Llandudno Junction
Llantwit Fardre
Llantwit Major
Locks Heath
Lytham St. Anne's

Mansfield Woodhouse
Marske-by-the-Sea
Melton Mowbray
Menai Bridge
Merthyr Tydfil
Merthyr Vale
Milford Haven
Milton Keynes
Milton of Campsie
Mountain Ash

Newark-on-Trent
Newbiggin-by-the-Sea
Newcastle-under-Lyme
Newcastle upon Tyne
Newport on Tay
Newport Pagnell
Newton Abbot
Newton Aycliffe
Newton-le-Willows

Newton Mearns
Newton Stewart
Norton Canes
Norton-Radstock

Ogmore Vale

Paddock Wood
Pembroke Dock
Penrhyn Bay
Port Glasgow
Port Talbot
Potters Bar
Poulton-le-Fylde
Princes Risborough

Radcliffe on Trent
Richmond upon Thames
Ross-on-Wye
Royal Tunbridge Wells

Saltburn-by-the-Sea
Seven Sisters
Shepton Mallet
Sonning Common
Southend-on-Sea
Sowerby Bridge
Stanford le Hope
Stansted Mountfitchet
Stockton Heath
Stockton-on-Tees
Stoke-on-Trent
Stoke Poges
Stourport-on-Severn
Stratford-upon-Avon
Sunbury-on-Thames
Sutton Coldfield
Sutton in Ashfield

Taff's Well
Telford Dawley
Tower Hamlets

Ushaw Moor

Virginia Water

Waltham Abbey
Waltham Forest
Walton-on-Thames
Wath upon Dearne
Welwyn Garden City
Westbury-on-Trym
Weston-super-Mare

Westward Ho!   Wimborne Minster
Whitley Bay   Woburn Sands
Wide Open   Wootton Bassett

Londonderry, in Northern Ireland, is known to some of the population as Derry.
    Furthermore, there is generally no hyphenation fornames beginning with the following words:

Bishop   Middle
Castle   Near
East   Nether
Far   New
Great   North
Greater   Old
High   St
Higher   South
Lesser   The
Little   Upper
Low   West
Lower   Y
Market   Yr
Mid

In some databases, these words may sometimes be found following the rest of the settlement name in this way:

    Tew, Great

Saint is always printed as St.

Administrative districts

England has 46 counties, Wales has 8, Northern Ireland 6 and Scotland has 12 regions. The Isle of Man and the Channel Islands are Crown Dependencies.
    You will often find the county name added to UK addresses. Some recipients like this, but it is really not necessary provided that the postcode is used.
    The following list of counties provides common abbreviations in brackets.

England

Avon   Essex
Bedfordshire (Beds)   Gloucestershire
(Royal) Berkshire (Berks)   Greater London
Buckinghamshire (Bucks)   Greater Manchester
Cambridgeshire (Cambs)   Hampshire (Hants)
Cheshire   Hereford & Worcester
Cleveland   Hertfordshire (Herts)
Cornwall   Humberside
Cumbria   Isle of Wight
Derbyshire   Kent
Devon   Lancashire (Lancs)
Dorset   Leicestershire (Leics)
Durham   Lincolnshire (Lincs)
East Sussex   Merseyside

Norfolk
Northamptonshire (Northants)
Northumberland
North Yorkshire
Nottinghamshire (Notts)
Oxfordshire (Oxon)
Salop
South Yorkshire
Somerset

Staffordshire (Staffs)
Suffolk
Surrey
Tyne and Wear
Warwickshire
West Midlands
West Sussex
West Yorkshire
Wiltshire (Wilts)

Wales

Clwyd
Dyfed
Gwent
Gwynedd

Mid Glamorgan
Powys
South Glamorgan
West Glamorgan

Scotland (Administrative Districts)

Borders
Central
Dumfries and Galloway
Fife
Grampian
Highland

Lothian
Orkney
Shetland
Strathclyde
Tayside
Western Isles

Northern Ireland

Antrim
Armagh
(London)Derry

Down
Fermanagh
Tyrone

Crown dependencies

Alderney
Guernsey
Isle of Man

Jersey
Sark

Counties may be written in addresses without the word 'shire', especially where the county is named after a town. Thus, Gloucestershire is often written as Gloucester, Oxfordshire as Oxford, etc. This is especially the case with the old Scottish counties, where the 'shire' is rarely used.

If you want to use counties in addresses, it is necessary to note a number of idiosyncratic differences between the existing administrative regions and the county names as used in addresses. These idiosyncracies are as follows:

1. In Scotland, the administrative regions which replaced the old counties in 1975 are not referred to at all by the Post Office. The old county names are still used. The old Scottish counties are as follows:

Aberdeenshire
Angus
Argyllshire
Ayrshire
Banffshire

Berwickshire
Buteshire
Caithness
Clackmannanshire
Dumfriesshire

Dunbarton	Peeblesshire
East Lothian	Perthshire
Fife	Renfrewshire
Inverness-shire	Ross & Cromarty
Kincardineshire	Roxburghshire
Kinross-shire	Selkirkshire
Kircudbrightshire	Stirlingshire
Lanarkshire	Sutherland
Midlothian	West Lothian
Morayshire	Wigtownshire
Nairnshire	

2. For London, the Post Office uses the pre-1965 boundary. So, for example, Harrow is addressed as Middlesex, and Sidcup as Kent. Middlesex no longer exists as a county but is still used in postal addresses.
3. The county name Greater Manchester is not used by the Post Office. Pre-1984 boundaries are used, thus, for example, Stockport, Cheshire.
4. Humberside is split into North Humberside (north of the River Humber) and South Humberside (south of the River Humber) for postal purposes.
5. The county name Hereford & Worcester is not used by the Post Office. The separate names Herefordshire and Worcestershire are used.
6. The county name Avon is not used by the Post Office.

London boroughs will often be found in addresses. In order to be able to recognize these, a list of the currently existing boroughs follows:

Barking and Dagenham	Hillingdon
Barnet	Hounslow
Bexley	Islington
Brent	Kensington and Chelsea
Bromley	Kingston upon Thames
Camden	Lambeth
City of London	Lewisham
City of Westminster	Merton
Croydon	Newham
Ealing	Redbridge
Enfield	Richmond upon Thames
Greenwich	Southwark
Hackney	Sutton
Hammersmith and Fulham	Tower Hamlets
Haringey	Waltham Forest
Harrow	Wandsworth
Havering	

Note that the boundaries and names of the counties are currently under review. North Humberside will shortly revert to being East Yorkshire, whilst South Humberside will rejoin Lincolnshire. It will therefore be necessary to check this information.

Vatican City
Città del Vaticano

Area: 0.44 sq. km (0.17 sq. miles)

Population: 752 (1988 estimate)

Population density: 1,709 per sq. km.

Currency: The Vatican has its own currency, and the monetary system is independent of that of Italy, although Italian Lira are valid within the Vatican. The Vatican coins are the gold lire 1000 (nominal), silver lire 500; 'Acmonital' lire 100 and 50, 'Italma' lira 10, 5 and 1, and 'bronzital' lira 20.

Languages

Latin is used for Church affairs, whilst the language used on a day-to-day basis is Italian.

Addresses

For details of address formats, please refer to the chapter on Italy.

Telephone numbers

The Vatican City forms part of the Italian Telephone system. The area code is 06 (shared with Rome and surrounds).

Appendix 1 Returns

Envelopes returned to the sender usually give the reason that they were undeliverable on a sticker or stamp on the envelope. A stamp will usually give the reason in the local language only, a sticker will give it in the local language and French. The following list provides a translation of these reasons for non-delivery. Note that not all reasons are applicable to all countries.

French	English	German	Spanish	Italian	Dutch
Absent	Absent			Assente	
Adresse Illisible	Address unreadable		Dirección ilegible		Onleesbaar adres
Adresse Inexacte	Incomplete address		Calle Desconocida	Indirizzo Inesatto	
Adresse Insuffisante	Insufficient address	Anschrift ungenügend	Dirección Insuficiente	Indirizzo Insufficiente	Ontoereikend adres(B) Onvolledig adres (NL)
Bureau Inexistant	No such Post Office				
Décédé	Deceased	Verstorben	Fallecido	Deceduto	Overleden
Déménagé/Parti	Moved/ Gone Away	Abgereist			
En voyage	Travelling	Verreist			
Inconnu	Not known	Unbekannt	Desconocido	Sconosciuto	Onbekend
Introuvable	Unfindable			Irreperibile	
Non admis	Non-admissible			Non ammesso	
N'habite plus à l'adresse indiquée	Does not live at this address				Woont niet meer op aangeduid adres
Non réclame	Not called for	Nicht abgeholt	No Reclamado	Non Reclamato	Niet afgehaald
Parti	Gone away			Partito	
Parti sans adresse	Gone away without leaving address		Partió sin dejar señas/ dirección		Vertrokken zonder adres
Parti sans laissez d'adresse	Gone away without leaving address	Unbekannt verzogen			
Raison sociale n'existe plus	Company closed	Firma erloschen			
Refusé	Refused	Verweigert	Rehusado	Rifiutato	Geweigerd
Rue Inconnue	Unknown street				
Rue/numéro inexistant(e)	Non-existant street/number				Straatnaam/huisnummer bestaat niet
Transféré	Moved			Trasferito	

▋ Bibliography

Alitalia, *Arrivederci*, III, 34, Rome, December 1992 .

Aulestia, Gorka and White, Linda (1992) *Basque – English, English–Basque Dictionary*, Reno, USA: University of Nevada Press.

Bartholomew & Co. Ltd. (1966), *Gazetteer of the British Isles*, Edinburgh.

Beard, Jonathan (1991), 'Computer Code Speaks in Many Tongues', in *New Scientist*, no. 1759, 9 March , p. 28.

Beckett, Kay (1991) 'Europe's Mailing Preference Services', *European Direct Marketing*, Issue 1, Summer, pp 8 & 12.

Belgisch Staatsblad, 15.10.91.

Blattberg, Robert C. and Deighton, John (1991), 'Interactive Marketing: Exploiting the Age of Addressibility', *Sloan Management Review*, Fall, pp 5-14.

Boer-Den Hoed, Dr. P.M. (1953) *Van Goor's Zweeds Handwoordenboek Nederlands-Zweeds*, Den Haag: Van Goor.

British Telecom (1990), *The Code Book, National and International Dialling Codes*, February.

Correos u Telégrafos (1992), *Guia Codigo Postal*, 1992, Madrid: Ministerio de Obras Públicas u Transportes.

Davies, John M. (1992) *The Essential Guide to Database Marketing*, Maidenhead: McGraw-Hill.

Deutsche Bundespost (1977) *Die Postleitzahl*.

Deutsche Bundespost (1993) *Das Postleitzahlenbuch, Alphabetisch geordnet*.

Deutsche Bundespost (1993) *Das Postleitzahlenbuch, Numerisch geordnet*.

Deutsche Telekom (1990) *Vorwahlnummern*.

Diccionario Empresarial Stanford (1990) Area Ed., Madrid: SA Expansion.

Dipartiment Tal-Posta (Malta) (1991) *Direttorju Tal-K dići Postale*, Valletta, Malta: Media & Graphic Services Ltd.

Dominicus, Jo (1981, 1991 edition) *Kanaaleilanden*, Haarlem: J.H. Gottmer.

Donovan, Judith (1989) *Back to Basics – an Introduction to Direct Marketing*, Hertford: *Direct Response Magazine*.

Fraser-Robinson, John (1989) *The Secret of Effective Direct Mail*, Maidenhead: McGraw-Hill.

Gobierno de Navarra/Nafarroako Gobernua (1986), *Ley de la Lengua Vasca / Euskarari Buruzko Foru Legea*.

Gorski, Debbie (1992) 'The I.T. Advantage', *Marketing Director International*, Vol. 3, No. 2, Autumn, pp. 87–90.

Guardian, 'On the Line' [Estonian international telephone code], 2.2.93.

Guardian, 4.8.93, p. 1.

Hammond, Robin (1981) *A German Reference Grammar*, Oxford: Oxford University Press.

Hughes, John (ed.) (1982) *The Mail Marketing File*, Mail Marketing (Bristol) Ltd.

James, Clive (1990), *May Week was in June*, London: Picador.

James, P.D.(1963) *A Mind to Murder*, London: Sphere.

Katzner, Kenneth (1977) *The Languages of the World*, London: Routledge & Kegan Paul.

Kompass Publishers (1987) *Kompass UK Register of British Industry and Commerce*, East Grinstead.

Kossman-Putto, J.A. and Kossman, E.H. (1989), *The Low Countries – History of the Northern & Southern Netherlands*, Rekkem, Belgium: Stichting Ons Erfdeel vzw.

L'Evenement, no. 357, 5–11 September 1991.

Mason, O. (1989), *Bartholomew Gazetteer of Places in Britain*, Edinburgh: Bartholomew.

Medhurst, Professor Kenneth (1982), *The Basques and the Catalans*, Minority Rights Group Report no. 9, London: Minority Rights Group.

Meijes Tiersman, Pieter (1985) *Frisian Reference Grammar*, Dordrecht: Forsi Publications.

Meio Caminho Andado (1991) *Lista do Código Postal 1991 ediça 2, Lisboa*, Correios e telecomunicaçõ es de Portugal.

Miles, Louella (1991) 'Direct Marketing in the United States', *European Direct Marketing*, Issue 1, Summer, pp. 15–16, 18.

Minority Rights Group (1991) *Minorities and Autonomy in Western Europe*, London: Minority Rights Group.

Nash, Edward L. (1993) *Database Marketing – The Ultimate Marketing Tool*, New York: McGraw-Hill, Inc.

Nederlandse Taalunie (1993) *Voorzetten 41 – Lijst van Landnamen – Namen van landen, alsmede opgave van de dararbij behorende bijvoeglijke naamwoorden en inwoneraanduidingen en van de namen van de hoofdsteden, Officiële schrijfwijze voor het Nederlandse taalgebied*, 's-Gravenhage: Stichting Bibliographia Neerlandica.

Nordiska DM-Dagar (1990) *Nordic D.M. Guide – Postal Opportunities in Direct Marketing*.

Office Fédéral de la Statistique, 1993, *Mémento Statistique de la Suisse 1993*, Bern.

Pebesma, H. (1982) *Van Goor's Klein Fries Woordenboek*, Ljouwert: Algemiene Fryske Underrjocht Kommisje.

Printronic International (1991), *E.C.-ing with Printronic International*, London.

PTT (Switzerland) *Numerisches Verzeichnis der Postleitzahlen /Liste des numéros postaux d'achemine-ment dans l'ordre numérique /Elenco dei numeri postali d'avviamento in ordine numerico*, Bern.

PTT (Switzerland) (1989) *Verzeichnis der Postleitzahlen/Liste des numéros postaux d'acgeminement/ Elenco dei numeri postali d'avviamento*, Bern.

PTT Post (Netherlands) (1978) *Postcodeboek*.

PTT Post (Netherlands) (1991) *Postcode, aanvulling nr. 24*.

PTT Post (Netherlands) (1993) *Postcode Databank*.

PTT Telecom (NL) (1989) *Buitenlandse Netnummers, juli 1989*, Den Haag.

The Reader's Digest (1966) *The Reader's Digest AA Book of the Road*, London.

Royal Mail International (1991), *Royal Mail International Business Travel Guide*, London: Columbus Press.

Royal Mail International (1992), *Royal Mail International Business Travel Guide 1992/93*, London: Columbus Press.

Società Italiana per l'Esercizio delle Telecommunicazioni p.a. (1988) *Prefessi Teleselettivi*, Torino.

Shaw, Robert and Stone, Merlin (1988) *Database Marketing*, Gower Business Enterprise Series, Aldershot: Gower.

Swedish Postoffice (1988) *Postnummerkatalog 1988*, Stockholm.

Van Goor (1984) *Van Goor's Noors-Nederlands Woordenboek*, Amsterdam: Van Goor Zonen.

Venâncio, Fernando (1983) *Basis Woordenlijst Portugees*, Muiderberg: Dick Coutinho .

Venâncio, Fernando (1989) *Basis Grammatica Portugees*, Schiedam: Blok Uitgeverij.

Venâncio, Fernando (1989) *Boa Sorte – Leer en Oefenboek Portugees 1*, Muiderberg: Dick Coutinho.

Visser-Boezaardt, ir. G. and Schram-Pighi, dr. L. (1980), *Prisma Woordenboek Nederlands Italiaans*, Utrecht/Antwerpen: Het Spectrum.

Vliegher, J. De (1991) *Gids voor Vaticaanstad*, Antwerpen/Baarn: Uitgeverij Hadewijck.

Wilson, Kathryn (ed.) (1991/92) *Marketing Without Frontiers*, London: Royal Mail International.

Wouters, dr. Herman (1976)*Volken en Stammen – Noordelijk Europa*, Amsterdam: Amsterdam Boek.

Wouters, dr. Herman (1977) *Volken en Stammen – Zuid-Europa en de Balken*, Amsterdam: Amsterdam Boek.

▌▌ Maps used

Bartholomew (1992) *Europe 1992 – Political Map of the New Europe*, Edinburgh.

Bartholomew (1991) *Planner's Counties & Regions Map of the British Isles*, scale 1:792,000, Edinburgh.

De Rouck Cartography (1993) *Administratieve Kaart van België en van Groothertogdom Luxemburg*, scale 1:300,000, Brussels, 5th edition.

Deutsche Bundespost (1993) *Postleitzahlen, Übersichtskarte der Postleiteinheiten*, scale 1:800,000.

Edizioni Uerre, *Italia Postale*, Umberto Ronca.

Falkplan-Suurland BV, *Gemeentekaart van Nederland*, scale 1:250,000, Eindhoven.

Jakez Derouet (1989) *Celtica*, Pluguvan, Brittany.

John Bartholomew & Son Ltd (1974) *The World Atlas*, Edinburgh.

Johnson & Perrott Ltd (1983) *Map of Ireland*, Ordnance Survey.

Kümmerley & Frey *Road Map of France*, scale 1:1,000,000.

Recta Foldex *France Administrative, Départements, Régions*, scale 1:100,000.

RV Reise- und Verkehrsverlag *Map of Postcode areas of Germany*, Berlin, scale 1:700,000.

Shell *Touring Map of Italy*.